American Conspiracies

AMERICAN CONSPIRACIES

Lies, Lies, and More Dirty Lies that the Government Tells Us

By Jesse Ventura
with Dick Russell

Skyhorse Publishing

Skyhorse Publishing books may be purchased in bulk at special discounts for sales promotion, corporate gifts, fund-raising, or educational purposes. Special editions can also be created to specifications. For details, contact the Special Sales Department, Skyhorse Publishing, 307 West 36th Street, 11th Floor, New York, NY 10018 or info@skyhorsepublishing.com.

Skyhorse® and Skyhorse Publishing® are registered trademarks of Skyhorse Publishing, Inc.®, a Delaware corporation.

www.skyhorsepublishing.com

10 9 8 7 6 5 4 3 2 1

Papserback ISBN: 978-1-61608-214-7

Library of Congress Cataloging-in-Publication Data

Ventura, Jesse.

American conspiracies : lies, lies, and more dirty lies that the government tells us / by Jesse Ventura, with Dick Russell.

p. cm.

Includes bibliographical references.

ISBN 978-1-60239-802-3 (hbk. : alk. paper)

1. Conspiracies--United States. 2. Conspiracy theories--United States. I. Russell, Dick. II. Title.

HV6285.V46 2010

973--dc22

2009052309

Printed in the United States of America

"A foolish faith in authority is the worst enemy of truth."

—*Albert Einstein*

CONTENTS

INTRODUCTION

WHY I'M WRITING ABOUT CONSPIRACIES IN AMERICA

First of all, let's talk about what you *won't* find in this book. It's not about how extraterrestrials are abducting human beings, or the Apollo moon landing being a colossal hoax perpetrated by NASA, or that Barack Obama somehow is not a natural-born American citizen. I leave these speculations to others, not that I take them seriously. What this book will delve into are a number of things you don't see on TV or read about in the papers. The fact is, the media—the fourth branch of government that our founding fathers anticipated would speak truth to power and keep our democracy on track—has at least since the assassination of President Kennedy systematically ignored any "conspiracy theory" that might rock the Establishment's boat. We are, excuse my French, in deep shit today because of this head-in-the-sand mentality.

Let's start out by defining what a conspiracy is. My 2,347-page *Webster's New Universal Unabridged Dictionary* says: "a planning and acting together secretly, especially for an unlawful or harmful purpose, such as murder or treason." Synonyms include plot, cabal, connivance, collusion. Hard to swallow? Think of the Roman senators who knocked off Julius Caesar in 44 B.C. But I guess we've come a long way since then, right? Think Operation Northwoods, circa 1962. We'll get to that in due course—*Seven Days in May*, that novel about a military takeover during the Kennedy years, wasn't far off the mark.

Clearly, there's something going on in our national psyche that the *New York Times* and the *Washington Post* don't want to examine. Look at the popularity of *The X-Files*, or Mel Gibson in the movie *Conspiracy Theory*. Not that I think we should all booby-trap our doors and hide behind our file cabinets, but sometimes those "lone nuts" turn out to be right! I'm tired of being told that anybody who questions the status quo is part of the disaffected, alienated element of our society that ought to wake up and salute the flag. Maybe being patriotic is about raising the curtain and wondering whether we've really been told the truth about things like September 11.

I guess my questioning of the "official" line goes back to my school days, being taught that we had to fight in Vietnam to stop the domino effect of Communism. That's what I learned in school, but my father—who was a World War II vet—took the exact opposite position at the dinner table. He said that was a load of crap, that the Vietnam War was all about somebody making big money off it. At first I thought my dad was crazy, because I could not believe they would lie to me in school. I fought with him over it, and he'd keep doing his best to debunk what I was saying.

When I, in turn, went into the service and learned a whole lot more about Vietnam, I had the good fortune to come home and tell my father that he was right. Especially growing up in the Midwest, you never even contemplate that your government might not be telling the truth. You don't realize until you get much older that government is nothing but people—and people lie, especially where money and power are concerned.

The next prong in the fork was, when I got out of the navy and went to junior college one year, Mark Lane came to give a talk and I happened to hear him that night. That was the first time I ever paid attention to someone saying that what they told us about President Kennedy's assassination might not be true. I'd been in junior high school when JFK was shot, and I remember the announcement over the loudspeakers and being sent back to our homerooms and then school was dismissed. Like most everybody else, I saw Jack Ruby shoot Lee Harvey Oswald on TV, but I never questioned the Warren Commission's report that this disaffected ex-Marine had acted alone.

After hearing Mark Lane that year, I was at the height of my wrestling career during the 1978 congressional hearings into the assassination and didn't really start delving into any of this until wrestling changed in the mid-1980s. All of a sudden, I was no longer driving to towns, but flying. Sitting on airplanes all the time becomes extremely boring, so I started reading. Besides Mark Lane's *Plausible Denial*, I remember Jim Marrs's *Crossfire* and then a whole bunch of other books. When I'd see anything about the Kennedy assassination in the bookstores, I'd buy it.

So as I got older and started looking back at the Sixties, where every assassin was supposedly a "lone nut," I began thinking how could that be? These nuts who never told anybody anything or planned with anyone else, but just felt the need to go out and commit murders of prominent individuals—John and Robert Kennedy, Martin Luther King and Malcolm X. The odds of that, I figured, simply defied all logic.

It made me wonder who's really running the show. Especially when you look at things they now admit never happened, like the Gulf of Tonkin incident that drew us into the Vietnam War. These things, as portrayed by our government and media, seem to be smaller segments of a bigger picture. It almost seems like a game of chess sometimes, where you don't understand the significance of one move until maybe a decade or two later and start to see the results of how things turned out differently.

You can bet that during my four years as the independent governor of Minnesota (1999 to 2003), I was shielded from plenty of information, because they figured this guy will come and go. At the same time, I had some personal experiences that would tend to make a sane public servant start looking over his shoulder. (As William Burroughs once said, "Paranoia is having all the facts.")

The first inkling that certain people inside the federal government were out to keep an eye on me came not long after I took office. Sometime early in 1999, I was "asked" to attend a meeting in the basement of the Capitol building, at a time when the State Legislature was not in session. I was informed that the Central Intelligence Agency (CIA) was conducting a training exercise that they hoped I'd be willing to participate in. Well, by this time I knew that the CIA's original mission statement from 1947 meant they were only supposed to operate outside the U.S. The FBI was the outfit with domestic jurisdiction. But, being an ex–Navy SEAL and a patriotic citizen, I basically felt I should cooperate. Besides, I was curious as to what this was really all about.

Down there in the bowels of the building, some "fledgling" CIA operatives sat waiting for me in a conference room. There were 23 in all; I counted heads. They ranged in age from right out of college to what looked like retired people, both men and women, a very diverse group. Your average middle-class neighborhood types—except all of them were with the CIA, which was kind of chilling when you think about it. I was placed in the middle of a big circle of chairs, and they all sat there staring at me, with notebooks on their laps.

Well, before they could start asking me questions, I said I had a few for them. First of all, what were they doing *here*, in the FBI's territory? Nobody seemed to want to say. Then I started going around the room, asking for their names and their job descriptions. Maybe three or four answered, but the others dummied up. Either they'd describe what they did without identifying who they were, or neither. Considering that I'm an elected governor, I thought this was not only rude, but rather brash. So I told the group, "Well, being that you're not being too cooperative with me, it's going to be difficult for me to cooperate with *you*."

They asked their questions anyway, and it was interesting. They all focused on how we campaigned, how we achieved what we did, and did I think we truly could win when we went into the campaign? Basically, how had the independent wrestler candidate pulled this off? Sometimes I answered and other times I didn't, just to mess with them a little. They remained very cordial and proper. Nobody raised their voice or made me feel I was being interrogated. But I've got to say, it was one of the strangest experiences of my life. I was baffled by the whole experience.

When I got home that day, I called my friend Dick Marcinko. He wrote all the *Rogue Warrior* books, created the anti-terrorist SEAL Team Six, and I figured he'd probably know more about how the CIA operates than anybody else I knew. Dick started laughing as I told him the scenario of what had happened. I asked why he thought this was so funny.

"Well, I'm not privy to exactly why they were there," he said, "but I could give you my educated guess." He went on, "They didn't see you coming. You were not on the radar screen. And all of a sudden, you won a major election in the United States of America. The election caught them with their pants down, and their job is to gather intelligence and make predictions. Now, next to Bill Clinton, you're probably the most famous politician in America."

Then Dick added this: "I think they're trying to see if there are any more of you on the horizon."

So were they trying to gather information to insure this would never happen again? I wondered: Was I that much of a threat?

Not too long after that meeting, I found out something else and it stunned me. I revealed this for the first time in my memoir, *Don't Start the Revolution Without Me!*, and it raised a lot of eyebrows. It just so happens there is a CIA operative inside every state government. They are not in executive positions—in other words, not appointed by the governor—but permanent state employees. While governors come and go, they keep working, holding down legitimate jobs but with a dual identity. In Minnesota, this person was fairly high up, serving at the deputy commissioner level.

I wasn't sworn to secrecy about this, but only my chief of staff and I were allowed to know his identity. I had to go meet with the person and later, when somebody else took the cover post for the CIA, I had to know who the new agent was. I still have no idea what they're doing there. Are they spying? Checking out what direction the state government is going in and reporting back to someone at headquarters in Langley? But who and for what purpose? I mean, are they trying to ferret out traitors in the various states? (Or maybe just dissidents—like me!)

Anyhow, I wasn't told the reason and was simply left to ponder how come our Constitution is being violated. Let's say it gave me pause. I've seen it firsthand. And that's another reason why I am writing this book, because I believe it's vital to our democracy to see the hidden pattern that's been undermining this country for most of my lifetime. The Bush Administration, which made lying into an "art form" that took us into the Iraq War, was in a way the logical extension of all the cover-ups, crimes, and conspiracies that preceded it.

Researching this book has been fascinating, but I wouldn't call it fun. When you look back on how the power brokers have deceived us over the years, it gets pretty damned depressing. Maybe that's why so many people prefer to remain in denial. The way I look at it, though, is that old truism from the Bible: "You shall know the truth, and the truth shall set you free." Until we come clean about our recent history, there's no way to move forward and return to the representative democracy that our forefathers intended America to be.

We'll start by looking back at the assassination of Abraham Lincoln. If you're like me, you certainly know the name of John Wilkes Booth—just like we do Lee Harvey Oswald (ever wonder why lone assassins always have middle names set down, too? Maybe so we'll get them firmly implanted in our minds?). But how many of us were taught that Booth had eight known coconspirators, and that it's never been resolved as to whether he may have been involved with someone in Lincoln's own circle?

Then we'll cut to the 1930s, when Franklin D. Roosevelt got elected in the midst of the Great Depression. That's when a cabal of wealthy industrialists using a veterans' front group embarked on a plot to get rid of FDR and institute a fascist-style regime in this country. They'd probably have succeeded, except they chose the wrong man to lead the way: Major General Smedley Butler, a true American hero who'd twice been awarded the Congressional Medal of Honor. Butler blew the whistle to Congress, which held hearings that exposed the whole scheme. And guess who was among the conspirators, along with J.P. Morgan, DuPont, and other titans of finance? None other than Prescott Bush, grandfather of George W. and father of George H.W. Prescott also happened to be a business partner and American banker for a German steel and coal baron who funded Hitler's rise to power!

I'm going to devote several chapters to the assassinations of the 1960s, because in my view the truth has been covered up about all of them. We'll start with the one I've studied the longest, and that's the conspiracy that took President Kennedy's life on November 22, 1963. I believe our country has never been the same since that terrible day, which established a precedent for treachery in our contemporary political life that we're still living with.

I don't believe you can ever form an opinion and say: this is absolutely what happened. That's one of the reasons the perpetrators succeed, because when the most powerful entity in the world is doing the covering up, it becomes extremely difficult to know that you can ever lay the truth completely bare. I think I probably read a scenario that's true, but there might be several others as provocative and just as well true. Or they might all be intertwined into one. The criticism of Oliver Stone's film *JFK* (which I've watched many times) is that he just threw all the mud at the wall to see which part sticks. Well, he *had* to. He was putting it all out there and letting you the viewer decide what you wanted to take home to the bank. It didn't make it any less of a great film because Oliver couldn't pinpoint exactly what went down.

One aspect I'll be scrutinizing, when it comes to Oswald, is whether there were in fact *two* of them. This is one of the most intriguing parts of the case, because it clears up the fact that a number of witnesses saw Oswald in different places at the same time. It also raises some huge questions about how the military and the CIA might have been using Oswald—and a look-alike—in their intelligence games. The use of "doubles" is a classic intel *modus operandi*.

The assassinations of Malcolm X (1965) and Dr. Martin Luther King Jr. (1968) also are not what the official versions would have us believe. When Malcolm X was gunned down in New York's Audubon Ballroom, it looked then like a clear case of a power struggle within the Black Muslims. The men convicted of the killing were all fanatic followers of Elijah Muhammad, from whom Malcolm had split away. We didn't know at the time about COINTELPRO and other secret FBI programs actively disrupting civil rights organizations. J. Edgar Hoover's FBI, it turns out, was extremely worried about an alliance between Malcolm and Martin. The night before his assassination, one of Malcolm's murderers is said to have met with an FBI undercover agent. And the CIA was heavily involved with shadowing Malcolm's every move.

In the case of Dr. King, his own family has said that they don't believe James Earl Ray committed the crime. The Kings, in fact, brought a wrongful death lawsuit that resulted in a jury returning a verdict in 1999 that governmental agencies were parties to a conspiracy! If you didn't hear about that, it's because nobody from the big media covered the proceedings. And O.J. Simpson's was the "trial of the century," with blow-by-blow TV coverage? Here our government declares a national holiday on Dr. King's birthday, at the same time it's still publicly proclaiming that he was killed by a lone racist! Maybe that's because we're really talking culpability by the police, military, FBI, and organized crime.

Robert Kennedy was assassinated two months after Dr. King, right after winning the California primary on the way to the Democratic nomination. Sirhan Bishara Sirhan, in front of many witnesses in the pantry of LA's Ambassador Hotel, fired a number of times at the senator and appeared to be the sole assassin. Well, turns out that Sirhan's gun held eight bullets but new audio testing on the only known recording of the shots indicates that there were at least ten fired. But if Sirhan *was* the assassin, to this day he doesn't have any memory of pulling the trigger. Even at his trial, lawyers wondered whether he'd been "programmed" through hypnosis or drugs or some combination. Was Sirhan part of MK-ULTRA, a grim CIA program to control human behavior where most of the records were destroyed in 1973? That's a question we'll look into later in this book.

Along comes Watergate, and ultimately the resignation of Richard Nixon. Assuredly a not-so-nice guy who obstructed justice and had his staff commit all manner of illegal acts, was dumb (or arrogant) enough to tape himself, and deserved to otherwise have been impeached and sent to prison if Gerald Ford hadn't pardoned him. But what if this outrageous chapter of our recent history has an even darker side? What if Nixon was set up? The tapes revealed his obsession with "the whole Bay of Pigs thing," which many experts believe was code for the Kennedy assassination. As president, he was demanding the CIA release to his White House all of its files on that period. Nixon was nothing if not self-protective, so he may have just wanted to know what dirt the spies had on *him*. Or maybe he wanted the goods on *them*. It's dog-eat-dog in his realm. This much I've figured out: a whole lot of the Watergate cast of characters tracks back to the JFK mystery, including some of the burglars who conducted the fateful break-in.

I know this next chapter might seem "on the fringe," but we've been sold at least a partial bill of goods on the infamous Jonestown "cult suicides" in 1978 where 900-some followers of Jim Jones met their demise in Guyana. The chief medical examiner in Guyana actually concluded that more than 700 of the victims had been *murdered*. Before he founded his People's Temple, Jones had some very suspicious ties to the CIA, as well as doing some informing for the FBI. Ever hear about the Jonestown survivors filing a $63 million lawsuit in October 1981? They were alleging that the State Department and CIA conspired to "enhance the economic and political powers of James Warren Jones," conducting "mind control and drug experimentation." Hold the Kool-Aid and read on!

What I regard as the first of *three* stolen presidential elections in our recent history happened in 1980. That's when Ronald Reagan's people made a secret deal with Iran to delay the release of those 52 American hostages being held over there. This is known as the "October surprise," because that's what the Republicans were afraid President Carter might pull off—free the hostages and win a second term. Instead, George H.W. Bush and about-to-be CIA director William Casey, among others, arranged to supply Iran with weapons and unblock their assets in U.S. banks. In exchange, the hostages got to stay a little longer under house arrest. Doesn't the timing of their release—twenty minutes after Reagan finished his Inaugural Address—kinda make you wonder? It sure did me, even at the time.

Next we'll take a look at our government "on drugs." At the same time Nancy Reagan was telling our kids to "just say no," America's backing of the Nicaraguan Contra movement was being funded mainly by cocaine traffickers and money-launderers. A report by the CIA's own Inspector General finally confirmed this in 1998, and showed that the operation tracked straight into Oliver North's office in Reagan's National Security Council—though, once again, the major media pretty much ignored the story. Of course, the drug trade had been part and parcel of our involvement in the Vietnam War, just as it is today in Afghanistan. The CIA's secret missions are all financed with drug money, because then they don't have to account for it. It's time to end this corruption once and for all, starting with legalization of marijuana!

You can't talk politics since the millennium without delving into the conspiracies that resulted in George W. Bush stealing two elections. We all know the Supreme Court handed him the presidency in 2000, by stopping the recount in Florida. All but forgotten, though, are the illegal actions taken before the election by brother Jeb (then Florida's governor) and Secretary of State Katherine Harris that deprived thousands of citizens of their right to vote. Not to mention the touch-screen voting machines, controlled by Republican bigwigs, that suddenly switched votes from Al Gore to Bush.

These machines perpetrated more widespread fraud in 2004. The exit polls and early vote counts showed John Kerry the clear winner in Ohio, until everything shifted around in the middle of the night. That's when a computer expert named Michael Connell, a crony of Karl Rove's, transmitted the vote count to private, partisan computer servers down in Chattanooga, Tennessee. Connell can't tell us about it, though. He was killed in the crash of his private plane soon after the 2008 election, when he was on the verge of blowing the whistle. Many suspect foul play—surprise!

If the Bush-Cheney crowd could thieve elections and bump off potential tattlers, what about September 11? I never wanted to believe anything different than we were told about what happened on that terrible day. Even though, having been in the military, I wondered right away—where were our jets to intercept the four hijacked planes? How could our air defenses have failed so badly? Since then, I've done considerable research into the events surrounding 9/11. In 2008 I spent weeks on the road, where my investigative team and I conducted interviews with witnesses for the pilot episode I'd contracted to do of a new series for truTV. And I've come to a frightening conclusion. Either the Bush Administration had advance knowledge and let the attack happen, in order to justify their future agenda including going to war against Iraq, or they orchestrated the terrorist plot themselves. I know that sounds radical, if not treasonous—but there's a whole "truth movement" out there that thinks the same thing, and is demanding answers. The 9/11 Commission, it's now abundantly clear, was involved in the same massive cover-up as the Warren Commission. Toward the end of this book, I'm going to tell you what I learned firsthand, and what I've determined to be the strongest evidence of a 9/11 conspiracy.

Now, thanks to those same Bush people, our economy has gone into a free fall and we're in the biggest crisis of that sort since the Great Depression. Is it a stretch to include how this came about in a book on conspiracies? I don't think so. Something definitely smells about how Bush Treasury secretary Henry Paulson ended up making Goldman Sachs—the company he served as CEO until 2006—the dominant player among investment bankers through the bailout. Then there's the role of the New York Fed under Timothy Geithner (now Obama's treasury secretary) when it came to loaning AIG billions to pay back certain "special" creditors. The company deemed "too big to fail" is, if truth be known, rotten to the core—and with longstanding ties to the CIA.

The simple fact is, for 20 years Wall Street was run by shady dealers who pushed the laws to their limits and then flouted them openly until they became blurred beyond any possibility of enforcement. The Securities and Exchange Commission, the government agency set up to regulate our capital markets, ended up totally captured by the financial elites. And the Federal Reserve that's supposed to safeguard our currency? Nothing but accomplices in the biggest swindle of all time! This is, to my thinking, about as big a conspiracy as you can imagine—and one with deep historical roots that need to be dug up and exposed.

We've got a Clean Air Act, how about a Clear-the-Air Act that gives us a fighting chance to restore the republic and the ideals we once stood for? In the concluding chapter of this book, I want to talk about my biggest fear—that certain people may be just waiting in the wings for enough disgruntled hungry citizens to rise up, so the real crackdown can begin. I'm sure that's not what President Obama *wants* to do, and I hope he's able to set us back on course, but the legal groundwork was laid under Bush for a whole new ball game. In fact, ten months before 9/11, Donald Rumsfeld approved an updated version of the army's so-called Continuity of Government plan—with ways and means to suspend the Constitution in the event of civil unrest. Secret memos drafted by Bush's team would allow a president to send the military to wage war against American citizens; to drag people from their homes and, without trial, hold them at some Guantánamo-type facility indefinitely. Basically, to kiss the Bill of Rights goodbye.

So brace yourselves, folks. Even with a change of administration for the better, we're not out of the woods. Like the poet Robert Frost once wrote, "The woods are dreary, dark and deep." And we'd better be prepared for a rough ride through the wilderness that's been closing in around us. That's why I'm putting together this book. We need to understand where we've been—and it's not a pretty picture—in order to know where we need to go.

When some people refer to me as a conspiracy theorist, I respond laughingly and say, "Well, the government is, too." For the most part, they've never proven any of their "theories." Right now I'm a skeptic about anything I read officially from the government. They don't tell the whole truth. They often seem to have an entirely different agenda. That's disheartening, to realize that what you read in the newspapers and the history books may not be accurate. I think the other side of the story needs to be published somewhere. And whether or not people believe it, at least it should be out there.

So let's begin with the hour of America's first great crisis, the Civil War, and what we need to remember about the assassination of our greatest president, Abraham Lincoln.

CHAPTER ONE

THE FIRST NOT-ALONE-NUT: JOHN WILKES BOOTH

THE INCIDENT: The assassination of President Abraham Lincoln at Ford's Theatre, in Washington, on April 14, 1865.

THE OFFICIAL WORD: The president was shot in the back of the head at point-blank range, by a prominent actor named John Wilkes Booth, who escaped on horseback and was later killed by a soldier while hiding in a barn. Eight coconspirators were also caught and found guilty by a military court.

MY TAKE: The plot is likely to have gone well beyond those who were rounded up, but except for Booth we don't hear much about *any* others in our history books. Besides leaders of the Confederacy, the conspiracy to kill Lincoln probably included people within his own cabinet.

"The dogmas of the quiet past are inadequate to the stormy present. The occasion is piled high with difficulty, and we must rise with the occasion. As our case is new, so we must think anew, and act anew. We must disenthrall ourselves, and then we shall save our country."
—Abraham Lincoln's Second Annual Message to Congress,
December 1, 1862

I had the occasion very recently to be sitting with my nephews, who are of later junior high or first-year high school age. They're here in Minnesota, part of the same public school system that I was. I wanted to get a sense of whether they're still learning the same things in the history books today.

So I asked them what they knew about the assassination of Abraham Lincoln. It was funny because one nephew immediately said, "Oh, we just got done with that," so it was fresh in his mind.

He basically related the same story I'd studied back in the 1950s. This actor named John Wilkes Booth came up behind President Lincoln in the theater, shot him in the back of the head, yelled something as he leapt down onto the stage, fell, and broke his leg. He then snuck away and they tracked him down later and set the barn on fire where he was hiding, then shot and killed him. That was the extent of it.

Well, after doing the research for this book, I knew differently. It's not even a theory. There were eight people tried and convicted by a jury and punished. Four of them were hung, and the other four sent to prison. All coconspirators of John Wilkes Booth. Why did my nephews not know a thing about that? Why is that eliminated from what's being taught, along with the fact that the plotters had also targeted the vice president and secretary of state on the same night that Lincoln was killed. Here was a classic case of a conspiracy going through the court system, yet my nephews today—just as I was earlier—are led to believe that Booth was a lone assassin who had no cohorts. It was just the action of a lone nut.

Our history textbooks and our schools are averse to telling the whole story. In the back of my mind, this raises the issue: is the Lincoln assassination a setup to where that becomes the norm for our way of thinking? That the only people who ever gun down our leaders are upset over a particular issue that compels them to kill? In this case, of course, Booth was a Southern sympathizer, angered about losing the Civil War. Later, Lee Harvey Oswald would be a die-hard Communist, James Earl Ray a jailbird racist, and Sirhan Bishara Sirhan a fanatic Palestinian. This becomes the pattern. I see the simplification as part of the dumbing-down of our people.

So what follows in this chapter is what my nephews *ought* to have been informed about. First, how far-reaching the Lincoln conspiracy really was remains unknown to this day. For sure, some of the evidence links the plotters to the Confederate leadership. But it also looks like Booth had advance information about Lincoln's movements from someone inside the president's cabinet. And Dr. Samuel Mudd, at whose house Booth took refuge afterwards, wasn't some kindly country doctor carrying out his Hippocratic Oath by setting the broken leg of a stranger. He'd been in the conspiracy up to his neck.

Unlike the assassins a century later, Booth was well-known around the country. He was an American matinee idol who made the then-princely sum of about $20,000 a year at the peak of his theater career. Lincoln even saw him once in a play at Ford's Theatre called *The Marble Heart*, and was so impressed he asked to meet Booth backstage. Booth declined.[1] Maybe he already had something else in mind.

As Lincoln once put it, "There are a thousand ways to getting at a man if it is desired that he should be killed." As early as when he took the train to Washington for his inauguration, a paramilitary group was prepared to kill him when his train stopped in Baltimore. The plan was discovered and Lincoln warned ahead of time, so he was already tucked away in a hotel in Washington. But he still resisted the idea of having bodyguards.[2]

The next plot we know about involved biological warfare. That's right, it's not a new idea. A group in Canada—which was a haven for Confederate spies—had the notion to spread clothing infected with yellow fever into certain Northern population centers. Lincoln was to receive a poisoned expensive dress shirt from an anonymous admirer. The whole scheme was pretty hare-brained and never got off the ground, but the Confederate leadership apparently knew about it and didn't bat an eye before it fell apart.[3]

Things got serious after some papers were found on the body of a Colonel Dahlgren, who was killed on a raid while trying to free some Union prisoners. The papers said that, once the Union made it into the Confederate capital, Richmond, "it must be destroyed and Jeff Davis and cabinet killed."[4] Of course, this could have been a made-up excuse. But Jefferson Davis is said to have had his agents prowling around the White House area by September 1864, monitoring Lincoln's movements. They were looking to kidnap the president and hold him hostage.

Booth hooked up with the conspirators somewhere around this time, after he joined a rebel spy network called Knights of the Golden Circle.[5] His first scheme was to abduct Lincoln from the presidential box at Ford's Theater, but the president didn't show up that night. Then, when Booth found out about Lincoln planning to visit some convalescing soldiers at a hospital on a sparsely traveled road, they decided to try to nab him from his carriage. Again, Lincoln changed his plans at the last minute. Instead—talk about ironies!—he went to give a speech at a ceremony held in the same hotel where Booth was living![6]

As late as the end of March 1865, Booth still had a kidnap operation in mind. In one of the books I read about the assassination, it was speculated that "the fall of Richmond and Lee's surrender may well have caused Booth to conclude that capturing Lincoln no longer had a strategic purpose."[7] Then there was another plot that didn't involve Booth—to blow up the White House during a meeting of the cabinet.

On the night of April 14, Booth met with three of his coconspirators around eight o'clock. This was the first any of them knew about something other than a kidnapping. George Atzerodt was to kill Vice President Andrew Johnson; Lewis Powell, accompanied by David Herold, was to take out Secretary of State William Seward at his home. They were all to make their escape from the Capitol on horseback into Confederate territory. [8]

The story goes that, before he went into the theater, Booth went to bolster his courage in a nearby bar, where a drunken customer told him: "You'll never be the actor your father was."[9] To which Booth replied: "When I leave the stage, I will be the most famous man in America."

Now here's the strange part. For Booth to fulfill his mission, "it required information that could only have come from the highest sources in Washington."[10] In the first place, Lincoln's attending a play that night hadn't been publicly announced. Carrying a single-shot derringer pistol and a knife, Booth had to walk through a crowded theater and then pass through two doors into the State Box. How could Booth have known that Lincoln had a substitute bodyguard that night who wouldn't be at his post at the fateful moment? Booth then stood behind the president without being seen by three other occupants, fired his one bullet, jumped onto the stage and shouted a message to the audience—"*Sic Semper Tyrannis!*" (As Always with Tyrants)—and escaped through a rear exit onto his waiting horse. "More than blind luck" had to be involved in "these skillfully timed movements and activities."[11]

At least this was the way that historian figured it. But, with Lincoln himself being so averse to bodyguards and protecting himself, he certainly wasn't surrounded by the security we have today. He didn't want it, and seemed resigned to the fact that if someone was going to kill him, they could. So to me, how hard could it have been to pull off, if you were a determined group of people?

At that same time on the other side of Washington, Lewis Powell broke into Secretary Seward's house and left him and four others bleeding from their wounds. David Herold took off before the mayhem ended. George Atzerodt got cold feet and never even tried to kill Vice President Johnson. (This has led some to believe, without any justification, that Johnson was involved in the conspiracy.) Booth and Herold then found refuge at a Maryland tavern run by Mary Surratt, who as an accomplice later became the first woman ever executed by the federal government. Her son, John Surratt, had also been part of the kidnapping plot.

Which brings us to the story of Dr. Mudd. In recent times, President Carter and President Reagan came under some pressure from Mudd's descendants and both all but declared Mudd innocent of any complicity.[12] Sorry, gang, but your ancestor got off easy. Remember, Booth had a broken leg from the moment he landed on the stage. He bypassed three other doctors along his escape route, to make straight for Mudd's house. Later the doctor claimed he'd never seen Booth before, and so was innocently providing medical care to an injured stranger who needed help. But I highly doubt Mudd was caught completely unaware when Booth rode up to his house. At the least, he certainly had knowledge of what was happening.

The truth that came out later was this: Mudd had introduced Booth to John Surratt the previous December of 1864. In fact, Mudd was "responsible for two key figures being added to Booth's team of conspirators."[13] Booth had earlier been a guest at the doctor's home. For the kidnap plot, Atzerodt claimed, Booth "sent provisions and liquor to Dr. Mudd's for the supply of the party on their way to Richmond with the president."[14] Even if Booth hadn't stopped off at Mudd's, there was plenty of evidence to have hauled in the physician as one of his cohorts in the Confederate underground.

After hiding Booth out, Mudd then bought him two full days head start by withholding information from the Union soldiers who were tracking Lincoln's killer. But Mudd and his wife couldn't get their stories straight, and ten days after the assassination, he was taken into custody. At the conspirators' trial, five witnesses (including the doctor's own wife) testified that Mudd had admitted knowing Booth's identity. Mudd escaped the gallows by a single juror's no vote.

After an epidemic of yellow fever struck the Florida Keys prison where he was sent, Mudd jumped in to provide medical service and ended up receiving high praise for his efforts. Andrew Johnson, during his last months as president, then gave Mudd an unconditional pardon in 1869. Mudd went home to his wife and four children, had five more kids and even tried to get elected to the state legislature, before he died from pneumonia just shy of his fiftieth birthday.[15]

Twelve days after the assassination, Booth and Herold were finally tracked down to the Virginia farmhouse of Richard Garrett. Herold came out of the burning barn and was tied to a tree. Supposedly Booth refused to come out and was shot in the neck by Sergeant Boston Corbett with a single bullet from a Colt revolver. Corbett, an eccentric religious fanatic, had violated orders to stay thirty feet away and make sure Booth was captured alive. At the time, Corbett was quoted as explaining: "It was not through fear at all that I shot him, but because it was my impression that it was time the man was shot; for I thought he would do harm to our men in trying to fight his way through . . . if I did not."[16]

Some, however, think Booth shot himself, and there was even a story that aired on NBC's *Unsolved Mysteries* that he'd actually gotten away! Here's how that one got started: Booth had been quietly buried under a dirt floor in an old penitentiary, and the secretive nature of his burial raised questions almost from the get-go. One of the Union soldiers who claimed to have been at the Garrett farm said it was somebody else's body.[17] Then in 1907, a Tennessee lawyer named Finian Bates wrote a book claiming that Booth safely made his way south, changed his name, and ended up in Oklahoma. The book sold an amazing 75,000 copies, and the lawyer had "Booth's body" mummified and took it on the road to exhibit to thousands![18] As late as 1994, some historians tried to have the "original" Booth exhumed for DNA tests, but that got rejected. The fact is, of nineteen people who viewed the body afterwards, all but one were in agreement it was Booth. You couldn't fake the letters "J.W.B." that had been scrawled in India ink on the back of his hand since he was a boy.

Besides that, there was a telltale scar, a plugged tooth, and that broken left leg with the old shoe.[19]

Which doesn't solve whether Booth was intentionally silenced before he could stand trial—and possibly implicate some higher-ups beyond the Confederate fanatics. Back in 1937, an amateur historian named Otto Eisenschiml published *Why Was Lincoln Murdered?*, maintaining that Secretary of War Edwin Stanton was involved in Lincoln's death. In more recent years, *The Lincoln Conspiracy* (1977) put forth a similar scenario.

For sure, Stanton hadn't started off as a big fan of Lincoln's. A year after the election, he'd spoken of "the painful imbecility" of the president. It's contended by a majority of historians that his contempt had eventually given way to respect and that Stanton became staunchly loyal and was always urging Lincoln to accept bodyguards. So, while a lot of the charges against Stanton don't seem to have a legitimate basis, from my reading it seems that some of them are worth considering.

First of all, to me, the planning of an assassination isn't going to be carried out by common everyday citizens who are unhappy with the rule of their country and take it upon themselves to change it. When you look at who killed Caesar, it was the Roman senators. If there is a conspiracy involved, it's going to include the highest levels. You always need to ask the question, who profits the most? I wouldn't rule out the Confederates, because you could understand the motive of revenge. Certainly the list of whom they'd most like to see die would be the people who directly led to their losing the war. But I tend to think there would also be some kind of help from the Union side. They can have ulterior motives, because politics is the name of the game. When you look at the two political parties today, they can be very cutthroat within their own ranks. Why would you expect anything different back then?

During the Civil War, Stanton was the second most important official in Washington—but somehow he wasn't included on Booth's target list. After the assassination, he not only made himself acting president but took charge of the investigation right away. "While others sat sobbing, he ordered a furious dragnet in which civil liberties were ignored and dozens of people were falsely arrested—none of whom had in any way aided the assassin."[20] In the wake of what had happened, that's not too surprising. What does raise my eyebrows is that, only a few hours after the assassination, seven names on Stanton's to-capture list were part of the earlier kidnap plots. Which leads you to conclude that the War Department must have had prior knowledge, at least about those.[21] And if they did, how come nobody had been arrested already?

Then there's the matter of Booth's diary. Yup, Oswald and Sirhan weren't the first assassins to set down their thoughts ahead of the deed. Booth's little red book was supposedly removed from his body after he was shot. The diary was taken to Washington and ended up in Stanton's custody, at which point it disappeared for a while. When it was located in time for the conspirators' trial that summer, Lafayette Baker—the fellow who gave the diary, intact, to Stanton—said somebody had removed eighteen pages. Others who'd seen the diary testified that the pages had already gone missing when Stanton received it. But those were all underlings of Stanton's at the War Department.

With Nixon, we'd have the infamous eighteen-minute gap in the White House tapes that his secretary Rosemary Woods, "accidentally" erased. In the same vein, who could have "erased" those eighteen diary pages of Booth's? One story that surfaced about this came from a congressman, George W. Julian, who said that when he got summoned to the War Department ten days after the assassination, he discovered Stanton pacing back and forth and saying, "We have Booth's diary, and he has recorded a lot in it." Julian claimed that Senator John Conness from California showed up and, as he was checking out the diary, started mumbling: "Oh my God, oh my God, I am ruined if this ever gets out!" Then, according to the congressman, Stanton issued instructions to put the diary in his safe.[22]

What's interesting is, Senator Conness was one of the so-called Radical Republicans, who wanted a much tougher Reconstruction policy toward the South than Lincoln was willing to go for. It was alleged that an envelope linking Conness to George Atzerodt, one of the conspirators, had been found in Atzerodt's room, but Stanton didn't choose to follow that up.[23] When Stanton died on Christmas Eve, 1869, it's pretty likely that a lot of secrets went with him.

This much we know for certain: Eight Lincoln conspirators were found guilty before a military court on June 30, 1865, and four of them were hanged—Powell, Herold, Atzerodt, and Mary Surratt. She was the least directly involved of any of them, but she owned the boardinghouse and tavern where the conspirators gathered—and she knew enough to have alerted the authorities about what was up. Her son, John Surratt, was a different story. He'd been deeply involved with Booth in the kidnapping plot. At first Stanton offered a $25,000 reward for Surratt's capture but, after his mother's hanging, seems to have lost interest. Surratt got to Europe before the Vatican corralled him, but he escaped. Eventually he did get caught and came back to be tried in a civil court. But the government didn't have the evidence to convict him on a murder charge.

So where did Surratt end up? As a respected tobacco farmer in Maryland who earned extra money giving lectures and married the second cousin of Francis Scott Key, who wrote "The Star Spangled Banner." Surratt lived to the merry old age of 74, when he died of pneumonia in 1916. He is said to have burned the manuscript of his autobiography a few days before that.[24]

One of the recent books has Booth portrayed as a rebel agent who, after Richmond fell, turned his thoughts from kidnapping to killing. A Confederate plot that went at least as high as their secretary of state, Judah Benjamin (who burned all his papers before he escaped to England and never returned), is today the most accepted of all the conspiratorial possibilities.[25] The "lost confession" of Atzerodt, talking about Booth's knowledge of a Confederate plan to blow up the White House, was discovered in 1977 and bolsters that theory.[26] Still, I wonder if it's a little too pat—kind of like the idea today that Castro had Kennedy assassinated in retaliation for the plots against him.

There are some other "out-there" theories, like Booth being a hired gun of big international bankers such as the Rothschilds, who didn't like the president's monetary policies. Or that the Vatican did it, because the totalitarian Popes considered Lincoln their enemy. If that piques your interest, you can try to find *Democracy Under Siege: The Jesuits' Attempt to Destroy the Popular Government of the United States: The True Story of Abraham Lincoln's Death.*[27] (I didn't look into that one.)

Even if Booth's was the only smoking gun, we can safely say that the first presidential assassination in American history involved much more than first meets the eye. Almost a century and a half later, historians are still uncovering new evidence about the plot. Clearly, with the conviction of eight other coconspirators, who knows how far it went? That was just where the buck happened to stop.

Just like it did a hundred years later with Lee Harvey Oswald.

WHAT SHOULD WE DO NOW?

Let's start by getting some honesty into our school textbooks about the conspiracy that resulted in the assassination of our greatest president. Our kids should know that groups can and have engaged in plots to pursue their own nefarious ends and undermine our democracy.

CHAPTER TWO

THE BIG-MONEY PLOT TO OVERTHROW FDR

THE INCIDENT: A coup attempt by some of the titans of Wall Street, to overthrow Franklin D. Roosevelt in 1934 and put a military man in charge of the country.

THE OFFICIAL WORD: The plotters were foiled when the man they selected, Major General Smedley Butler, blew the whistle to Congress.

MY TAKE: This was an attempt to turn America into a fascist country run by corporate powers, but it's been ignored in most official histories of the Great Depression.

"The liberty of a democracy is not safe if the people tolerate the growth of private power to a point where it becomes stronger than their democratic State itself. That, in its essence, is Fascism—ownership of government by an individual, by a group or by any controlling private power."

— Franklin D. Roosevelt

I would think that a coup to overthrow our government and turn us into a fascist state ought to make it into our history books. That way, we could read about it and hopefully learn from it, so that we don't live to repeat it. But this certainly wasn't taught in any public school curriculum that I saw. You learned about Franklin D. Roosevelt and the New Deal. Never did I hear about leaders of business during that era literally setting out to have a coup! I don't consider myself dumb or not well-read, but researching this book is the first I've come across this story. That was when I found a book originally published in the Seventies called *The Plot to Seize the White House*,[1] by an investigative journalist named Jules Archer. Yet back in the 1930s, the plot had been fully documented in congressional hearings, although in the end they decided not to name certain names. It was also documented by some of the big media, even though they downplayed the whole thing.

I find it interesting that we do learn about some traitors in American history—Benedict Arnold and Aaron Burr come to mind—but, once again, they're more of the "lone nut" variety. Rich and powerful titans of finance wouldn't stoop to such a thing, right? Well, if it hadn't been that they tried buying off the wrong man to be their puppet, quite possibly we'd have been living in a country not that far removed from Hitler's Germany or Mussolini's Italy. That man was Major General Smedley Darlington Butler, one of the great unsung heroes in our history—but he's not exactly a household name, is he?

A little background first: FDR, after getting elected in 1932 in the midst of the Great Depression, started implementing his New Deal. He took on the stock speculators and set up new watchdog agencies. He put a stop to farm foreclosures, and made employers accept collective bargaining by the unions. And he took the country off the gold standard, meaning that more paper money could be available to create jobs for the unemployed and provide loans. That outraged some of the conservative financiers. FDR went even further and started talking about raising their taxes to help pay for these programs. So the oligarchs of finance hated him and everything he stood for on behalf of the common man. They considered the new president a traitor to his own class, namely them. Within a year of FDR's taking office, they'd started hatching a plan to get rid of him.

The plotters' idea was to enlist a military man who was popular with veterans from the First World War. Many veterans were disgruntled because they'd never been paid the bonuses promised them when the war ended. When their "Bonus Army" protested by camping out in Washington in 1932, Smedley Butler had shown up to support their cause. He was the most decorated Marine in American history. And when another general, Douglas MacArthur, led a charge to destroy the veterans' tent city under orders from President Hoover, Butler got so pissed off that he switched parties and voted for FDR in the election that year.

But maybe the coup-makers didn't know that when they decided Butler was the man to lead their takeover of the government. Or maybe they figured that, with enough money and the temptation of running the country, anybody was corruptible. The idea was to create havoc by Major General Butler leading a veterans' march on Washington. Pressured by these events, FDR, so they thought, would be convinced to name Butler to a new cabinet post as a Secretary of "General Affairs" or "General Welfare" (Homeland Security would have to wait awhile longer). Eventually, the president would agree to turn over the reins of power to Butler altogether, under the excuse that his polio was worsening, and would become a ceremonial figurehead.

The whole notion seems pretty far-fetched today, especially given what we know about the integrity of Roosevelt through the Depression and World War II. Apparently though, the Wall Street group thought they could pull it off. But they sure didn't do enough homework on the military man they thought would play along, Smedley Butler. He'd grown up in a politically prominent Quaker family in Pennsylvania, and gotten his baptism-under-fire with the Marines at Guantánamo during the Spanish-American War. During his distinguished service, he would come under fire more than 120 times and receive 18 decorations, including three Medals of Honor.

As a good soldier, Butler followed orders. The Taft Administration asked him to help rig elections in Nicaragua, which he later admitted doing. In what was then called "dollar diplomacy," Butler also helped American business interests maintain their hold on other Latin American countries. If that's all they knew about Butler, it's understandable that the conspirators against FDR might figure he'd play along.

But he'd given a speech to an American Legion convention, the year before FDR was elected, that clearly showed he'd had a change of heart. When the Legion first formed in the 1920s, most veterans had no clue that big corporations were backing it to use later in breaking strikes. It turned out that one of the Legion's main founders was Grayson Murphy, who ran one of Wall Street's big brokerage firms along with being director of a Morgan bank, Guaranty Trust. His name would soon surface as one of the financiers who wanted to remove FDR from power.

In his speech, Butler decided to give the Legion veterans some insight into how things worked.

"I spent 33 years being a high-class muscle man for Big Business, for Wall Street and the bankers," Butler said. "In short, I was a racketeer for capitalism. I helped purify Nicaragua for the international banking house of Brown Brothers in 1909–1912. I helped make Mexico and especially Tampico safe for American oil interests in 1916. I brought light to the Dominican Republic for American sugar interests in 1916. I helped make Haiti and Cuba a decent place for the National City [Bank] boys to collect revenue in. I helped in the rape of half a dozen Central American republics for the benefit of Wall Street.

"In China in 1927 I helped see to it that Standard Oil went its way unmolested. I had a swell racket. I was rewarded with honors, medals, promotions. . . . I might have given Al Capone a few hints. The best he could do was to operate a racket in three cities. The Marines operated on three continents."

In another talk, Butler told veterans that war was "largely a matter of money. Bankers lend money to foreign countries and when they cannot repay, the President sends Marines to get it. I know—I've been in eleven of these expeditions." Butler also told the vets not to believe "the propaganda [that] capital circulates" in the controlled press. In 1932, the year after he gave that speech, at the age of fifty, Butler retired to civilian life. He handed out maps to his house to Marines who'd served under him, in case they ever needed anything.

Butler speculated privately that the unsuccessful assassination attempt on Roosevelt a few weeks before his inauguration might have been orchestrated by a big-business cabal. Now members of that same elite circle decided that Butler, not MacArthur, was the military man best able to lead their coup attempt. One day, they had a bond salesman named Gerry MacGuire approach him. Butler quickly smelled a rat, but decided to play along until he could figure out what was really going on. Over the course of some months, Maguire courted him. His employer turned out to be Legion sponsor and financier Grayson Murphy.

There were some important people, MacGuire told Butler, who wanted to establish a new organization in the U.S. They had money, lots of it, $3 million in working capital and as much as $300 million that could be tapped into. Butler realized the truth of this when some captains of industry came together and announced formation of a new American Liberty League in September 1934. The organization said its goals were "to combat radicalism, to teach the necessity of respect for the rights of persons and property, and generally to foster free private enterprise." Backers included Rockefellers, Mellons, and Pews. Also two unsuccessful Democratic presidential candidates, John W. Davis (an attorney for the Morgan banking interests) and Al Smith (a business associate of the DuPonts). At first Butler couldn't believe even Smith could be involved, until he suddenly published a scathing attack on the New Deal.[2] (I guess you could say not a whole lot has changed with our two-party system.)

Butler had once served with a fellow named Robert S. Clark, an heir to the Singer Sewing Machine fortune and a wealthy banker. He now paid a visit and put forward more of the plan to Butler, who remembered Clark saying: "You know, the President is weak. . . . He was raised in this class, and he will come back. . . . But we have got to be prepared to sustain him when he does." So Butler was their choice to lead the takeover.

I view Smedley Butler as someone who'd read the Constitution and followed the law. He didn't have to be in FDR's camp to realize that what he was being asked to do was wrong. FDR was the commander-in-chief of the country, and we have a system for how we exchange our leaders. That system is the vote and the election.

Butler brought a reporter friend in on the conspiracy, so it wouldn't be just his word against the plotters. They worked together on gathering more background. Around Thanksgiving in 1934, the McCormack-Dickstein Committee of the House of Representatives took Butler's testimony behind closed doors. The next day, the *New York Times* ran a two-column headline on the front page: "Gen. Butler Bares 'Fascist Plot' To Seize Government by Force.'" Butler was struck by how the paper played it. The gist of his charges was buried deep inside, while most of the article consisted of denials and outright ridicule from some of the prominent people he'd implicated. *Time* magazine followed up with a front-page piece headlined "Plot Without Plotters." It caricatured Butler riding a white horse while asking veterans to follow him. "No military officer of the United States since the late tempestuous George Custer has succeeded in publicly floundering in so much hot water as Smedley

Darlington Butler," the article said snidely. (Are we surprised that FDR started his "Fireside Chats" so he could go straight to the people, and over the heads of media barons like Luce and Hearst?)

The House committee went ahead and commenced a two-month-long investigation. It verified an $18,000 bribe offer to Butler, and came up with a number of other facts to verify his story. The VFW Commander, James Van Zandt, revealed that he had *also* been approached by "agents of Wall Street" to lead a Fascist dictatorship. Even *Time*, which twelve weeks before had made fun of the plot idea, came out with a small-print "footnote" that the committee was "convinced . . . that General Butler's story of a Fascist march on Washington was alarmingly true."

After that, though, the committee's investigation came to a sudden stop. They never called any of the big financiers for questioning. In fact, when the transcript of the committee's interview with Butler appeared, all the names he'd named were deleted. Some said that the names were omitted at the request of a member of FDR's cabinet, who didn't want to embarrass the two former Democratic presidential candidates that Butler identified. FDR never made any comment on the plot, so we can't know what he might have said behind closed doors. Maybe he figured, now that this was public knowledge, he didn't need to pursue it further. Maybe he dismissed the plan as a preposterous idea. For whatever reason, the Justice Department avoided any steps toward fuller investigation. That caused Roger Baldwin of the ACLU to issue an angry statement: "Not a single participant will be prosecuted under the perfectly plain language of the federal conspiracy act making this a high crime." (Does this remind anyone of the current administration not wanting to prosecute the Bush people for their involvement in torture?)

When Jules Archer interviewed John McCormack in 1971, the former House Speaker claimed he couldn't remember why his committee had stayed away from implicating the bankers and corporate presidents. McCormack did say: "If the plotters had got rid of Roosevelt, there's no telling what might have taken place. They wouldn't have told the people what they were doing, of course. They were going to make it all sound constitutional, of course, with a high-sounding name for the dictator and a plan to make it all sound like a good American program. A well-organized minority can always outmaneuver an unorganized majority, as Adolf

Hitler did. . . . The people were in a very confused state of mind, making the nation weak and ripe for some drastic kind of extremist reaction. Mass frustration could bring about anything."

Even though this happened more than 75 years ago, it's worth paying attention to where the plot came from—and how its would-be perpetrators haven't necessarily gone away but only taken on different faces. Let me start to explain that by telling you about a book called *Tragedy and Hope: A History of the World in Our Time*. It was written by a Georgetown University professor named Carroll Quigley, a well-connected academic who had many friends and associates among the "elite" class. One of his students was Bill Clinton. In *Tragedy and Hope*, Quigley wrote:

"There does exist, and has existed for a generation, an international Anglophile network which operates, to some extent, in the way the radical Right believes the Communists act. In fact, this network, which we may identify as the Round Table Groups, has no aversion to cooperating with the Communists, or any other groups, and frequently does so. I know of the operations of this network because I have studied it for twenty years and was permitted for two years, in the early 1960s, to examine its papers and secret records. I have no aversion to it or to most of its aims and have, for much of my life, been close to it and many of its instruments. . . . in general my chief difference of opinion is that it wishes to remain unknown, and I believe its role in history is significant enough to be known."[3]

Quigley says it all began with a wealthy Englishman named Cecil Rhodes, who'd worked with financiers like the Rothschilds to gain a monopoly over South Africa's diamonds and gold. "The Rhodes Scholarships, established by the terms of Cecil Rhodes' seventh will, are known to everyone. What is not so widely known is that Rhodes in five previous wills left his fortune to form a secret society, which was to devote itself to the preservation and expansion of the British Empire."[4]

Funding for "the widely ramified activities of this organization" later came from groups "associated with J.P. Morgan, the Rockefeller and Whitney families." In looking to expand after the First World War, front organizations were set up—the Royal Institute of International Affairs in London and, in New York, the Council on Foreign Relations (CFR), "a front for J.P. Morgan and Company in association with the very small American Round Table group."[5] The CFR in 1928, according to Quigley's list, had John W. Davis as its president—the very same fellow who, along with Morgan and others, established the American Liberty League that tried to use General Butler in the plot against FDR. Also among the CFR's leading lights was attorney Allen Dulles, future director of the CIA and member of the Warren Commission to investigate JFK's assassination. And "closely allied with this Morgan influence were a small group of Wall Street law firms" that included another future Warren Commission member, John McCloy. Same cast of characters, from FDR to JFK.

The goal of this cabal of global financiers, writes Quigley, was "nothing less than to create a world system of financial control in private hands able to dominate the political system of each country and the economy of the world as a whole. This system was to be controlled in a feudalist fashion by the central banks of the world acting in concert, by secret agreements arrived at in frequent private meetings and conferences. Each central bank... sought to dominate its government by its ability to control treasury loans, to manipulate foreign exchanges, to influence the level of economic activity in the country, and to influence cooperative politicians by subsequent economic rewards in the business world."[6]

Then there was this: "The American branch of this 'English Establishment' exerted much of its influence through five American newspapers (the *New York Times*, the *New York Herald Tribune*, the *Christian Science Monitor*, the *Washington Post*, and the lamented *Boston Evening Transcript*)."[7]

Quigley's book is back in print today, but when it first appeared in 1966, it didn't stay long on bookstore shelves. The professor came to believe it had been "suppressed," because "it apparently says something which powerful people do not want known."[8]

As I've expanded my study of conspiracies, I find that I'm often getting the same information from two separate sources. Let me insert here something about the Bilderbergs. For a TV series I'm doing on conspiracies, we interviewed a fellow named Daniel Estulin, an investigative journalist from Spain who's been researching the Bilderberg secret society for more than 17 years. It turns out that the wealthiest CEOs of the world have been coming together with the political elite from Europe and America since 1954, when they first met at the Bilderberg Hotel in a little Dutch town called Oosterbeek. The Bilderberg deep pockets reach back centuries, to royalty who still believe they're the entitled ones and the rest of us are merely cannon fodder. Banker David Rockefeller, at the 1991 Bilderberg meeting, is said to have argued for one world government "of an intellectual elite and world bankers."[9] But I was told that, within this group, David Rockefeller is a waiter. Meaning, at his level, he would bring the other members drinks as mid-level help. The others are much more powerful.

To get a sense of the continuity among the power brokers: In *Tragedy and Hope*, Quigley doesn't mention Prescott Bush—the first President Bush's father—or George Herbert Walker (President Bush's grandfather), but both of them were among the right-wing elite on Wall Street during FDR's day. In 2007, an American investigative journalist named John Buchanan found documents from the McCormack-Dickstein Committee in the National Archives. These directly linked Prescott Bush to the power brokers (Morgan, DuPont, Remington, and others) who were behind the plan to get rid of FDR. This got some play in the U.K., but not a word in the mainstream American press.[10]

But if you check out Kevin Phillips's book on the Bush family, *American Dynasty*, you can find some interesting cross-references. Dating back to the First World War, George Herbert Walker (Prescott's father-in-law) was involved with "a frequently collaborative group of moneymen— Averell Harriman, Percy Rockefeller at National City Bank, and others at Guaranty Trust—who had large international plans."[11] (Remember that one of the anti-FDR coup leaders had ties to Guaranty Trust). In 1919 National City Bank "joined in setting up the new W.A. Harriman and Company, soon to be under George Walker's presidency" and including Remington's Samuel Pryor as "part of this cabal."[12] Five years later, Harriman and Walker established the Union Banking Corporation (UBC) in New York "on behalf of the politically active German steel baron Fritz Thyssen"—a major funder of Hitler's Nazi Party.[13] Prescott Bush and a number of his Skull and Bones pals from Yale "came together under one roof through the Brown Brothers Harriman merger in 1931."[14]

Phillips doesn't bring the Smedley Butler story into his book, but he goes on to say: "Unfortunately, we have no reliable way of knowing exactly why, after 1933, men like Averell Harriman, George Walker, and Prescott Bush, the Dulles brothers, James Forrestal, Henry Ford, and several

Rockefellers maintained investment relationships with Hitler's Germany, in a few cases up to (and even after) Pearl Harbor."[15]

"By the late 1930s, Brown Brothers Harriman . . . and Dillon Read were two notable active investors in a Germany rapidly rearming under Adolf Hitler." Prescott Bush "handled much of the German work at Brown Brothers Harriman," working closely with Wall Street lawyers Allen and John Foster Dulles. Prescott was also a director of the UBC bank "that Brown Brothers Harriman ran for the German Thyssen steel family. . . . In 1941, the *New York Herald Tribune* had featured a front-page story headlined 'Hitler's Angel Has $3 Million in U.S. Bank'" that Thyssen was possibly holding for "Nazi bigwigs." In October 1942, the federal government then "seized the assets of the Union Banking Corporation" under the Trading with the Enemy Act.[16]

Prescott Bush went on to be a U.S. Senator from Connecticut; the Dulles brothers ran the CIA and the State Department under Eisenhower; Averell Harriman ended up governor of New York. "It is almost as if these various German embroilments, despite their potential for scandal, were regarded as unfortunate but in essence business as usual," Kevin Phillips writes.[17]

So maybe that's how the FDR plot was conceived, too—"business as usual," which the president's New Deal was obstructing. Smedley Butler did his best to issue the warning. Lecturing around the country as spokesman for the "forgotten veteran," the general accused the big industrialists of bloating themselves on the blood of the soldiers in the First World War. He pointed out that DuPont's profits had soared from only $6 million before the conflict, to $58 million in the course of it. Similar huge jumps were made by companies like Bethlehem Steel and International Nickel. Munitions, as the "war to end all wars" proved, was a mighty profitable enterprise.

Butler also asked a question, in his book *War Is a Racket*, that I've thought about a lot in terms of today: "How many of these war millionaires shouldered a rifle?" His idea was: "Let the officers and directors and the high-powered executives of our armament factories and our steel companies and our munitions makers and our ship-builders and our airplane builders . . . as well as the bankers and the speculators, be conscripted—to get $30 a month, the same wage as the lads in the trenches get."[18]

Do you think we'd have gone to war in Iraq if Dick Cheney and his Halliburton buddies were subject to Butler's idea? The "Fighting Quaker, as he was called, died in 1940, so he never lived to see America enter the war against Germany and Japan. Today we owe the man a great debt, as someone courageous enough to blow the whistle on the big-money forces out to undermine our democracy. Too bad there wasn't another Smedley Butler around when George W. Bush stole two presidential elections. That's a story we'll get to, in due course.

Getting back to the Bilderbergs and the scary notion: is this attempt to control the world real? I don't think it's necessarily a case of a dozen guys sitting around a table deciding our future. But I do think that these power brokers, bankers, money men of the world, have the power to *try* to control the direction we're going. Can they guarantee it? Never, because you've always got the human element, and they don't seem to want to rouse the ire of the masses. They're sneakier than that.

I found it interesting that, they same day that the Bilderberg expert, Daniel Estulin, was to meet with me in New York, our filming schedule got thrown off. I had to wait an extra day because he happened to be on the no-fly list. It took 24 hours for him to be cleared and come talk to me. I was trying to figure out why they would deem this guy a terrorist. I mean, he's a writer. Who would have the power to put him on that list? What are the qualifications? Like Shakespeare once put it, "Oh, what a tangled web we weave."

It makes me want to run to the Baja for six months and get away from it all. But by the time I'm ready to go, I'll probably be on the no-fly list, too! I'll keep you posted.

WHAT SHOULD WE DO NOW?

We need real heroes for our young people to emulate, individuals who weren't afraid to take a stand for the sake of our country. The story of Major General Smedley Butler needs to be as widely known as those of Washington and Lincoln. If this means making us think about the fact that wealthy people can sometimes be out for evil purposes, so be it. I'd rank Professor Quigley as a hero, too, for his willingness to expose the secret machinations of the rich and powerful. Again, let's revise our history textbooks!

CHAPTER THREE

THE KENNEDY ASSASSINATION: BIGGEST COVER-UP OF MY LIFETIME

THE INCIDENT: The assassination of President John F. Kennedy, riding in his limousine in Dallas, on November 22, 1963.

THE OFFICIAL WORD: Lee Harvey Oswald, an ex-Marine and Communist sympathizer, shot the president twice from behind, firing a rifle from the sixth-floor window of the Texas School Book Depository. He was captured later that day in a theater, and killed two days later by Jack Ruby.

MY TAKE: The cover-up of what really happened to JFK starts with the Warren Commission's "lone assassin" conclusion, and continues to this day with the help of the big media. A second gunman assassinated the president from the grassy knoll, while Oswald was set up as the fall guy. The perpetrators behind Oswald are tied into the CIA, the Pentagon, and the Mob, along with right-wing extremists who tried to make it look like Cuba was behind it. Oswald himself was part of an intelligence operation that involved a look-alike "double."

"In the councils of government, we must guard against the acquisition of unwarranted influence, whether sought or unsought, by the military-industrial complex. The potential for the disastrous rise of misplaced power exists and will persist. We must never let the weight of this combination endanger our liberties or democratic processes. We should take nothing for granted."

—Dwight D. Eisenhower in his Farewell Address as president, 1961

There are two official government reports on the assassination of President Kennedy, and they directly contradict each other. The first was, of course, the *Warren Commission Report*, which concluded that a disgruntled Marine-turned-Communist named Lee Harvey Oswald took out JFK on his own, using an old Italian-made rifle and connecting with two out of three shots in 6.3 seconds from a sixth-floor window. The second was a report fifteen years later by the House Select Committee on Assassinations, concluding that JFK was "probably" eliminated as part of a conspiracy.

Somehow, that one keeps slipping through the cracks. Maybe it's because the Justice Department never investigated it and came to a real conclusion. As it is, every time a new book comes out that supports the Warren Commission, the big media reviewers tell us this puts all the rumors to rest for good. I'm talking about Gerald Posner's *Case Closed* (1993) and then Vincent Bugliosi's 1,600-page tome, *Reclaiming History* (2007). Vince is a good friend of mine, and a prosecutor for whom I have great respect, but in this case it's beyond me how he can buy into the lone-nut scenario. Other new books like *Brothers*, *Legacy of Secrecy*, and *JFK and the Unspeakable* barely merit a mention; anything raising the specter of a plot gets quickly relegated to the stack of books-to-be-ignored.

So let's start with a serious look at the overwhelming physical evidence that Oswald couldn't have been acting alone. First of all, what about the so-called "magic bullet" that moved all around and caused seven separate wounds in President Kennedy and Governor Connally? When this bullet just happened to turn up on a stretcher at Dallas's Parkland Hospital, there weren't any bloodstains on it. Although the bullet appeared to be undamaged, the one that hit Connally left behind some permanent lead in his wrist. According to Dr. Cyril Wecht, former President of the American Academy of Forensic Scientists, these two facts simply don't add up. Without the "magic bullet," the idea that Oswald killed the president falls apart.[1] (Of course, if you challenge the status quo like Dr. Wecht eventually they'll come after you, as the Justice Department did. For sending personal faxes and giving students permission to study autopsies, Dr. Wecht found himself facing numerous criminal charges. He was forced to resign as a county coroner in Pittsburgh and spent $8 million on legal fees before the Justice Department dropped most all its charges against him in 2008.[2]

A total of eighteen witnesses at Parkland Memorial Hospital that day—most of them doctors—all described a bullet wound that blew away where the back of JFK's head should have been. But somehow, the autopsy photos that got entered into evidence don't show that wound. Of course, Dr. James Humes, the navy physician who led the autopsy at Bethesda Naval Hospital, admitted later that he burned both his autopsy notes *and* the first draft of his report.[3] Somehow, the president's brain disappeared, too.

What gets me is that John Kennedy's body was illegally removed from the city of Dallas, where by law the autopsy should have taken place. Texas law in 1963 required that the autopsy of anyone murdered in the state had to take place *within* its borders. The only exception was a murder that happened in a place owned, possessed, or controlled by the federal government—which wasn't the case here. In fact, the Dallas County medical examiner, Dr. Earl Rose, tried to enforce the law when the Secret Service was removing the president's body from Parkland late that afternoon for immediate return to Washington. Dr. Rose was overruled by the Dallas district attorney, Henry Wade. So did the feds simply come in and say, this is what's going to happen? Why don't they have to abide by the same laws as the rest of us? This set a terrible precedent that happened again after September 11, but I'll get into that later.

As for the famous Zapruder film: anybody can see that JFK's head is thrust violently backward when the fatal shot strikes him. Despite all the claims to the contrary, this supports someone firing from the front, most likely the grassy knoll. A number of experts say that the film was definitely altered—and we've recently learned that it went to a CIA lab run by Kodak in Rochester, New York, the weekend of the assassination![4] When *Life* magazine published stills from the Zapruder film not long after the assassination, they were printed out of order. Kinda makes you wonder about the media again, doesn't it?

Did you know that not a single fingerprint was found on Oswald's alleged murder weapon? When the FBI did a nitrate test on Oswald, it came up positive for his hands but negative for his face. Which means that he maybe fired a pistol, but not a rifle, that day. After Oswald was killed by Jack Ruby, the Dallas Police did come up with a palm print on the Mannlicher-Carcano—but this was after the FBI's top fingerprint analyst had dusted the whole rifle and said he found nothing of importance.[5]

During my first year as governor, I caused a pretty big stir when I told an interviewer from *Playboy* that I did not believe the official conclusion on Oswald. I think I may have been the highest-ranking official who ever said that, at least publicly. I started by simply applying common sense. If Oswald was who they told us he was—a Marine private who gets out of the Marine Corps and decides to defect to the Soviet Union at the height of the Cold War, then comes back home with a Russian wife and docs minimum-wage jobs—why would any records need to be locked away in the National Archives because of "national security" for 75 years? As a Navy SEAL, I had to have top secret clearance. That was higher than Oswald's, and I know a few secrets, but not enough to endanger national security. Yet in Oswald's case, hundreds of documents were withheld.

When I was traveling around the country to promote my first book, the publisher said I could go to either Houston or Dallas. I said, "Give me Dallas." With my apologies to readers who may already have read this story in my previous book, as well as the one about my meeting with Fidel Castro, I feel like these are too important to leave out of what I've learned about JFK's killing. First a cop gave me the tour of the police headquarters basement where Jack Ruby shot Oswald. The eerie part was, there was the elevator we all saw on TV—and down on the floor, almost on the exact spot where Oswald lay dying, the tile has oil on it that still looks like blood.

From there I went to Dealey Plaza and took my time walking the picket fence on the grassy knoll, where a second gunman most likely was firing from. That was eerie, too. Then I went to what's now the JFK Museum inside the Texas School Book Depository, where the curator, Gary Mack, met my party. The actual supposed sniper's nest on the sixth floor is sealed off. But you can go to the next window, which would seem to be an easier shot, because you're eight feet closer to where the president's motorcade passed and at basically the same angle. I didn't see how three shots could possibly have cleared the branches of an oak tree and lined up on the presidential motorcade.

After my book signing was over, we headed out to Dallas's Love Field airport. At the time, I was smoking cigars, so they found me a restricted area outside where I could light up. I remember it was a beautiful day, and we were all laughing and making small talk. As it came time for me to put out my cigar and board the plane, the police officer who'd been our guide all day took me off to the side.

He said, "Be very careful, Governor. You are a high-profile person who might say things that certain people don't want brought to light."

That made my head spin a little. If there was nothing to hide about the assassination, how could my making comments about it forty years later affect anybody? In hindsight, I wish I'd canceled the flight and gone to the policeman's home that night. I wanted to ask him, "Why are you warning me about this? What do you base it on, or won't you tell me?" But I had the strong impression he didn't want me to know.

Then, my last year in office, in 2002, I had an even more powerful experience when I got the opportunity to meet Fidel Castro. A few of America's sanctions against Cuba dealing with food and agricultural products had finally been lifted, so Minnesota was able to put together a trade mission for humanitarian purposes. President Bush was very opposed to my going along, but I decided it was my right as an American citizen. We now know that Robert Kennedy, on December 12, 1963—less than a month after his brother's assassination—had sent a memo to Dean Rusk asking the secretary of state to get rid of the restrictions on American travel to Cuba, because this was inconsistent with our belief in freedom. It took almost a half-century more for his daughter, Kathleen Kennedy Townsend, to push the Obama Administration to go forward on this—which it seems is finally going to happen. I guess I was a few years ahead of my time.

I'd grown up in fear of Fidel Castro. I was young when his revolution took place in 1959, but I remember the propaganda. I vaguely recall hearing about the Bay of Pigs invasion, because it dominated the news when I came home from school. As a kid, the name fascinated me. Why would they name a place after pigs? As an adult, when I started reading books trying to figure out what really happened to President Kennedy, Castro and Cuba of course loomed large: Oswald and his Fair Play for Cuba Committee, his attempt to get a visa to Cuba on a trip to Mexico. So Cuba had intrigued me for years, though I never dreamed I'd have a chance to actually go there, much less to spend an hour with Castro himself.

The last day of our visit, around noon, Castro was waiting for me in a room at the trade fair. I've never known a handshake like Castro's. He comes up to me, winds up, pulls back his hand all the way to his shoulder, and thrusts it out with great excitement. We sat down in two chairs right across from each other. He had his interpreter along, and some of his security people.

The first words out of his mouth were, "You are a man of great courage."

I was puzzled by this and said, "Well, Mr. President, how can you say that? You don't know me."

He looked back at me and said, "Because you defied your president to come here." I guess he has pretty good "intel."

And I looked right back at him and said, "Well, Mr. President, you'll find that I defy most everything."

Castro laughed. Who knows, maybe he felt this was something we had in common.

The whole conversation, on my part, was in English and interpreted to him by a lady in Spanish. But I don't think he really needs her. Because now and then, I'd say something that was funny and he'd laugh before the interpretation happened. As good as Castro is at masking the fact, I think he understands English very well. Let's put it this way: I'm sure he does English far, far better than I do Spanish.

We covered a lot of ground in our conversation. Just as I have great pride in Minnesota, he has the same for Cuba. He was extremely proud of the fact that they have the highest literacy rate of any Latin-American country in the hemisphere. He's also proud that they have the best medical care. I found him very engaging. He's a master of hyperbole. I told him that I felt the U.S. boycott was wrong. It did nothing positive for either of our countries, and it was time for America to get over it. His questions of me were mainly about my political future. He was interested in the fact that I was an independent and didn't belong to either of the two major parties. A kind of rogue element being the governor of a state.

Time passes very quickly when it's only an hour and you're sitting with Fidel Castro. He's so perceptive. At one point I glanced at my watch and immediately Castro said, "I'm sorry, do you have to be somewhere?" I said, "No, sir. But I'm only here a short time with you, and there are some personal questions I wanted to ask you before our hour is up. So I was just checking my watch to see how much more time I had. So—can I ask you one?"

His answer was, "Ask me anything you'd like."

I told him about how I was only twelve years old when John F. Kennedy was killed. And how later, as an adult, I started studying the murder. I told him that I came to not believe the Warren Commission, or what my country has portrayed as what happened. I said, "Naturally, in studying this, there are a few scenarios where you come up very strongly as being a part of it, that Oswald was somehow linked to you. You were around back then, and much older than I was, and more involved—I would like to know your perception of what happened to John F. Kennedy."

For the next twenty minutes, I couldn't stop him from talking. First of all, he said it was an "inside job," meaning that the assassination was orchestrated from within the United States. He very intently stared at me and said—which also told me that he was aware of my military background—"You know as well as I do, Oswald couldn't make the shots." Then he went on to explain the reason he knew that. During the Cuban Revolution, he was the main guy who taught and carried out sniper work. Knowing all he did about this, he knew Oswald couldn't have accomplished the job with the antiquated Mannlicher-Carcano rifle that he used.

Then Fidel described why it was an inside job. First of all, he said, he was very close to the Soviet Union at that time. "The Soviets didn't do it," he stated emphatically. In fact, the Kremlin leaders had told him about Kennedy: "You can talk to this man." Apparently the Russians were pleased that Kennedy had enough of an open mind to at least consider their side's position, on Cuba and other matters. Besides, neither country wanted another nuclear confrontation like the Cuban Missile Crisis.

Secondly, Castro said, "*I* didn't do it." Again his gaze was penetrating. He went on, "I'm not suicidal crazy. Why would I destroy my Cuba, the country I love so much. If I would have ordered Kennedy killed, and the United States found out, we wouldn't exist anymore. They would have unleashed everything they had on us, and basically blown us off the face of the earth. Why would I take that risk?"

It made sense to me. Not only that, but look who was waiting in the wings—Lyndon Baines Johnson. I didn't see his becoming president as a positive for Fidel Castro.

He also recalled for me how, at the moment Kennedy was killed, he was meeting in Havana with a French journalist named Jean Daniel, whom Kennedy had personally sent to see him. Castro felt very strongly that

Kennedy was considering a change in policy towards Cuba. I could tell that he felt Cuba was worse off without Kennedy alive.

He said again, "It was completely an inside job. It was done by people within the United States of America."

I wanted to ask for specifics—it felt like he knew some—but our time was up.

That last night, I turned to my Cuban bodyguards and asked them to take me out for a night on the town. They took me to the infamous Club Havana. It's a beautiful nightclub, maybe the biggest one in Cuba, with a Vegas-type entertainment show where they bring out Latino comedians, a variety of different musical acts, and have beautiful Cuban girls who dance in their feathered native costumes.

The night wore on. Castro apparently has informants everywhere. One of them came up and whispered something to my bodyguard, who then told me. It seems that some CIA operatives were tailing me. I thought to myself—is that for my benefit, or for theirs? Am I in some type of danger that they need to be following me around? I don't think so. I doubt that Fidel Castro would want an American governor coming to harm on his island, when I'm there on a mission of good will. So I ruled out that somehow the CIA were hanging around to protect me, especially considering I had my own armed bodyguards plus the three assigned by Fidel.

The Cubans had only one question: Did I want to lose them? If this made me uncomfortable, they would help me get rid of these guys and we could go on about our business. I said, "No, we're not going to even acknowledge that they're here. Who cares, we're not doing anything wrong. There's nothing they'll be able to blackmail me with, or take back to the U.S. about any misbehavior on my part. Let's ignore them, they're not going to ruin our night."

So we ended up going to another club, and I don't know if we were followed there or not. The subject was never brought up again. It could be the Cuban security team decided on a means to lose them on the way; I never inquired. What I did do was put this incident on file in the back of my mind.

When I came back to the States, a week or so later I had a two o'clock meeting penciled in on my schedule—but whom I was supposed to meet with was blank. That's very unusual for a governor's public schedule. So I asked my chief of staff, "What's the deal with the two o'clock meeting?" He rolled his eyes and said, "CIA."

I expected it, because they have their jobs to do. I had been with Castro and why wouldn't they want to debrief me? And that's precisely what it was. The two agents from the CIA came into my office—one of them I'd already met, shortly after I became governor—and they very respectfully gave me the old "Twenty Questions" routine. They went through their litany, and I answered them as honestly as I could. Typical intelligence questions: What did Castro's health appear to be like? Was he in control of all his faculties? Did he seem bright for his age?

I said I felt that he was very much in control. His mental capacity seemed to be right-on. I offered a few opinions. I told them, "I know his mom lived to be a hundred, so it's in his genes, and looks to me like he just might make it. Do I think this guy is gonna die within the next couple of years? I'd have to tell you no, he looks fit as a fiddle for his age."

Their faces were expressionless. They said they were finished, and thanked me. I looked coldly at them and said, "You're done. You're all done?"

They said yes.

I said, "You're sure? There's no other question you want to ask me, there's nothing you want to tell me, anything like that?"

"No, sir, we're all done."

In that case, I wanted to send them back with something to think about. "Well," I said, "I have something that I want to tell *you*, and I'll leave it up to your discretion who should hear this. You take it to whoever you think is appropriate. A need-to-know basis."

They feigned being very surprised and said, "Governor, we don't understand what you're talking about."

I said, "Well, here's what I'm talking about. If you or your people ever put a tail on me again, and don't tell me beforehand, and I discover it—you're gonna find the tail floating in the river."

They looked at me in seeming astonishment. They looked at each other and pretended they didn't have a clue as to what I was talking about.

I said, "That's fine. If *you* don't get it, you can take it and tell it to somebody that does. I'm sure somebody upstairs, above you, knows exactly what I'm talking about—*if* you don't. So you be the judge, like I say take it to where it needs to go."

I've often wondered how far it went. Did it get to George Tenet, who was the director of the CIA at the time? To George Bush? Dick Cheney? Or maybe it didn't even leave the room. Maybe they didn't even bother with passing along my little message, I don't know. But at least I got it off my chest, and let them know that the next time they try to fool me, they ought to do a better job.

One night after I got back to Minnesota, I had dinner with Jack Tunheim. He was a Minnesota federal judge who, after Oliver Stone's *JFK* film came out, was put in charge by President Clinton of reviewing the still-classified assassination archives for potential release. Tunheim told me that, in following up on the intelligence side, he'd encountered some of the shadiest characters that he'd ever come across. The judge also told me I had great knowledge of the case, and that I was on the right track.

On the fortieth anniversary of the assassination on November 22, 2003, I decided to go to Dallas again to pay my respects. I'd left office the previous January. I was the only elected official who spoke in Dealey Plaza that day. No one else even bothered to show up. This speaks volumes to me. Does our government still have a collective guilty conscience when it comes to John F. Kennedy?

When I ended up teaching at Harvard in 2004, I decided to focus my next-to-last class on the Kennedy assassination. I knew that was a gutsy move to make at the Kennedy School of Government. I hadn't wanted to try it too soon because, if Harvard objected, I didn't want to go through a big fight. Anyway, I got away with it. My guest speaker was James Fetzer, a University of Minnesota Duluth professor and former Marine who's an expert on the ballistics evidence that shows it had to be more than just Oswald shooting.

I noticed there were people in my class that day who'd never attended any of the others. They were too old to be students. Their sole purpose in being there was apparently to debunk any conspiracy theories. They didn't completely disrupt the class, but they would speak out of turn and insinuate that it was un-American and undermining our great country by bringing up the past and questioning the integrity of all those great men on the Warren Commission. Never question your government was the message. So where did these people come from? I suspect they were plants, sent in by somebody in the Bush Administration.

So that's my personal experience with the assassination of JFK. What I respect most about the man is that he was willing to grow and change his views while in office, for the sake of the greater good. Without his going up against the generals who wanted to attack Cuba and take out the Soviet missiles in the fall of 1962, I wouldn't be sitting here today writing this book. We'd have all been victims of a nuclear holocaust. But because Kennedy wasn't afraid to take on the powers-that-be—not just the military madmen but the CIA, the Mafia, and the right-wing Texas oilmen, among others—he made enemies. So many enemies that it's almost impossible to sort out which one eventually killed him.

The conclusion of Robert Blakey, who ran the House investigation back in the late 1970s, was that the Mob was most likely behind the assassination. On this question, I have to defer to what Kevin Costner said in Oliver Stone's *JFK* movie: "I don't doubt their involvement . . . but at a lower level. Could the Mob change the parade route . . . ? Or eliminate the protection for the president? Could the Mob send Oswald to Russia and get him back? Could the Mob get the FBI, the CIA, and the Dallas Police to make a mess of the investigation? Could the Mob get the Warren Commission appointed to cover it up? Could the Mob wreck the autopsy? Could the Mob influence the national media to go to sleep?"

Now let's run down some comments made by government officials at the time, most of which haven't been made public until recent years.

President Johnson, on the telephone recordings made of his White House conversations: "I never believed that Oswald acted alone, although I can accept the fact that he pulled the trigger."[6] However, he also told his friend and Warren Commission member Richard Russell, the senator from Georgia, that he didn't believe in the single-bullet theory.

President Nixon, on the White House tapes, talking about the Warren Commission: "It was the greatest hoax that has ever been perpetuated."[7]

FBI Director J. Edgar Hoover, responding to the question, "Do you think Oswald did it?": "If I told you what I really know, it would be very dangerous to this country. Our whole political system could be disrupted."[8]

Warren Commission member Hale Boggs: "Hoover lied his eyes out to the Commission—on Oswald, on Ruby, on their friends, the bullets, the gun, you name it."[9]

Senator Russell: "[I] never believed that Lee Harvey Oswald assassinated President Kennedy without at least some encouragement from others . . . I think someone else worked with him on the planning."

Who was this guy Oswald anyway? A lot more than a 24-year-old loner, that's for sure. Does it make sense that this Marine radar operator who arrives in Moscow in 1959 offering secrets to the Russians then comes home married to a colonel's niece and never gets debriefed by the CIA—let alone charged with a possibly treasonous act? The Warren Commission knew, from Texas Attorney General Waggoner Carr *and* District Attorney Henry Wade, that Oswald apparently was FBI informant No. 179 and was making a couple hundred dollars a month in wages from the Bureau![10] Wade's source said that Oswald had a CIA employment number as well.

Of course, we can't know for sure which Oswald this was. Let me explain. At the time the Warren Commission places Oswald on a bus heading to Mexico City to try and get a visa to Cuba, he was also in Dallas with two Latinos at the door of Silvia Odio. Later on, as the assassination date approaches, he's supposedly target-practicing at firing ranges and driving a car like a maniac—except he doesn't know how to drive or have a license. Well, how could Oswald be in two places at once? Maybe there were *two men*, and one of them was setting up the other as the fellow who'd take the rap for the assassination.

This question of double identity has been around since 1967, when Richard Popkin published a little book called *The Second Oswald*. A decade after that came Michael Eddowes's best-seller, *The Oswald File*. His hypothesis was that the Marine Oswald went to the USSR, but a different "Oswald" came back—actually a Russian spy who then killed the president. In 2003 came John Armstrong's exhaustively researched *Harvey and Lee*, where the premise is that two males who looked very much alike were groomed from an early age as part of a CIA operation.

Here's what Armstrong concluded was going on. "In the early 1950s, an intelligence operation was underway that involved two teenage boys—Lee Oswald from Fort Worth, and a Russian-speaking boy named

Harvey Oswald from New York. Beginning in 1952, the boys lived parallel but separate lives—often in the same city. The ultimate goal was to switch their identities and send Harvey Oswald into Russia, which is exactly what happened seven years later."

Armstrong's evidence is impressive, including contradictions in Oswald's school records between the Warren Commission and the New York courts; a "Lee Oswald" in New York simultaneously with a "Harvey Oswald" in Stanley, North Dakota; an Oswald employed at the Pfisterer Dental Lab in New Orleans while another was in the Marines in Japan. How else do you explain the FBI swooping down on Dallas's Stripling Junior High the day of the assassination and seizing all "Oswald's" school records, as assistant principal Frank Kudlaty remembered, during years when he was officially attending a different school?[11]

The way Armstrong pieced it together, when Harvey went to Russia, Lee stayed in New Orleans and Florida associating with Cuban exiles and their CIA handlers. And, as the fateful day approached in Dallas, Lee was used to impersonate Harvey in a series of events aimed at setting up Harvey as the assassin and falsely implicating Cuba as being behind the whole thing.

I realize this sounds like something out of the most bizarre sci-fi novel, but there's quite a bit already in the existing record that supports such a possibility. It turns out the Warren Commission never saw a memorandum that Hoover sent to the State Department nine months after Oswald's "defection," dated June 3, 1960. Hoover wrote that "there is a possibility that an impostor is using Oswald's birth certificate."[12] After this memo surfaced when a researcher stumbled across it in the National Archives in 1975, Warren Commission investigator W. David Slawson was asked about it by the *New York Times*. Slawson said: "I don't know where the impostor notion would have led us, perhaps nowhere, like a lot of other leads. But the point is, we didn't know about it. And why not? It conceivably could have been something related to the CIA. I can only speculate now, but a general CIA effort to take out everything that reflected on them may have covered this up."[13]

Now think about this: there are almost 50 separate instances of U.S. government files—from the CIA, FBI, Secret Service, Military Intelligence, Dallas Police, and Warren Commission testimony—where

"Lee" and "Harvey" are transposed. In quite a few of these, the original file identifying a "Harvey Lee Oswald" was altered after the assassination to read "Lee Harvey Oswald."[14] Which raises the obvious question: was there an intelligence operation involving one Oswald who identified himself as Lee, and another who called himself Harvey?

When Oswald's older brother, Robert, showed up at the Dallas Police station not long after he was told about Lee getting arrested, the very first question the FBI posed to him was: "Is your brother's name Lee Harvey Oswald or Harvey Lee Oswald? . . . We have it here as Harvey Lee." Robert replied, "No, it's Lee Harvey Oswald."[15]

The first Dallas Police memo generated that day also designated the fellow as "Harvey Lee Oswald." An army cable sent from Fort Sam Houston to the U.S. Strike Command at McDill Air Force Base in Florida started out: "Following is additional information on Oswald, Harvey Lee." By the time the Secret Service interviewed Oswald's widow, Marina, three days after the assassination, you'd think they'd have the name right. But the way they phrased it to Marina went: "After you married Harvey, where did you and Harvey maintain your address or residence?" And the Secret Service report of its interview with William Stout Oswald said he "stated that although Harvey Lee Oswald is said to be his second cousin, he had never met him nor had he known Harvey was also employed by the William B. Reily Coffee Company."

This weird pattern had been going on for a long time. When Oswald was living in Russia, a March 2, 1961, memo from the U.S. Passport Office to the State Department Security Office "requested that the recipients advise if the FBI is receiving info about Harvey on a continuing basis." Soviet records only deepen the mystery. Oswald was known to sometimes use the nickname of "Alik" with people he knew over there. When he was hospitalized in Minsk for an adenoid operation, he's variously listed as "Harvey Alik Oswald," "Harvey A. Oswald," and "H.A. Oswald." The name "Lee" doesn't appear on any of the hospital files.

A CIA document dated three days after the assassination says: "It was partly out of curiosity to learn if Oswald's wife would actually accompany him to our country, partly out of interest in Oswald's own experiences in the USSR, that we showed intelligence interest in the Harvey story." I found that phrasing rather odd. Back in Texas on Thanksgiving

Day, 1962, Oswald entered his name as "Harvey" in his half-brother John Pic's address book. This is despite the fact that a guy named J.E. Pitts who served with him in the Marines remembered that Oswald "had an intense hate for anyone that called him by the nickname of 'Harve' or by his middle name of 'Harvey' and he wanted to fight anyone that did it."[16]

Okay, now let's turn to the question of Oswald's height. The *Warren Report* has Oswald standing 5-feet-9-inches tall, the height recorded by the Dallas police after his arrest and during the autopsy on his body after Ruby shot him. The commission's 26 volumes of testimony and exhibits have 12 different documents recording that same height. These are all heights for Oswald in the United States after he came back home in 1962. The 5-foot-9 is on all of his employment applications, including the one at the Texas School Book Depository, and also how he was measured by the New Orleans police after getting arrested during a street confrontation with some anti-Castro Cuban exiles on August 9, 1963. It's also the height listed earlier when he finishes his Marine boot camp, on December 28, 1956.

But what the Warren Report *doesn't* say is that, on documents concerning his discharge from the Marines and his travels overseas after that, he's listed as 5-foot-11. Not just once, but three times over 11 days in September 1959 by a doctor and two other Marines. He's 5-foot-11 on his passport when he goes to Russia, and an application he makes to get admitted to Albert Schweitzer College in Switzerland. A total of eight documents in the Warren volumes have an Oswald two inches taller than the guy who got arrested on November 22, 1963.

When the police checked Oswald's wallet on the afternoon of the assassination, they found both a 1959 Marine Selective Service System Registration card and a Department of Defense Identification Card listing his height as 5-11. In the same wallet was a counterfeit Selective Service System Registration card under the fictitious name of "Alek James Hidell." Hidell's height was listed as 5-9.[17]

It gets stranger. Before he was buried, Oswald's body was unattended when an FBI team came to spend quite a bit of time checking it over carefully and taking another set of prints, according to the *Fort Worth Press*. When an FBI agent looked up Oswald's early medical history, a mastoidectomy and operation scar were noted on his Marine Corps health records, from a procedure he'd undergone at the age of six. But the post-mortem report of November 24, 1963, didn't list any scar or bone removal. Paul Groody, the funeral director who buried Oswald, recounted a story years later. Secret Service agents, he said, had come to ask him questions about some marks on Oswald's body and told Groody, "We don't know who we have in that grave."[18]

Richard Helms, who was then in charge of clandestine operations for the CIA, sent a memo to the FBI on February 18, 1964. Helms was interested in a scar that Oswald was supposed to have had on his left wrist, after he allegedly attempted suicide in Moscow in 1959. Helms requested any FBI information, "including the undertakers, copies of any reports, such as autopsy or other, which may contain information pertinent to this point. . . . The best evidence of a scar or scars on the left wrist would of course be direct examination by a competent authority and we recommend that this be done and that a photograph of the inner and outer surfaces of the left wrist be made if there has been no other evidence acceptable to the [Warren] Commission that he did in fact attempt suicide by cutting his wrist." A week later, two Dallas FBI agents contacted C.J. Price, the administrator at the Parkland Memorial Hospital where Oswald's autopsy took place. Price said "he failed to observe any scar on Oswald's wrist." Nor did anyone else, as far as he knew. According to a memo by Warren Commission investigator Slawson (March 13, 1964): "The CIA is interested in the scar on Oswald's left wrist. . . . The FBI is reluctant to exhume Oswald's body as requested by the CIA."[19]

The new book, *JFK and the Unspeakable,* contains a fresh interview that brings even more credence to the "double Oswald" scenario. Author Jim Douglass tracked down a fellow named Warren (Butch) Burroughs, who was running the concession stand at the Texas Theater where Oswald was apprehended. He says Oswald came in sometime between 1:00 PM and 1:07 PM, which is several minutes *before* Oswald supposedly shot and killed policeman J.D. Tippitt seven blocks away. Burroughs sold him popcorn at 1:15 (the very moment of Tippitt's slaying).

Most stunning of all was Burroughs's revelation that, a few minutes after the cops came rushing in to surround Oswald and half-drag him out the front of the theater, a second man who "looked almost like Oswald, like he was his brother or something," was arrested and taken out the *back* of the theater.[20]

Burroughs wasn't the only witness to this. Bernard Haire, who owned Bernie's Hobby House two doors east of the theater, had also seen police bring "a young white man . . . dressed in a pullover shirt and slacks" out the rear door of the theater, where he was driven off. Told that Oswald had been brought out the front, Haire was bewildered and said "I don't know who I saw arrested."[21]

You've also got witnesses at the Book Depository building seeing Oswald walk out the front and get driven off in a car, and more witnesses seeing him go out the back and take a bus. There are more witnesses inside the building who claim to have seen Oswald in two places at once. So there's quite the possibility that both of them, Lee and Harvey, were in the book depository at the same time.

My hunch is that they were both part of a false defector program that James Angleton and his friends in counterintelligence were running out of the CIA. While Harvey was over in Russia, Lee was working with anti-Castro Cubans in Florida planning to bump off Castro (he was seen by a number of people down there at the same time). Harvey, the wimpy-chinned one in the photographs, was married to Marina. Lee, the thick-necked one, was used to set up Harvey. I believe it's Harvey laying in the grave, and whatever happened to Lee, I have no idea.

In Armstrong's book, there's also the matter of the two mothers. Apparently the real Oswald mother was quite an attractive tall woman, but then you've also got short, dumpy Marguerite. What proves to me that she was a fraud? In one interview she gave, she had Lee's birthday wrong. I don't know of a woman who's ever given birth to a child that can't remember the day.

I can't end this chapter without a few words about the national media's role in the cover-up.[22] The very first dispatch out of Dallas on November 22, 1963, came from the *Associated Press*: "The shots apparently came from a grassy knoll in the area." That was the news in most of the early reports, though it was soon replaced by the Texas School Book Depository.

Dan Rather, who was a local newsman in Dallas at the time, was the first journalist to see the 20-second-long "home movie" taken by dressmaker Abraham Zapruder. Rather then told a national TV audience that the fatal shot drove the president's head "violently forward," when the footage showed just the opposite! Later on, in his book *The Camera Never Blinks*, Rather defended his "mistake" saying it was because his watching the film had been so rushed.

But nobody could question this at the time, because Time-Life snapped up the Zapruder film for $150,000—a small fortune back then—and battled for years to keep it out of the public domain. The *Life* magazine publisher, C.D. Jackson, was "so upset by the head-wound sequence," according to Richard Stolley, who was then the magazine's L.A. bureau chief, "that he proposed the company obtain all rights to the film and withhold it from public viewing at least until emotions calmed."

We didn't find out until 1977, when Carl Bernstein of Watergate fame wrote a piece for *Rolling Stone* on "The CIA and the Media," why *we* should have been upset about C.D. Jackson. Bernstein explained: "For many years, [Time-Life founder Henry] Luce's personal emissary to the CIA was C.D. Jackson, a Time, Inc., vice president who was publisher of *Life* magazine from 1960 until his death in 1964. While a *Time* executive, Jackson coauthored a CIA-sponsored study recommending the reorganization of the American intelligence services in the early 1950s." He also "approved specific arrangements for providing CIA employees with Time-Life cover. Some of these arrangements were made with the knowledge of Luce's wife, Clare Boothe." (Mrs. Luce was a member of the Committee to Free Cuba, and right after the assassination started putting out information connecting Oswald to Cuba—information she received from a group of CIA-backed Cuban exiles that she supported. The CIA still won't release its files about that group.)

Life published a story headlined "End of Nagging Rumors: The Critical Six Seconds" (December 6, 1963), that claimed to show precisely how Oswald had succeeded in hitting his target. Supposedly based on the Zapruder film, the magazine said that the president had been turning to wave to someone in the crowd when one of Oswald's bullets hit him in the throat. But guess what? That sequence is nowhere to be seen in the film.

From the get-go, Oswald was damned as guilty by the media. The headline in the *New York Times*: "Career of Suspect Has Been Bizarre." In the *New York Herald Tribune*: "Left Wing Lunacy, Not Right is Suspect." In *Time* magazine: "Evidence Against Oswald Described as Conclusive."

Here's what media critic Jerry Policoff later had to say: "Thus, the press' curiosity was not aroused when a 7.65 caliber German Mauser mutated into a 6.5 caliber Italian Mannlicher-Carcano; or when the grassy knoll receded into oblivion; or when an entrance wound in the President's throat became an exit wound (first for a fragment from the head wound and then for a bullet from the back wound); or when a wound six inches below the President's shoulder became a wound at the back of the neck. The press was thereby weaving a web that would inevitably commit it to the official findings."

Three months before the *Warren Report* appeared in September 1964, the *New York Times* ran a Page One exclusive: "Panel To Reject Theories of Plot in Kennedy Death." They then printed the whole report as a 48-page supplement, and collaborated with Bantam Books and the Book-of-the-Month Club to publish both hardcover and paperback editions. "The commission analyzed every issue in exhaustive, almost archaeological detail," according to reporter Anthony Lewis.

The *Times* also put together another book, *The Witnesses*, which contained "highlights" from testimony before the Warren Commission. All these were aimed at shoring up the lone-gunman notion. In one instance, a witness who reported having seen a man with a rifle on the sixth floor had other portions of his testimony eliminated—namely, that he'd actually seen *two* men but been told to "forget it" by an FBI agent. Witnesses like Zapruder, who believed some of the shots came from in front, were left out entirely.

Life magazine devoted most of its October 2, 1964, issue to the *Warren Report*, assigning commission member (and future president) Gerald Ford the job of evaluating it. In 1997, the Assassination Records Review Board would release handwritten notes by Ford, revealing that he had misrepresented the placement of the president's back wound—raising it several inches to suggest he'd instead been struck in the neck—in order to make it fit the theory that a single bullet had hit both Kennedy and Connally. Otherwise, the entire lone-assassin notion would have collapsed.

That same issue of *Life* underwent two major revisions *after* it went on sale. One of the articles was illustrated with eight frames from the Zapruder film. But Frame 323 turned out to contradict the *Warren Report*'s conclusion about the shots all coming from the rear. So the issue was recalled, the plates broken and re-set (this was all pre-computer), and Frame 313 showing the president's head exploding became the replacement. A second "error" forced still another such change. When a Warren Commission critic, Vincent Salandria, asked *Life* editor Ed Kearns about this two years later, Kearns wrote back: "I am at a loss to explain the discrepancies between the three versions of LIFE which you cite. I've heard of breaking a plate to correct an error. I've never heard of doing it twice for a single issue, much less a single story. Nobody here seems to remember who worked on the early Kennedy story. . . "

And so it went. Skeptics of the *Warren Report* were often labeled "leftists" or "Communists." After Mark Lane's book *Rush to Judgment* and Josiah Thompson's *Six Seconds in Dallas* came out in 1966 questioning the official version, and became best-sellers, the *New York Times* decided to conduct its own investigation. One of its unit, Houston bureau chief Martin Waldron, later said they'd found "a lot of unanswered questions" that the paper then wouldn't pursue. "I'd be off on a good lead and then somebody'd call me off and send me out to California on another story or something. We never really detached anyone for this. We weren't really serious."

Life magazine also took a fresh look at the case. "Did Oswald Act Alone? A Matter of Reasonable Doubt," an article in the November 26, 1966 issue was headlined. A reexamination of the Zapruder film, the magazine said, had reached the conclusion that the single-bullet theory didn't hold up and a new investigation was called for. This was to be the first of a series of articles but, in January 1967, editor Richard Billings says he was informed that "It is not *Life*'s function to investigate the Kennedy assassination." That was the last time they'd challenge the Warren Commission's findings. Billings resigned from the magazine and took a job with a newspaper in St. Petersburg, Florida. In 1967, led by Dan Rather, CBS News did a four-part study that again upheld the *Warren Report*. Warren Commission member John McCloy was the network's behind-the-scenes advisor.

Another decade went by before the Bernstein piece in *Rolling Stone* showed just how strongly these news organizations were all tied to the CIA. "By far the most valuable of these associations, according to CIA officials, have been with the *New York Times*, CBS and Time Inc.," Bernstein wrote. "Over the years, the [CBS] network provided cover for

CIA employees, including at least one well-known foreign correspondent and several stringers; it supplied outtakes of newsfilm to the CIA. . . . A high-level CIA official with a prodigious memory says that the *New York Times* provided cover for about ten CIA operatives between 1950 and 1966."

Bernstein's article began by describing how Joseph Alsop, a leading syndicated columnist, had gone to the Philippines in 1953 to cover an election, at the CIA's request. It would be Alsop, transcripts of President Johnson's taped telephone conversations later revealed, who first urged LBJ to form the Warren Commission to answer any unresolved doubts about the assassination. "Alsop is one of more than 400 American journalists who in the past twenty-five years have secretly carried out assignments for the Central Intelligence Agency, according to documents on file at CIA headquarters," Bernstein wrote. "Journalists provided a full range of clandestine services—from simple intelligence-gathering to serving as go-betweens with spies in Communist countries."

The article went on: "James Angleton, who was recently removed as the Agency's head of counterintelligence operations, ran a completely independent group of journalist-operatives who performed sensitive and frequently dangerous missions; little is known about this group for the simple reason that Angleton deliberately kept only the vaguest of files."

Among the CIA's most valuable relationships in the 1960s, Bernstein continued, was a *Miami News* reporter who covered Latin America named Hal Hendrix. He regularly provided information about individuals within Miami's Cuban exile community. He was the conduit through which the CIA passed word to then-Senator Kenneth Keating that the Soviets were putting missiles in Cuba in 1962, and got awarded the Pulitzer Prize for his coverage of the Missile Crisis. On the afternoon of the assassination, another reporter, Seth Kantor, has said that Hendrix provided him considerable yet-unrevealed information about Oswald's history—including his supposed defection to Russia and his activities with the Fair Play for Cuba Committee. The setup seems to have been "on," and it involved the media.

The cover-up still does. After the House Assassinations Committee concluded late in 1978 that the president "was probably assassinated as a result of a conspiracy," the *New York Times* buried the story—"Experts

Say That Second Gunman Almost Certainly Shot at Kennedy"—on page 37, right alongside the classified ads. Later, a *Times* editorial said that the committee seemed "more interested in inflaming than informing." And whenever there were intimations of conspiracy in the media, the finger pointed elsewhere—like a CBS documentary, "The CIA's Secret Army," which strongly hinted that Fidel Castro had ordered Kennedy's murder in retaliation for the attempts on his own life.

When Oliver Stone's movie *JFK* came out in 1991, the strongest attacks came from news outlets and journalists "with the longest records of error and obstruction in defense of the flawed Warren Commission inquiry."[23] Are we surprised? They'll cheerlead for Posner's and Bugliosi's books, but I'll bet you a free lunch they're not going to be reviewing this one anytime soon.

WHAT SHOULD WE DO NOW?

One lesson we can take away from the tragedy in Dallas is that the federal government shouldn't be allowed to supersede state and local laws, when it comes to having an "official" investigation into events as momentous as a presidential assassination or a terrorist attack. We also need to pay close attention to how our big media stopped doing their job as the eyes and ears of our democracy, refusing to acknowledge that something might be going on beyond a "lone nut" assassin. The pattern of denial continues, and we the people must demand thorough investigation and honest, unbiased information.

CHAPTER FOUR

THE ASSASSINATION
OF MALCOLM X

THE INCIDENT: Malcolm X was gunned down, execution-style, while giving a speech inside the Audubon Ballroom in Harlem, on February 21, 1965.

THE OFFICIAL WORD: His killers were Black Muslims loyal to Elijah Muhammad, who was involved in a power struggle with Malcolm X.

MY TAKE: Malcolm X was set up to die by elements of the CIA and FBI, who had him under constant surveillance and were afraid that he and Dr. Martin Luther King Jr. might form an alliance.

"It's a time for martyrs now. And if I'm to be one, it will be in the cause of brotherhood. That's the only thing that can save this country. I've learned it the hard way—but I've learned it. And that's the significant thing."—Malcolm X, talking to his friend Gordon Parks, two days before he was killed.[1]

Let me start with my perception of Malcolm X when I was growing up. I was terrified of him. He was this black man with an "X" attached to his name. The TV announcers portrayed him as some crazy revolutionary who wanted to kill every white man on the planet and take control. It was only when I read his autobiography in the late Eighties or early Nineties, and learned more about him and what he went through, that I came to look upon him as one of my heroes.

Sure, he'd gone the wrong way a couple of times in his life and there was a time when I probably should have feared Malcolm. But in the end, he was a brave, good man who had the ability to grow and change. After being as low as you could go, he was saved in prison by turning to religion through the Nation of Islam. Later, that became his prison and he had to break free again. He went to Mecca and had that huge transformation and admitted he was wrong, that we shouldn't segregate by color. Then to have him return to America and shortly thereafter be gunned down and silenced, I think did a terrible disservice to humanity.

I was wrestling in Atlanta when I first read *The Autobiography of Malcolm X*. I remember I was so moved by it, that I went out and bought one of those beautiful ball caps that had the "X" on it, standing for Malcolm X. I would wear that hat while taking the train downtown to the TV studio. Of course, it's predominantly black people that ride the rail in Atlanta. They'd kind of give me a double-take, like they didn't know what to think. As Jesse the Body, I could get away with it. People knew I could take the most bizarre positions and make them look normal. But I'd always chuckle to myself to watch the reaction of black people seeing this big white guy wearing a Malcolm X cap. I often sat and thought, do they think I'm just naïve and stupid? Or do they maybe think I know and understand, and there's a reason I'm wearing it? Because I'm a bit of a revolutionary myself, who can relate to him, in a humble way.

Malcolm X was only 39 when he died in a hail of shotgun and pistol fire, executed inside the Audubon Ballroom after giving a speech in Harlem. Clearly, by some of the things he said in the last month or so of his life, Malcolm knew it was inevitable. He told Alex Haley, who worked with him on the autobiography, that he didn't believe he'd live to see the book published. And he didn't. He was murdered on February 21, 1965, only a little more than a year after JFK's assassination. Since the gunmen were all part of the Black Muslims, and loyal followers of Elijah Muhammad, it was pretty much accepted that Malcolm X was the victim of a bitter feud between the two leaders. Today, we know that what happened on that Sunday afternoon was a whole lot bigger than that.[2]

After his pilgrimage to Mecca, Malcolm was no longer preaching what some had called his "message of hate." He'd already broken away from Elijah Muhammad, who was an advocate for a separate black state. He was forming alliances with revolutionary leaders in Africa and elsewhere—even making friends with Che Guevara, another of my heroes—and talking about civil rights as a human rights issue that the United Nations should take up. It looked like Malcolm X and Dr. Martin Luther King Jr. might even come together in a powerful alliance. I can imagine there were people in high places, like J. Edgar Hoover at the FBI, who didn't want that to take place. And I could certainly see where the status quo might decide, "This isn't going to happen, and we're going to make sure of that."

We've come a long way since those days in terms of race relations, but in the 1960s integration was still only beginning—the Voting Rights Act hadn't even become law when Malcolm X was alive. Those were the years of the Freedom Riders getting the crap beat out of them when they rode buses into the South, and "Bull" Connor fire-hosing African-Americans down in Birmingham, and James Meredith having to walk a National Guard gauntlet just to enroll at the University of Mississippi. It was a tempestuous period in our history, and Malcolm X was right at the forefront.

The FBI had been watching Malcolm as far back as 1950, when he was still in prison for grand larceny and first discovered the Nation of Islam [NOI].[3] When he was paroled after serving six years, he soon became a leading spokesman for Elijah Muhammad. In 1957, when the police beat a Black Muslim badly in Harlem and reluctantly agreed to hospitalize him thanks to Malcolm X's insistence, with a simple wave of his hand Malcolm had stopped what might have been a bloody riot of some 2,600 people. "No man should have that much power," a police inspector said.[4] Not surprisingly, the FBI's COINTELPRO agents were soon all over him. After Hoover learned that Malcolm would be Elijah Muhammad's likely successor, one COINTELPRO file said bluntly: "The secret to disabling the [NOI] movement, therefore, lay in neutralizing Malcolm X."[5]

In 1958, a fellow named John Ali was an adviser, friend, and housemate to Malcolm X. Five years later, he became National Secretary of the Black Muslims. When Elijah Muhammad left Chicago and moved to Phoenix because of his failing health, John Ali took over handling the group's finances and administration. At the same time, unbeknownst to the Muslims, he was working closely with the FBI. The main man he was keeping an eye on was Malcolm X.[6]

Isn't it interesting that for many of our public figures who've been killed—I'm thinking of John Lennon, Malcolm X, and Dr. King—they all seem to be under surveillance first and then assassinated later. Viewing it from a military standpoint, that would be the Standard Operating Procedure you'd expect: heavy surveillance to learn how you live, what way would be best to do it, how do we set up the patsy and get away with it? Look at it this way—if they're following these people around, wouldn't it turn up that somebody else was doing the same thing? But turning up the killers never seems to happen, does it?

By 1963, Malcolm was being pushed out of the Muslim hierarchy. The FBI, using informants and wiretaps to keep up with the rift, started spreading tales about Elijah Muhammad having affairs with young women—The FBI pretending it was Malcolm X doing the rumormongering. After Malcolm made comments about "chickens coming home to roost" following Kennedy's assassination, Elijah Muhammad seized the opportunity to suspend him for 90 days. At that point, FBI agents came around with a bribe offer that Malcolm refused. Not long after that, he was warned about a plot to wire his car to blow up as soon as he started the engine.

On March 8, 1964, Malcolm X announced he was leaving the NOI and founding a new mosque in New York. A few weeks later, he and Martin Luther King met for the one and only time in Washington, where they were both attending a Senate hearing on civil rights legislation. They spent time together on the Capitol steps, finding common ground. King said soon after that, unless Congress moved quickly, they could expect that "our nation is in for a dark night of social disruption."[7] Malcolm X was saying: "We need to expand the civil-rights struggle to a higher level—to the level of human rights."

Then he went off to Mecca. While he was gone, the NYPD's unit known as BOSSI (Bureau of Special Service and Investigation) was busy infiltrating Malcolm X's new mosque and passing along information to the FBI and CIA. The fellow in charge of the operation was Anthony Ulasewicz, who later became President Nixon's private detective for purposes of undercover ops and gained infamy during Watergate.[8] He brought onboard a 25-year-old black detective named Gene Roberts, a martial arts expert who joined up with Malcolm X as a bodyguard. "When he came back from Mecca and Africa, I went wherever he went, as long as it was in the city," Roberts said later.[9]

Toward the end of May 1964, the five men who'd be directly involved in assassinating Malcolm X met for the first time. They were part of a paramilitary training unit, known as the Fruit of Islam, based out of Newark, New Jersey.[10] That summer, when Malcolm left on an extended trip to Africa, John Ali said on a Chicago call-in radio station: "I predict that anyone who opposes the Honorable Elijah Muhammad puts their life in jeopardy."[11]

The CIA was aware that Malcolm was putting together information for African leaders at the second conference of the Organization of African Unity (OAU) in Cairo. One informant report claimed he was out "to embarrass the United States" by telling Africa about our "ill treatment of the Negro." Malcolm knew he was being shadowed by government agents, telling a friend that "our Muslims don't have the resources to finance a worldwide spy network."[12] While he was eating at the Nile Hilton, he recognized the waiter as a man he'd seen before in New York. Malcolm was rushed to a hospital just in time to have his stomach pumped. The doctor said there'd been something toxic in the food. By then, of course, the waiter had disappeared. Malcolm recovered, and urged the OAU leaders to consider African-American problems like their own and talk about this at the U.N.

The State Department then alerted President Johnson of an informant's report that Malcolm X and related "extremist groups" were receiving money from certain African states to ignite race riots. Johnson asked Hoover to look into this, and the State Department sent a memo to Richard Helms, the man in charge of clandestine operations at the CIA. The FBI told the CIA that the charges were trumped up. But Helms went ahead and authorized increasing surveillance on Malcolm X.[13] Over at the FBI, Director Hoover wrote in a memo: "There are clear and unmistakeable signs that we are in the midst of a social revolution with the racial movement at its core. The Bureau, in meeting its responsibilities in this area, is an integral part of this revolution."[14]

John Lewis, the future congressman, was part of SNCC (the Student Non-Violent Coordinating Committee) at the time, when he happened to run into Malcolm X in Nairobi. Lewis remembers Malcolm telling him "in a calm, measured way he was convinced that somebody wanted him killed."[15] He kept extending his stay abroad, before finally flying back to the U.S. Louis X, known today as Louis Farrakhan, released a public statement: "Such a man as Malcolm is worthy of death." Years later, Farrakhan admitted to filmmaker Spike Lee that he'd "helped contribute to the atmosphere that led to the assassination of Malcolm X."[16]

As Malcolm's influence grew, the CIA and FBI were only too happy to take advantage of the worsening divide between him and the followers of Elijah Muhammad. Malcolm seemed resigned to this. "Those talks [overseas] broadened my outlook and made it crystal clear to me that I had to look at the struggle in America's ghettos against the background of a worldwide struggle of oppressed peoples," he told a friend. "That's why, after every one of my trips abroad, America's rulers see me as being more and more dangerous. That's why I feel in my bones the plots to kill me have already been hatched in high places. The triggermen will only be doing what they were paid to do."

Alex Haley said that "Malcolm X complained repeatedly that the police would not take his requests for protection seriously." One headquarters officer put it like this: "The guy had a bad [rap] sheet. You don't offer somebody like that protection."[17] As 1965 began, he was being shadowed at every stop by potential assassins. John Ali was there waiting for his arrival in L.A., along with a group from the NOI. In Chicago, fifteen NOI members hung around outside his hotel. When Malcolm X flew to Paris to give a talk, the French authorities wouldn't let him enter the country. Later, a journalist named Eric Norden found out from a diplomat "that the CIA planned Malcolm's murder, and France feared he might be liquidated on its soil."[18]

On February 4, 1965, Hoover sent a "confidential" memo that outlined Malcolm's travel plans to Helms at the CIA and intel experts with all three branches of the military. At the same time, Elijah Muhammad was writing: "Malcolm—the Chief Hypocrite—was beyond the point of no return." On February 14, Malcolm's house was firebombed. He managed to get his pregnant wife, Betty, out along with their four daughters, into the 20-degree temperature outside. The NOI started a rumor that he'd burned his own house to get publicity. When a fireman left a bottle of gasoline on the dresser to make it look like that, Malcolm knew the plot against him went beyond the NOI.[19] The truth was, the main man spreading the rumor (Captain Joseph X) had been part of the firebombing team.

By now, Gene Roberts, the security guard sent in as an infiltrator by the NYPD, had become a friend and admirer of Malcolm X. "I learned to love the man; respect him. I think he was a good person." So when he observed a false disruption scene in the audience at one of Malcolm's talks, Roberts called his supervisors and said: "Listen, I just saw the dry run on Malcolm's life," adding that he thought it might happen at the Audubon Ballroom the next Sunday.[20] "And they said, okay, we'll pass it on," Roberts remembered. "What they did with it I don't know . . . I don't think they really cared." The same day of Roberts's alert, Malcolm X said to a friend: "I have been marked for death in the next five days. I have the names of five Black Muslims who have been asked to kill me. I will announce them at the [Sunday] meeting."[21]

Malcolm X didn't carry a gun. He even ruled against anybody getting searched before being allowed in to his last speech. That Sunday morning, he was awakened by a phone call to his room at the New York Hilton: "Wake up, brother," the voice said. Malcolm called his sister, Ella, in Boston, and told her: "I feel they may have doomed me for this day."[22]

Five men from Newark Mosque 25 had checked out the Audubon Ballroom's floor plan at a dance there on Saturday night. The next afternoon, the men entered the ballroom with their weapons concealed under their coats. Talmadge Hayer sat in the front row left, carrying a .45 automatic; next to him was Leon Davis, with a Luger. A few rows behind them sat William X with a sawed-off, double-barrel shotgun. The organizer of the killing squad, Benjamin Thomas, was next to him. Toward the back of the ballroom, Wilbur X waited to start the disturbance that would divert everyone's attention.

Before he came onstage, Malcolm X told his aides that what was happening to him lately went far beyond what the NOI alone could do. He walked out to a standing ovation. When he soon heard what seemed like a fight, he left the podium and went to the front of the stage. "Now, now, brothers break it up. Hold it, hold it," he said. Those were his last words. Bodyguard Gene Roberts, seated toward the back, recognized the tactic he'd seen before and headed down the aisle. In the rear, Wilbur X threw a smokebomb. The audience started screaming. William X, from fifteen feet away, made a circle in Malcolm X's chest with a dozen shotgun pellets. Hayer and Davis then riddled his body with shots from their pistols. As Hayer ran for the exit, Roberts grabbed a chair. Hayer fired again, hitting his suit jacket but not penetrating Roberts' body, who then knocked Hayer down with the chair. When he rose limping, another security guard shot him in the left thigh. Outside, the gunman found himself surrounded by an angry crowd that started beating him. The one policeman stationed in the vicinity then pulled Hayer away and shoved him into a cop car. Onstage, Roberts found a hint of a pulse and tried to resuscitate Malcolm X, but couldn't do it.

All the assailants except Hayer escaped. Two New York enforcers for the NOI were hauled into custody a week after the assassination. The three of them went on trial a year later. Some questionable witnesses, contradicting testimony they'd given to a grand jury, claimed they'd seen them all shooting. On the stand, Hayer confessed to his own role and truthfully said that the other two were not involved. But he wouldn't name the actual coconspirators, so his testimony was dismissed. All three were convicted and received life prison sentences. The FBI had kept close tabs on the trial, their main concern being to protect from exposure the informants and undercover agents they'd planted in Malcolm's organization.[23]

It wasn't until the late 1970s that Hayer named the others involved, hoping to get the House Committee on Assassinations to conduct a new investigation. That didn't happen, and the other killers have never been brought to justice. As of 1989, Leon Davis was still living in the vicinity of Paterson, New Jersey. William X (Bradley) was doing time in Bergen County for another crime, but refused to talk to an author who tried.[24]

There is also a confidential FBI report to Hoover about a witness who said: "John Ali met with Hayer the night before Malcolm X was killed."[25] It's a known fact that John Ali "had come in from Chicago on February 19th, checked into the Americana Hotel in midtown Manhattan and checked out on the evening of February 21"—meaning he'd arrived just in time for the final rehearsal of the murder.

When Leon Ameer, a 32-year-old aide to Malcolm X, went to the FBI about ten days after the assassination to talk about a conspiracy that included elements of the government, he was found dead a few days later in his Boston apartment. First it was ruled a suicide, then a drug overdose, and finally "natural causes."[26]

The official history is that Malcolm X's was a "revenge killing" by men connected to Elijah Muhammad. But notice how nearly all of them were never caught, only the one guy that got injured. All signs point to a conspiracy that went way beyond the Nation of Islam. We didn't know at the time about the CIA's "Executive Action" program to get rid of certain foreign leaders. For years, the agency had been plotting to assassinate Castro. In 1960 they'd come up with a plan to kill the Congo's Patrice Lumumba by infecting his toothbrush with a fatal disease. At least eight foreign heads of state were targeted during those Cold War years, and five of them died violent deaths. Given this fact, how can we not believe they'd also go after an "undesirable" like Malcolm X?

WHAT SHOULD WE DO NOW?

Let's focus on rethinking the meaning of surveillance. Certainly in the case of Malcolm X, as well as Dr. King, being shadowed by government agencies seemed to lead inevitably to their deaths. There is too much secrecy in our government, and surveillance today is even more widespread than it was then, at a considerable waste of taxpayer dollars. Let's also teach our young people that a willingness to change your attitude, as Malcolm X was willing to do, is a mark not of weakness but sometimes of greatness.

CHAPTER FIVE

THE MURDER OF DR. MARTIN LUTHER KING, JR.

THE INCIDENT: Martin Luther King was shot and killed standing on the balcony of the Lorraine Motel in Memphis, on April 4, 1968.

THE OFFICIAL WORD: James Earl Ray, a racist and escaped convict, shot King from the window of a rooming house across the street, fled the scene, and was arrested two months later in London, after which he pled guilty to the murder.

MY TAKE: Ray was another "patsy," like Oswald, who had evidence planted to incriminate him while the real killer fired from behind some shrubs. The links to King's assassination trace to people in the Mob, the military, and the right wing.

"He who passively accepts evil is as much involved in it as he who helps to perpetrate it. He who accepts evil without protesting against it is really cooperating with it."

—Dr. Martin Luther King, Jr.

In 1968 I was living a sheltered life in south Minneapolis, enjoying being a kid with my GTO and playing defensive end on my undefeated high school football team. There were never any racial tensions at my school. My best black friend in a predominantly white school was elected Winter Sports King. To me, Dr. King was a TV personality, whom you always saw walking arm-in-arm in front of a group of people and they had a cause. At the time, protests were peaking against the Vietnam War. But I was the flag-waving young American, being naïve and believing what I was taught in school, the domino effect of Communism and all that. After I graduated, I joined the navy.

So, while I remember being shocked by Dr. King's assassination, Minneapolis didn't see much if any rioting as happened in other cities. Two months later, when James Earl Ray was picked up in London and charged with the killing, I accepted what the authorities said and figured justice would be served. It was many years later when I began to question the official line. This happened in 1997, when King's son, Dexter, met face-to-face with Ray in a Tennessee prison. Ray was dying of liver disease. I read about Dexter King asking him point-blank, "Did you kill my father?" Ray answered him, "No, I didn't." And Dexter King said, "I believe you, and my family believes you."[1] I thought, wow, if that's the case, then there's a lot more to Dr. King's killing than meets the eye.

Then, in 1999, the King family brought a wrongful death lawsuit in a Tennessee Circuit Court. A nearly month-long trial ensued. Seventy witnesses were called. It took the jury only two and a half hours to come back with a verdict that Dr. King was assassinated by a conspiracy that included agencies of his own government.[2]

In the wake of the O.J. Simpson trial where TV had gavel-to-gavel coverage, you'd think the media would have been all over this. Trial of the century, maybe? Not so. I read where only one Memphis TV reporter, and one freelance journalist, covered the whole proceeding. I consider this another indictment of our media. Because O.J.'s trial, regardless of what a major personality he was and how entertaining it was to everyone, didn't affect anyone really. Not to the level of Martin Luther King's killing, which affected masses of people and had a far-reaching impact on society as a whole. Has the United States been so "dumbed down" that people are more concerned about the titillating news of a celebrity sports star and his murdered white girlfriend, than about the killing of a great leader like King? (If you want to find out what happened at the trial, the entire 4,000-word transcript is at www.thekingcenter.com.)

Let's start with a little context for what happened in the early evening of April 4, 1968, when a single shot struck Dr. King as he was standing on the balcony of the Lorraine Motel. He'd just come from leading a peaceful march of Memphis sanitation workers who'd gone on strike. Very soon he was planning to go to Washington for the Poor People's Campaign, prepared to inspire massive civil disobedience and shut down the Capitol if that's what it took to put poverty on the front burner. He was also going beyond civil rights and speaking out strongly against the Vietnam War.

A year to the day before his death, Dr. King called the U.S. government "the greatest purveyor of violence in the world today." In essence, Dr. King said things just as inflammatory as Obama's minister, Reverend Wright. I think King would probably be locked up for talking like that now. We have streets named after him, and a holiday in his name—how come we're not listening to what he said? We completely ignore the very teachings he taught and the honesty that he showed. We also ignore that the powers that be got rid of him.

The FBI's attempt to destroy Dr. King as the leader of the civil rights movement involved "attempts to discredit him with churches, universities, and the press,"[3] the Senate's Church Committee concluded a decade later. Walter Fauntroy was a colleague of Dr. King's who served 20 years in Congress and, between 1976 and 1978, was chairman of the House sub-committee looking into the assassination. Their report concluded that Ray did assassinate King, but that he probably had assistance. "It was apparent that we were dealing with very sophisticated forces," Fauntroy testified at the civil trial, saying he'd found electronic bugs on his TV set and phone. Fauntroy later said that, after he left Congress, he found information from Hoover's logs, showing that the FBI director had a series of meetings with persons involved with the CIA and military intelligence (MI) in the three weeks before King's assassination; also that there were MI agents as well as Green Berets in Memphis the night he was shot.[4]

So was James Earl Ray, a petty crook who escaped from a Missouri prison a year before the murder, a patsy like Oswald? Supposedly, he fired from the bathroom window of a rooming house a little more than 200 feet away. A tenant on the second floor said he heard a shot "and saw a man fleeing down the hallway from the direction of the bathroom," according to the House committee report. Ray went down some outside stairs and jumped into his white Mustang in an alley. Along the way he allegedly dropped a bundle that happened to include a Remington 30.06 rifle, some binoculars, and a sales receipt for ammunition. Ray's prints were on the rifle, which had one spent shell in the chamber.

Isn't it interesting how these lone-nut assassins seem to incriminate themselves in advance with dumb moves? I suppose they wouldn't want to be seen walking with the weapon, which could draw attention, but why on earth leave a weapon behind with your fingerprints all over it? Wouldn't you have a predetermined place where you're going to ditch it? Certainly not out in the open where anyone could find it! Or, in the case of Oswald, taking the rifle to the other side of the floor and tossing it behind some book boxes. What gets me is, the assassins are so "successful" in accomplishing the mission, but then utterly inept in the evacuation from the mission. They leave clues that point straight to themselves, and seem to always get caught fairly easily. Here they supposedly did all this sophisticated stuff up until it came time to pull off the killing. Yet it's like they never planned for the escape. I guess we're supposed to believe their minds are so focused on delivering the death blow that escape never enters into the plan. Then after they shoot, it's "oh, well what do I do now?" In the case of Oswald, it's run home and then go to the movies!

Later, Ray claimed that somebody else had left behind the bundle so as to incriminate him. In fact, one witness, Guy Canipe, said the package was actually dropped in the doorway to his store about ten minutes *before* the shot was fired. Makes a little more sense, doesn't it? Another witness, Olivia Catling, saw a fellow in a checkered shirt running out of the alley beside a building across from the Lorraine soon after the killing, who went screaming off in a green '65 Chevy. Ray, though, fled the scene in a white Mustang.

Judge Joe Brown, the first judge on the King family's civil case, spent two years examining technical questions about the murder weapon, and said that "67% of the bullets from my tests did not match the Ray rifle." When he called for more tests, he was taken off the case for showing "bias" by a Tennessee appeals court. "What you've got in terms of the physical evidence relative to ballistics is frightening," he said later. "First, it's not the right type of rifle. It's never been sighted in. It's the wrong kind of scope. With a 30.06, it makes a particularly difficult shot firing at a downward trajectory in that circumstance." Above all, according to Brown, "Metallurgical analysis excludes the bullet taken from the body of Dr. King from coming from the cartridge case they say was fired in that rifle."[5]

The actual sniper seems to have fired from behind some tall shrubs facing the second floor motel balcony. A Memphis newspaper reporter named Wayne Chastain had arrived at the scene within ten minutes. He was told by two witnesses, King's chauffeur and a lawyer, that the shot came from those bushes. Andrew Young told the FBI that he heard a sound like a firecracker come from the bushes above the retaining wall across the street from the motel.

By the next morning, according to the Reverend James Orange, an associate of King's, "the bushes were gone. The authorities were said to be cleaning up the area."[6] Why in all these cases does the government come in and make the most cardinal error you possibly could—and that is, disturb the crime site! When there's a violent crime, they're not supposed to do that! It's one of the first procedures any cop is taught, basic Police 101. So who gives the order to do this? Don't any of them sit and wonder, why are we not doing this according to the book, but instead breaking a cardinal rule of police work. But when there's an assassination, all local and state laws go out the window, and authority comes down from above about what's to happen. Isn't that the fox guarding the chicken house? The feds doing all the investigating and questioning just reeks of potential abuse.

So Ray has a car waiting to drive away in, then goes up to Canada and overseas, where he ends up getting caught two months later at the London airport. All by himself, right? No one aiding or abetting him in any way, shape, or form. Like Judge Joe Brown put it: "You want to say that a three-time loser, an escaped convict with no obvious financial resources and no technical knowledge, is going to not only miraculously learn how to become a good marksman: This one individual is able to acquire the resources to get identities of deceased individuals, come up with very good forgeries for passports and fake identification, and somehow acquire funds for a very expensive itinerary and travel schedule? Now, be real! . . . what you've got in this case was a stooge whose task was to throw everybody off the trail."[7]

While he was being held in a British jail before getting extradited, Ray told an officer that he'd expected to profit from being involved in the killing; later, he testified to the House committee that he figured he'd only be charged with "conspiracy." His second attorney, Percy Foreman, convinced Ray to cop a plea or else face the death penalty. Foreman later said he didn't give a damn whether there was a conspiracy or not, and never asked Ray about it. Ray reluctantly agreed to plead guilty, but pretty soon felt he'd been hung out to dry. When he died in prison in 1998, he was still saying he was innocent.

It would be a stretch to say that Ray wasn't involved at all. For one, there was big money being floated by Klan types that he certainly could have heard about. The question is, who was directly involved with Ray, and how far did the plotting go? But—no trial. Why aren't we having trials in such high-profile cases even when the guy pleads? It should go ahead anyway, just for the country's peace of mind. Then we'd know, well, he was tried and convicted and there was no evidence of a conspiracy. Or let the chips fall where they may, let the trial show enough evidence to get a couple more indictments. Just because you get a plea, isn't there any suspicion that someone is doing that to cover up for someone else? Is this guy simply falling on the sword?

In a book published in 2008, *Legacy of Secrecy*, we finally learned about a 1968 Justice Department memorandum that got withheld from congressional investigators. Based on confidential information from informers, including a "well placed protégé of Carlos Marcello in New Orleans," the memo says, "the Cosa Nostra [Mafia] agreed to 'broker' or arrange the assassination [of King] for an amount somewhat in excess of three hundred thousand ($300,000) after they were contacted by representatives of 'Forever White,' an elite organization of wealthy segregationists [in the] Southeastern states. The Mafia's interest was less the money than the investment-type opportunity presented, i.e., to get in a position to extract (or extort) governmental or other favors from some well placed Southern white persons, including the KKK and White Citizens' Councils."[8]

The memo was based on sources located by a journalist named William Sartor. The FBI didn't show much interest in going after his leads, but Sartor had uncovered information about a pre-assassination meeting between Ray and three of Marcello's associates in New Orleans—after which Ray left town with $2,500 cash and a promise of $12,000 more "for doing one last big job in 2 to 3 months."[9] Turns out that journalist Sartor was in Texas in 1971, preparing to interview a nightclub owner linked to Marcello, when he was found murdered.[10]

That same Justice Department memo stated that one participant in the plotting was "Frank [C.] Liberto . . . a Memphis racketeer and lieutenant of Carlos Marcello." What's noteworthy about this is that Liberto's name came up in recent years with two other people tied to the King case. One was Lloyd Jowers, who owned Jim's Grill across the street from the Lorraine Motel. In 1993, facing a possible indictment by Ray's last attorney, William Pepper, Jowers went public with Sam Donaldson on ABC's *Prime Time Live*.

Jowers said he'd been asked to help in the King plot by a gambling associate of his, a Memphis produce dealer named Frank Liberto who had a courier deliver $100,000 for Jowers to hold at his restaurant.[11] Jowers claimed Liberto told him that there would be a decoy, apparently Ray, and that the police "wouldn't be there that night." We know from other research that four tactical police units pulled back from the vicinity of King's motel on the morning of the assassination, making it much easier for an assassin to get away.

In a taped confession he later gave to King's son, Dexter, and ex–U.N. Ambassador Andrew Young, Jowers elaborated that planning meetings for the assassination had taken place at his restaurant. The plotters included three Memphis cops he knew, and two men who he believed were federal agents. Shortly before the assassination, Jowers was promised a substantial sum if he'd receive a package and pass it along to someone else. When it arrived he opened the package, found a rifle inside, and stashed it in a back room until another man came to pick it up on the day of the murder. Jowers said he had been instructed to be standing outside his back door that night at 6 PM. That was when one of the same Memphis policemen handed him a still-smoking gun, which Jowers broke down into two pieces, wrapped in a tablecloth, and hid in his shop until it was picked up the next day.[12]

This crucial bit of information was contradicted by another witness, who indicated Jowers was in deeper than that. This witness testified at the King family's civil trial that a deceased friend, James McCraw, more than once asserted that Jowers had given him the rifle, rolled up in an oil cloth, right after the shooting and told him "to get it out of here now." Supposedly McCraw did, tossing the rifle off a bridge into the Mississippi River.[13] Jowers was deemed, at 73, too ill to testify at the trial, so the transcript of the interview he'd done with Sam Donaldson was read to the jury.

Frank Liberto, the Mob-connected produce dealer named by Jowers, was also implicated by John McFerren, a store owner who said he came to Liberto's warehouse to pick up some produce about 45 minutes before King was shot. He overheard Liberto on the phone saying, "Shoot the son-of-a-bitch on the balcony." A café owner friend of Liberto's testified at the 1999 civil trial that Liberto flatly told her he "had Martin Luther King killed." The friend's son backed up her testimony: "[Liberto] said, 'I didn't kill the nigger but I had it done,'" and that Ray "'was a front man, a set-up man.'"[14] Liberto was dead by the time of the civil case.

At the same trial, quite a few witnesses also backed up Ray's story of a mysterious figure he knew as "Raul," whom he'd first met in Montreal three months after he escaped from prison. Ray had long claimed that it was Raul who gave him funds to purchase the rifle and the Mustang and then set him up in Memphis. The House committee had concluded that Ray's story was "not worthy of belief, and may have been invented partly to cover for help received from his brothers John and Jerry." But from a series of photographs shown him by attorney Pepper, Jowers picked out a passport photo of Raul as the guy who'd brought him the rifle to hang onto before the assassination. Glenda Grabow, who'd known Raul as a gunrunner, testified he'd once flown off the handle and told her that he'd killed Dr. King.[15]

It so happens that the Army's 111th Military Intelligence (MI) Group was keeping King under round-the-clock surveillance during the garbage strike in Memphis that spring of 1968. One of the MI guys, Marrell McCollough, was undercover with the Memphis police—and, according to Jowers, was also involved in the planning sessions for the assassination. A repeat of the kind of thing we saw with Malcolm X. In a famous photograph, McCullough was also the man seen checking Dr. King for a pulse on the motel balcony. Attorney Pepper's investigation found that McCullough went on to work for the CIA in the 1970s.[16]

In a speech given in 2003, Pepper said he'd come to believe that "a back-up operation" also involved a Special Forces unit known as Alpha 184.[17] Here's what he reported being told by an informant, a former Navy Intel guy, about a six-man sniper team: "King was never going to be allowed to leave Memphis. If the contract that was given didn't work these guys were going to do it. The story they told was that the six of them were briefed at 4:30 in the morning at Camp Shelby. They started out around 5 o'clock. They came to Memphis. They were briefed there. They took up their positions.

"At the briefing at 4:30 they were shown two photographs who were their targets. One was Martin King and the other was Andrew Young. . . . But they never got the order. Instead they heard a shot. And each thought the other one had fired too quickly. Then they had an order to disengage. It was only later that they learned that, as they call it, 'some wacko civilian' had actually shot King and that their services were not required."[18]

Carlos Marcello was also said to be "involved in a joint venture with the 902nd Mililtary Intelligence Group," splitting the profits after receiving stolen weapons and arranging to get them shipped into Latin America.

Now let's look at another strand in this spiderweb—the ultra-right. Soon after the assassination, a judge in Miami's Dade County, Seymour Gelber, wrote the U.S. Attorney General's office. Gelber said that an investigation ought to look at three men with a history of racial violence and a plot against Dr. King's life in 1964.[19] The FBI, within 48 hours, had gotten other leads that pointed to Sam Bowers, leader of the White Knights, and his associates in the Klan. FBI field offices were starting to check all this out, when Hoover ordered it be put on hold because they'd identified a fingerprint and were pursuing one fugitive (Ray).[20]

When Ray abandoned his car in an Atlanta housing project the morning after the assassination, he was overheard making a phone call to a partner of the notorious Georgia racist Joseph Milteer.[21] Before he died in a fire in 1973, Milteer's name never surfaced in connection with the King case. But Milteer was the likely fundraiser for Ray, as a conduit to the Marcello organization. Consider this curious fact: Ray's third attorney (after he'd already pled guilty) was a fellow named J.B. Stoner, who also happened to run the militant National States Rights Party. The same man who said, before Ray was apprehended, that "the white man who shot King . . . should be given the Congressional Medal of Honor and a large annual pension for life."[22] Stoner and Milteer were cronies. When Stoner became Ray's lawyer, he casually tossed it out that Hoover and the FBI might be behind the assassination. It gets even stranger. One of Ray's brothers ended up working for Stoner for more than a decade. When Stoner ran for governor of Georgia in 1970, he served as his campaign manager—until Stoner got trounced by Jimmy Carter.[23]

There's one other weird aspect we need to consider. While temporarily in Los Angeles early in 1968, Ray got into practicing self-hypnosis. Besides seeing a "psychologist-hypnotist," he visited "seven other psychiatrists, hypnotists, or scientologists."[24] One of these was "head of the International Society of Hypnosis," who later said that Ray was "impressed with the degree of mind concentration which one can obtain."[25] This was a German-born fellow named Xavier von Koss, who recommended several books on hypnosis that Ray was carrying when he got arrested in London. Von Koss seems to have also been involved in intelligence work.[26] According to one of Ray's brothers: "When Jimmy left Los Angeles he knew he was going to do it."[27] Meaning, be involved in the plot to assassinate Dr. King.

A recent book by Ray's brother, John Larry Ray, alleges that when Ray was in the army in the late 1940s, he did some moonlighting for the new CIA and the FBI—and was part of the Agency's early attempts to control human behavior that later became known as MK-ULTRA. Brother John recalls Ray telling him "that he thought the feds were messing with his mind. . . . My brother was a changed man when he returned from Germany [in 1948]. To be frank, he seemed drugged, even though I never saw him take anything. My dad and other family members commented that 'he must be on goof balls.' Also, he seemed easily persuaded to do things he never would have done before."[28]

In 1970, when Congressman Mendel Rivers tried to get Ray's entire army file, he received a response from Major General Kenneth Wickham that this would not be possible: "This is particularly true since there are medical aspects that cannot be disassociated from any discussion of Mr. Ray's military background." [29]

Ray's brother also describes an encounter in Montreal with a CIA asset who had ties to the Klan, Jules Ron "Rocco" Kimble, an identities specialist who got Ray his alias as "Eric S. Galt." Kimble said that "an older man came out from McGill University's Allen Memorial Institute to hypnotize" both Ray and him. Verification for this, as far as Kimble, came from Royal Canadian Mounted Police files. At that time, there wasn't any public knowledge about Dr. Ewen Cameron's mind-control experiments being conducted at McGill under the CIA's MK-ULTRA Sub-project 68.[30]

Early in 1968, Ray "began writing certain phrases over and over on paper. These are included in the FBI file on the assassination. [Robert Kennedy's assassin] Sirhan did the same thing. One of the phrases James wrote was, 'Now is the time for all good men to come to the aid of their country.'"[31]

Was that somebody's idea of a bad joke? I never believed *The Manchurian Candidate* was more than fiction until I got into doing this book. But there are records that prove MK-ULTRA did exist, it's undeniable. Then when you start looking at these different assassinations and how the assassins acted and reacted, you start to wonder. During the course of filming the TV show on conspiracies, we brought in an innocent person who had volunteered and put him under hypnosis with an expert. We went through a whole scenario where the guy comes out the door, starts walking and talking with me about baseball, then gets a call on his cell phone. All he needed to hear was a particular word, and that would cause a subconscious reaction to where he'd start limping, although he'd deny he was doing it. In his mind, he's not limping because he's been *told* that he's not.

Then we put him back in the room, and the hypnotist asked us, "Do you want him to remember this or not?" We chose that he not remember, because we wanted to see what would happen. When he came out of the hypnotic state, he swore to us that he'd only been in the room for a couple of minutes, when it was really nearly an hour and a half. When we told him the various things he'd done, you could clearly see that he did not believe us. Then we told him to look at his watch. That's when he freaked out, realizing how much time had passed.

So I've witnessed hypnosis firsthand. I was told that pretty much anyone who's willing can be hypnotized, because it comes from within, and the hypnotist is just someone who leads you down the path. Some people accept it more than others. To get someone to the level of an assassin, it would require you to work with them for more than a year. The hypnotist also said, "Remember this, a military man is much more predisposed to be a Manchurian Candidate than a civilian, because when you get indoctrinated into the military, you are told there are times when killing may be necessary. And that's already settled in your mind, so you might not have such an adverse reaction under hypnosis."

It's impossible to say whether the self-hypnosis that James Earl Ray was practicing, and what his brother is now claiming, actually fell under the CIA's MK-ULTRA program or something similar. But we shouldn't rule it out. Since the congressional committee's report already concluded that Ray probably had help, and the King family's court case saw a jury return a verdict of conspiracy that included *agencies of our government*, wouldn't you say that justice for Dr. King remains a long way from being served?

WHAT SHOULD WE DO NOW?

I fault the media again here, for giving us the sensational gavel-to-gavel coverage of the O.J. Simpson trial, while ignoring matters of true national importance like the civil case brought by members of the King family. I also wonder when we'll call for accountability of law enforcement agencies that seem in such a hurry to remove evidence from a crime scene, as they did in Memphis and would do again in Los Angeles and after 9/11.

CHAPTER SIX

THE ASSASSINATION OF
ROBERT KENNEDY

THE INCIDENT: Robert F. Kennedy was assassinated in the pantry of the Ambassador Hotel in Los Angeles on June 5, 1968, after winning the California primary and seeming to clinch the Democratic nomination for president.

THE OFFICIAL WORD: Sirhan Bishara Sirhan, a young Palestinian opposed to Kennedy's policy toward Israel, fired a pistol eight times from a few feet in front of him, was taken into custody immediately, and pled guilty to the murder.

MY TAKE: Sirhan didn't have enough rounds in his gun to make all the bullet holes found by police, so there was a second gunman firing from behind. Sirhan was hypnotically "programmed," using methods developed by the CIA, to take part in the murder.

"A revolution is coming—a revolution which will be peaceful if we are wise enough; compassionate if we care enough; successful if we are fortunate enough—but a revolution is coming whether we will it or not. We can affect its character; we cannot alter its inevitability."
— from a speech by Robert Kennedy in the U.S. Senate,
May 9, 1966

At the time Robert Kennedy was gunned down in the pantry of the Ambassador Hotel in L.A. on June 5, 1968, I viewed it more as a copycat political murder—this young Palestinian, Sirhan Sirhan, who didn't like

Kennedy's policies toward Israel, much like five years earlier Oswald had been a disgruntled Communist. It was now a trend, a cycle, where if a Kennedy decided to run for president, some idiot would put an end to it. At that point, I still didn't believe the government would lie to me. This was before my doubting of the Warren Commission, which didn't start until I got out of the military and heard Mark Lane speak. Later, the death of Robert Kennedy became the turning point where I felt either their father Joe had done something that was never going to be forgiven, or there certainly were forces out there ensuring another Kennedy would never occupy the White House. To say that my trust of the Establishment had deteriorated would be an understatement.

Robert Kennedy was only 42 when he was assassinated and, having just won the California primary, was on his way to the Democratic nomination and likely the presidency. He would have begun withdrawing our troops from Vietnam and saved thousands of American lives. He'd already been talking with his aides about reopening the investigation into who killed his brother. I think it's safe to say that, if he'd lived, we'd have a different kind of country than what we've become. Robert would have led a "compassionate" revolution—because he was a man not only of courage, but of compassion.

That night in the Ambassador Hotel, it seemed a pretty open-and-shut case that Sirhan was another "lone nut." After all, he was wrestled to the ground after firing his .22-caliber revolver from a few feet in front of Kennedy. The police soon found a diary, in which Sirhan wrote over and over that "RFK must die." We soon learned he'd been stalking the senator, which again raises the question in my mind as to how come nobody in authority picked up on Sirhan as a potential threat. The curious thing, even at his trial, was that Sirhan had no memory of committing the killing. He still doesn't.

Let's start by looking at the physical evidence. First of all, Sirhan's revolver held only eight rounds and he never had time to reload. But a reporter's recording has what audio expert Philip Van Praag has determined are *thirteen* shots in a little more than five seconds.[1] Two of those are what forensic experts call "double shots," meaning they happened so close together that there's no way they came from the same gun. In pictures taken in the pantry later that night, you can see some policemen looking up at what they later said was a bullet hole in a ceiling panel. The trouble is, that's *behind* where Sirhan was shooting from.[2] The L.A. County coroner, Thomas Noguchi, said almost right away that the fatal shot had come from less than an inch away from Kennedy's head, behind the right ear. That, of course, also rules out Sirhan.[3]

You'd think some of this might have come up at Sirhan's trial. But his defense attorneys decided not to challenge any evidence, because their claim was that Sirhan had "diminished capacity" (a nice way of saying he was crazy) and they were looking to get him a life sentence instead of the death penalty. Again, once he pled guilty, there was no real trial with witnesses who might contradict the official story. After a judge approved a citizen's petition to reinvestigate the firearms evidence, in 1977 the L.A. district attorney's office wrote that "the apparent lack of reports, both written and photographic, either made . . . and destroyed, or never in existence, raised serious doubts as to the substance and reliability of the ballistics evidence presented in the original Sirhan trial."[4]

So, if not Sirhan, then who killed RFK? Well, several witnesses saw a security guard who was standing behind Kennedy draw his gun, and one witness even said that he fired it. This was a fellow named Thane Eugene Cesar. He was a plumber by trade, who'd been hired part-time by Ace Security less than a week before the assassination, his assignment being to guard the pantry that night. One of Cesar's first statements to the police was that he'd been holding Kennedy's arm when "they" shot him. Not "he," but "they." He said when he saw Sirhan's gun, he reached for his own. But the LAPD never asked to see his gun, or even to ask him what kind it was.[5]

Years later, he passed a polygraph overseen by author Dan Moldea, who called Cesar "an innocent bystander caught in the crossfire of history."[6] Well, maybe he was. Or maybe not. Acoustics expert Van Praag did tests on an H&R 922 pistol of the type that Cesar had on him, and concluded that an H&R 922 had been fired at the same time as Sirhan's.[7] Then, too, besides Sirhan and Cesar, *another* man with a gun was mentioned by several more witnesses. Conceivably, that person could have gotten in between Kennedy and the security guard to fire the fatal shot, as RFK was falling back from Sirhan.[8]

The strongest evidence that Sirhan had accomplices are no less than fourteen witnesses who all talked about a girl in a polka-dot dress. A 20-year-old Youth for Kennedy volunteer immediately reported seeing such a girl, both to the press and the police. Earlier in the night, Sandra Serrano said, she'd observed a young woman dressed in a white dress with black or dark-blue polka dots, walking up a back stairway of the hotel. She was with two men, one well-dressed in a white shirt and gold sweater, and the other rather disheveled and short with black bushy hair, who was likely Sirhan.

Then, after the assassination, Serrano saw the same girl, running down a fire escape out of the hotel and shouting, "We shot him! We shot him! We shot Kennedy!" Later, an LAPD interrogator put heavy pressure on Serrano to recant her story, which she did at the time. But when Serrano was interviewed again 40 years later, she stuck to what she'd originally said. And she wasn't the only one who reported seeing something like this. Police Sergeant Paul Sharaga, who was in the hotel's back parking lot six minutes after the shooting, also heard a young couple run past yelling about having killed Kennedy.[9] He put out an APB. But Sharaga said, when he went to look for the three copies he made of his report two weeks later, they had vanished.[10]

Sirhan himself said: "I met the girl and had coffee with her. She wanted heavy on the cream and sugar. After that I don't remember a thing until they pounced on me in that pantry."[11] Could it be that the girl said some key word or phrase that triggered his amnesia?

According to the LAPD logs, the cops were looking for two suspects besides Sirhan within minutes of the assassination. Then they stopped searching within the hour, because "they only have one man and don't want them to get anything started on a big conspiracy. This could be somebody that was getting out of the way so they wouldn't get shot."[12] Huh? That makes no sense at all for an honest investigator to reason.

The fact is, the LAPD had a long history of a "special relationship" with the CIA, from helping out with clandestine activities to training certain officers for double duty. When they formed Special Unit Senator (SUS) to look into the assassination, the two main cops through which all information flowed both had ties to the CIA. "In retrospect it seems odd that . . . policemen who doubled as CIA agents occupied key positions in SUS, where they were able to seal off avenues that led in the direction of conspiracy."[13] They also badgered any witness who didn't support the Sirhan-did-it-alone scenario.

Manuel Pena, a multilingual fellow who'd done special ops for the CIA, saw all the SUS reports and was the man responsible for approving all interviews. His partner, Sergeant Enrique "Hank" Hernandez, handled all the polygraph work, which he'd also done in Vietnam, South America, and Europe. Both Pena and Hernandez had been undercover CIA with the Agency for International Development (AID). Later, Hernandez started his own security firm and got rich handling big government contracts.[14]

As soon as Sirhan's trial ended, the LAPD got busy destroying evidence, including the ceiling panels and door frames from the pantry that they'd taken pictures of showing extra bullet holes. Their rationale, when asked later, was these were "too large to fit into a card file"! Once again, we've got the authorities destroying evidence at a crime scene, just like with the King case. They also burned some 2,400 photographs, supposedly all duplicates, but we know some important ones are still missing—like the pictures taken by a 15-year-old kid named Scott Enyart. He was standing on a table so he could get a good view of Kennedy as he came in and took three rolls of Kodak film that the cops confiscated afterwards and said he could get back—if he came around in twenty years! Enyart had to fight in court to eventually be returned only 18 prints (no negatives), which were then promptly stolen out of the back seat of a car.[15]

Also gone missing were "X-rays and test results on ceiling tiles and door frames, spectrographic test results [for bullets], the left sleeve of Senator Kennedy's coat and shirt, the test gun used as a substitute for Sirhan's gun during ballistics tests, and results from the 1968 test firing of Sirhan's gun." Tapes of key interviews that raised the question of conspiracy disappeared, too.[16]

When the LAPD declassified more files in 2008—forty years too late!—a fuller picture of Sirhan started to appear. He was raised a Christian, wanted to be a jockey, and spent a good bit of time betting on horses at the Santa Anita racetrack. He wanted to make a bundle of money, and seems to have had some gambling debts. His personality appeared to change after he fell off a horse in September 1966. That's when he began developing a curiosity about mysticism, such as the Rosicrucians, and got into learning self-hypnosis. Toward the end of 1967, Sirhan pretty much dropped out of sight for three months. His mother was worried because she didn't know where he'd gone. When he finally did come home, his interest in hypnosis escalated.[17] At the same time, somebody put Sirhan under clandestine surveillance for reasons that were never explained. Some 16-millimeter footage taken of Sirhan late in 1967—by whom or for what purpose we don't know—later showed up in a drawer of a private detective's office.

In mid-February 1968, Sirhan bought a .22-caliber Iver-Johnson, the pistol he would use the night of the assassination, for twenty-five bucks on the street. A gunshop owner remembered him coming in with several other people asking for "armor piercing ammunition," for another weapon he doesn't seem to have owned.[18] So it sure looks like somebody was prompting Sirhan. He was also seen stalking Kennedy on two other occasions, both times with a young female companion (at a luncheon May 20 and a downtown L.A. rally four days after that). And he was seen doing target practice at tin cans with a young brunette and a tall guy who had sandy-colored hair.[19]

What does it all add up to? A few weeks before RFK's assassination, the *Providence Evening Bulletin* ran a story headlined—"'To Sleep': Perchance to Kill?" It told of a visiting professor of psychology at Rhode Island College, who had been a leading adviser to the military since the 1930s on the possible applications of hypnosis. Dr. George H. Estabrooks was quoted that "hypnotism is widely used by intelligence agencies of the United States and other countries." He went on to say that the key to creating an effective spy—or assassin—revolved around splitting someone's personality: "It is like child's play now to develop a multiple personality through hypnosis."

The professor added that Lee Harvey Oswald and Jack Ruby "could very well have been performing through hypnosis. They would have been perfect cases but I doubt you will find anyone admitting this possibility, especially in the *Warren Report*." Estabrooks concluded by referring to the novel and film, *The Manchurian Candidate*, as putting forth an "entirely possible" scenario.[20]

The Manchurian Candidate had been a best-selling book in 1958, later made into a movie by John Frankenheimer (who, ironically, was a good friend of Robert Kennedy's and had him as a houseguest right before the assassination). It's about a soldier who gets "brainwashed" by the Communist Chinese during the Korean War, then later is used in a domestic assassination plot against an American presidential contender. This was regarded as pretty wild fiction at the time. Nobody knew until the late 1970s that both the military and CIA had been experimenting for years with drugs, hypnosis, and other means to figure out how to alter human behavior.

Back in 1954, a CIA study had raised the question: "Can an individual of (deleted nationality) descent be made to perform an act of attempted assassination involuntarily, against a prominent (deleted) politician or if necessary, against an American official." After being drugged, the subject would perform the deed "at some later date," after which "it was assumed the subject would be taken into custody by the (deleted) government and thereby 'disposed of.'"[21]

In June of 1960, the CIA under the MK-ULTRA program had "launched an expanded program of operational experiments in hypnosis in cooperation with the Agency's Counterintelligence [CI] staff." The program had three goals: "(1) to induce hypnosis very rapidly in unwitting subjects; (2) to create durable amnesia; and (3) to implant durable and operationally useful posthypnotic suggestions."[22]

So what do we have in the case of Sirhan? A year before the government's mind control efforts became public, a nationally-recognized expert in hypnosis, Dr. Herbert Spiegel, had this to say: "I've gone over the data very carefully on Sirhan and my hypothesis is that someone. . . programmed him to be there and fire that gun. . . . I know from his lawyer that he appeared at another political rally that night in the Ambassador Hotel, for some right-wing school superintendent. Here's what Sirhan reports: 'I'm in this rally and I ask myself, what am I doing here? So I leave. Then I go back to my car and the next thing I know there's a gun on the seat. And I don't know where that gun came from. Then all of a sudden, I'm in the kitchen.' And he has no recall of how he went from that car into the hotel kitchen. If he was drunk or under drugs, which is possible, it would not be as easily recoverable. But if he were in a trance state and programmed, it is recoverable."[23] Meaning, an expert like Spiegel could still "unlock" Sirhan's mind today, if he were allowed into Pleasant Valley State Prison.

Sirhan showed a number of signs of being in some weird zone that night at the Ambassador. A Western Union operator had seen him standing transfixed in front of a teletype machine.[24] Other witnesses observed his intense concentration in the pantry, and his almost super-human strength when being wrestled down, despite a "very tranquil" look on his face. Policeman Art Pacencia noticed that the pupils of Sirhan's eyes were dilated, which is another indication of a hypnotic state. Just as Oswald was when questioned about the assassination of JFK, Sirhan was oddly detached during that first long night of interrogation.

It could be, of course, that Sirhan was in a state of shock after the assassination. But Dr. Bernard Diamond was hired by Sirhan's defense team to check out his mental state, and Diamond put him under hypnosis. Sirhan turned out to be such an easy subject, "going under" so fast and so deeply, that Diamond had trouble keeping him awake. (I've learned that a rapid induction like this is a sure sign of someone having been hypnotized before.) Diamond could actually get Sirhan to climb the bars of his cell like a monkey, or sing a tune in Arabic. When he once asked Sirhan who killed Senator Kennedy, the response came back: "I don't know I don't know I don't know." Yet strangely, on the opening day of the trial, Sirhan got up and started shouting how he wanted to be executed because he'd killed the senator "willfully, premeditatedly, with twenty years of malice aforethought." Which was the real Sirhan?

On the witness stand, Dr. Diamond testified that he was surprised how easy it was to hypnotize Sirhan, but believed Sirhan had basically programmed himself through studying texts on self-hypnosis. The "automatic writing" found in Sirhan's notebooks, he said, "is something that can be done only when one is pretty well trained."[25]

Another expert called in was Dr. Eduard Simson-Kallas, the chief psychologist at San Quentin when Sirhan was being held there. Simson-Kallas thought Sirhan was an ideal "Manchurian Candidate": "He was easily influenced, had no real roots, and was looking for a cause."[26] Once, Sirhan told him: "Sometimes I go in a very deep trance so I can't even speak . . . I had to be in a trance when I shot Kennedy, as I don't remember having shot him."[27] But after Sirhan asked Simson-Kallas to hypnotize him and see what he could find out, the San Quentin warden terminated their visits. Simson-Kallas ended up quitting his job at the prison. Even Roger LaJeunesse, the FBI's liaison to the L.A. County prosecutor, told journalist Robert Blair Kaiser: "The case is still open. I'm not rejecting the Manchurian Candidate aspect of it." J. Edgar Hoover told the *Washington Post* that the interviewer had "manufactured" the quote, but Kaiser had it on tape. [28]

Dr. Spiegel thinks there were probably "one senior programmer and many accessories."[29] A couple names of hypnosis experts have surfaced over the years as being possible Svengalis behind Sirhan. Both did work for either the CIA or FBI and claimed to have been technical advisers on *The Manchurian Candidate* movie. Both are now dead. One was Dr. William J. Bryan, who phoned the KABC radio station not long after the assassination and said that the suspect had probably been acting under post-hypnotic suggestion. Bryan, the founder and executive director of the American Institute of Hypnosis, was known for hypnotizing the Boston Strangler, Albert De Salvo, after his arrest, to see what the mass murderer might reveal. (Strangely, again, De Salvo's name appears in Sirhan's notebook, even though Sirhan didn't have the foggiest idea who he was.) In 1977, Bryan is said to have told a researcher who asked him about Sirhan and programming, "I'm not going to comment on that case because I didn't hypnotize him." After Bryan was found dead in his Vegas hotel room in 1977, supposedly of natural causes, some call girls came forward saying he'd once bragged of having hypnotized Sirhan. [30]

In the same league as Bryan was Dr. William Kroger, a world authority on hypnosis who consulted for the FBI and the LAPD, and who died in 1996 at almost ninety. While alive, he was referenced in Philip Melanson's book on the assassination under the pseudonym of Jonathan Reisner. Kroger and Bryan each "had an interest in the links between mystical orders and hypnosis, as well as in the uses of auto-hypnosis."[31] Melanson made it clear that he suspected "Reisner" as the man who programmed Sirhan. In the two years before Kroger died, my coauthor on this book conducted a couple of interviews with the man. Although Kroger denied having anything to do with Sirhan, he did admit knowing Jack Ruby and Sam Giancana, as well as George White, the chief field officer for the CIA's MK-ULTRA program.[32]

One clue to Sirhan's "handlers" might be the lawyers who took his case for free. One was Grant Cooper, a well-known L.A. criminal attorney. Sirhan selected his name, and that of Russell Parsons, right away from a list provided by the ACLU—a list Sirhan had asked for. Parsons did legal work for the mob, having been Mickey Cohen's counsel. Cooper, at the time, was defending one of mobster Johnny Rosselli's pals in a cheating scandal at the Friar's Club.[33]

Cooper gave Sirhan the motive that he was angry at RFK for giving jets to Israel. Prior to this, there was "not a single reference to Zionism, Israel, Palestine, [or any of] the terms Sirhan would spout at his trial as propelling him to murder."[34] Years later, Sirhan said that "Cooper sold me out."[35] During conversations with his attorney, Sirhan once asked Cooper, "If I got the money, where is it?"[36] In the strange notebooks he kept before the assassination, there were references to a figure of $100,000. Also, at least a dozen times, the notation: "Please pay to the order of Sirhan," always on the same pages where he scrawls things like "RFK must be be be disposed of."[37]

So it looks like somebody was telling Sirhan he'd be getting paid handsomely for the deed. One fellow he knew by an alias of Frank Donneroumas had hired Sirhan to exercise and groom horses at the racetrack. The first place he worked was "a Syndicate meeting place," and another track where Sirhan worked "was frequented by some of the nation's most infamous racketeers." Donneroumas's real name was Henry Ramistella, with a record of narcotics violations in both New York and Florida.[38]

It's been long known that Teamster boss Jimmy Hoffa had made threats against RFK. Joseph Marcello, brother of New Orleans Mob boss Carlos Marcello, can be heard telling an informant on tape, when the subject of the Kennedys came up: "We took care of 'em, didn't we?" There's also a file on a Roy Donald Murray, who was overheard by cops saying that he'd pledged some Vegas funds for a Mob contract on Robert Kennedy.[39]

Same as with his brother's assassination, it's hard to conceive that the Mob had enough power to pull this off without government help. Of course, it's possible they knew of MK-ULTRA and of the hypnosis experts, and paid one of those guys to program Sirhan—knowing the CIA and FBI would want to keep that from being exposed. But it still smells to me like there was intelligence involvement. CIA agent David Morales, who hated the Kennedys, allegedly once told his attorney: "I was in Los Angeles when we got Bobby." Morales had once come up with a similar scenario for assassinating Castro in a pantry.[40]

Can we still get to the bottom of what happened? Maybe, if Sirhan's mind can be "de-programmed." That's what his new attorney, William Pepper, wants to do. He was James Earl Ray's last attorney, too, and he's pushing to start new psychological evaluations of Sirhan with an expert in regression therapy. [41] I'd like to be a fly on the wall for that one, because recently I had a personal experience with a guy who claims to be a programmed "Manchurian Candidate."

I was filming an episode about "Big Brother" for my new TV series when I met with him in the basement of a parking garage, very much like Deep Throat in *All the President's Men*. He says that his father was in the CIA, and he was taken as a "candidate" at the age of six, selected partly because of his nationality (he's an American Indian). He says his parents didn't have a choice. The only reason he knows today is, he was in a bad car wreck. He had to get a full-body MRI, where they discovered four different implants.

The accident also jostled him to the point where he's getting his memory back about what was done to him, and what *he's* done. I asked him point-blank, "You have killed people?" He said, "Yes, I have." He told me he was fourteen when he was first sent to do "ops." He keeps referring to "we," meaning that there are way more than him. He said, "We're all getting together now because we want our lives back." They're going to go public. "That's one of the reasons I did the interview with you, because we think we might want to have you with us," he said. I told him, "I don't know if I've got *that* much courage." He said, "Well, we just feel that we need someone with credibility to stand there with us and say, 'Listen to what these people have to say, they're not all crazy. Or if they are, they were made to be that way.'"

Is this man a real "Manchurian Candidate"? Or is he nuts and making it all up? Like my son said, maybe he had something traumatic happen to him as a kid that set this off. Well, maybe, but whatever happened, *he* believes it. There's no doubt in my mind about that, from the stories he told me. Also, he had a handler, a girl who accompanied him. She said, "I'm one, too. I know his case, and I'm also here to control his multiple personalities. We get strength through each other."

Being left with the impression of how strongly he believes this, then clearly I could see him being able to perform an act of violence. How do I feel about the government—or whoever it is—doing something like this to someone? They should be in jail. These are evil people who don't belong out in society, because obviously they have no regard for another human life. Or are these people so callous that, looking at the "big picture," they view a body or two as simply collateral damage? They're beyond human feelings? If some have to be destroyed to achieve the goal, it's better for the mass of humanity. I don't fit into that mold. These are the types of things you attribute to the Nazis. Sure, some were exceptionally intelligent, but they were an empire based and designed on evil.

If Robert Kennedy had survived the first attempt on his life, and tried to implement all that he wanted to do, he'd have been "killed again." All the people making money off the Vietnam War, would they let the golden goose be stopped? And to reopen his brother's case? I compare this to President Obama's inaugural address. When I heard him give that dynamic speech the day he took office, I turned to my wife and said, "If he attempts to do all this, he's going to be killed." Where he wanted to tread, the same as Bobby Kennedy—you're talking about powerful forces involved in evil, who don't sweat one more piece of collateral damage.

That's a terrible thing to realize. The things I'm learning about, I come home at night and wonder, why do I need to know this? I was better off being ignorant. Meeting with a man who considers himself a "Manchurian Candidate"—what we talked about scares you, whether you believe it or not. It scared me. And I don't scare easily.

WHAT SHOULD WE DO NOW?

If the assassination of Robert Kennedy tells us anything, it's that even apparently obvious things are not always what they seem. Here we had what appeared to be an open-and-shut case with Sirhan Sirhan as the perpetrator. It's almost unthinkable, in polite society, to consider that his mind may have been manipulated by unscrupulous people using techniques out of the Dark Ages. But MK-ULTRA's existence is a proven fact, and should not be forgotten.

CHAPTER SEVEN

WATERGATE REVISITED: THE CIA'S WAR AGAINST NIXON

THE INCIDENT: The Watergate burglars broke into the Democratic National Committee headquarters on June 17, 1972, were taken into custody by police, and discovered to have ties to the Nixon White House.

THE OFFICIAL WORD: President Nixon authorized the break-in, along with other "dirty tricks," and then covered this up, leading to his resignation on August 9, 1974, before he could be impeached.

MY TAKE: Nixon was involved in a power struggle with the CIA, trying to pry loose what their files contained on the Kennedy assassination. He was taken down by "double agents" who were actually working for the CIA, who intentionally got themselves caught. Many of the Watergate cast track back to who killed JFK.

"In a time of deceit, telling the truth is a revolutionary act."

—George Orwell

At this point in my life, I guess the word "astounding" should not be used, because I've been astounded by so many other things. But it was astounding to realize that Richard Nixon could actually have been set up by some of the Watergate burglars, whose loyalty was really to the CIA. When you look at some of the data, you realize this possibility exists. Watergate was an attempt to get him *out* of the White House, because he was going where other powerful people didn't want him to tread.[1]

The official history, of course, is that the break-in on the night of June 17, 1972, into the Democratic National Committee headquarters at the

Watergate complex, was simply the latest in a long line of "dirty tricks" authorized by President Nixon. It just happened to be the time that his henchmen got caught. Ultimately, Watergate came to refer to the many illicit activities and the cover-up that led to Nixon's resignation in August 1974. That's the basic storyline of Woodward and Bernstein in *All the President's Men*, and most other accounts. Nixon was the bad-guy who got carried away with his thirst for power, and that's that. But maybe it's as Watergate burglar G. Gordon Liddy once said: "The official version of Watergate is as wrong as a Flat Earth Society pamphlet."[2]

Let's start with the fact that Nixon had been haunted by the specter of the Kennedys ever since losing the election to JFK in 1960. He even happened to be in Dallas on November 22, 1963, for a Pepsi-Cola Bottler's Convention! If Robert Kennedy hadn't been assassinated, he'd have been the likely Democratic contender against Nixon in 1968, and quite likely Nixon would have lost. So what if, after his election, his obsession resulted in the beginning of a carefully orchestrated plan to get rid of Nixon?

What if it all tracked back to the assassination of John F. Kennedy almost a decade earlier? What if the Watergate backstory is really about what Nixon knew, or wanted to know, about who killed JFK?

Maybe Nixon was determined to find out what the CIA possessed about the assassination, out of curiosity and for his own purposes. He could then use that knowledge against the powerful Agency, if he had to. Or maybe Nixon himself knew something about the assassination, and was paranoid that the CIA might have the same secret knowledge. This knowledge could lead back to him, or people he knew. I'm not sure which it was, but I'll bet it was one or the other. And the CIA was determined to stop his quest.

Let's start with a story that H.R. Haldeman, Nixon's chief of staff, related in his memoirs. Soon after taking office in 1969, the president called him into the Oval Office and officially asked Haldeman to get hold of any and all documents from the CIA that pertained to the Bay of Pigs. This was the first of many occasions that Nixon referred to that historical event, when the CIA sent an invasion force of Cuban exiles to try to overthrow Castro in April 1961. This plan had been in the works before JFK took office and, when it failed, Kennedy threatened to "scatter the CIA to the four winds." Now that Nixon was president, why should he desire to learn everything he could about "the whole Bay of Pigs thing," as he put it during one of his taped Oval Office conversations. Haldeman makes the startling assertion in his book that "in all of those Nixon references to the Bay of Pigs, he was actually referring to the Kennedy assassination."[3]

Around the middle of '69, Haldeman remembers Nixon domestic adviser John Ehrlichman dropping by to talk about Nixon's demand for CIA records. "'Those bastards in Langley are holding back something," Ehrlichman said. "They just dig in their heels and say the President can't have it. Period. Imagine that! The Commander-in-Chief wants to see a document relating to a military operation, and the spooks say he can't have it. . . . From the way they're protecting it, it must be pure dynamite."[4] At that same time, CIA Director Richard Helms—who'd been in charge of clandestine ops when JFK was in power—was on his way over to the White House. Ehrlichman believed that "the president is going to give him [Helms] a direct order."

But after a long private conversation between Helms and Nixon, Ehrlichman said the president instructed him "to forget all about that CIA document. In fact, I am to cease and desist from trying to obtain it."[5]

That little story is a volume-getter to me. First, it makes me wonder how much stonewalling takes place at the highest levels of government by subordinates? The CIA is supposedly the president's intelligence-gathering arm and answerable to him. What's gone wrong with our country when his guys are now keeping information from the boss? What gives them the right to make that kind of command decision? I can understand, in certain instances, giving the boss plausible denial if you're doing something underhanded. But by the same token, people are going to question who's actually running the show.

During these same early months of Nixon's presidency, the Howard Hughes empire was imploding in Las Vegas. Hughes had gotten billions in secret contracts from the CIA over the years, and let his Medical Institute serve as one of their front companies. Hughes also gave Nixon, among other politicians, plenty of under-the-table funds. At the end of 1970, suddenly Hughes disappears. His top aide, Robert Maheu, thinks the billionaire has been kidnapped. Maheu gets forced off the Hughes Tool Company board, and he stashes a bunch of documents and tapes in the safe of his pal Hank Greenspun, the editor of the *Las Vegas Sun*.

What might have been in those documents and tapes? One of the Watergate burglars, James McCord, later said he'd been part of a plot to steal some stuff from Greenspun's safe. When the Senate Watergate Committee demanded that Greenspun show them those documents, the publisher got a court order to stop it. We still don't know what they contained, but one clue emerged in a column by Jack Anderson early in 1971 that tracked right back to the "whole Bay of Pigs thing."[6]

"Locked in the darkest recesses of the CIA is the story of six assassination attempts against Cuba's Fidel Castro," the article began. It went on to detail how Hughes's man Maheu had teamed up with mobster Johnny Rosselli to work with the CIA on a "hush-hush murder mission." Anderson speculated that, after the CIA-Mob plots supposedly stopped in the spring of 1963, Castro had sought revenge on JFK. This was the first time any details such as these had hit the news.

Hughes had brought Rosselli into his own organization when he moved into the Mob's Las Vegas territory. Rosselli was tight with Sam Giancana and Santos Trafficante Jr., a couple of the gangsters who have since been linked to JFK's assassination. And a friend of Rosselli's, Jimmy Starr, later told the mobster's biographers: "What I heard about the Kennedy assassination was that Johnny was the guy who got the team together to do the hit." We know today that certain people in the CIA wanted to pin the blame for JFK's murder on Castro, to take the heat off themselves. We also know today that Nixon, while he was Vice President under Eisenhower, was the liaison to the CIA in the first assassination attempt against Castro. But that secret, like the others, was still way below the radar when Nixon was in office.

So, on the very day that column by Jack Anderson came out, Haldeman asked John Dean (the White House counsel) to make an inquiry into the relationship between Maheu, Hughes, and a guy named Lawrence O'Brien. Remember that name? It was O'Brien's office that the burglars broke into at the Watergate. At the time, he headed the Democratic National Committee, so people presumed Nixon's team were looking for dirt on the dems. But O'Brien was not only a former staff assistant to the Kennedy brothers, but also an old friend of Robert Maheu's. Two weeks after Robert Kennedy's assassination, Maheu had arranged for O'Brien to hire on as a consultant to the Hughes organization. Then when Hughes vanished and Maheu got purged, O'Brien went with him. As a White House aide wrote to John Dean on February 1, 1971: "Mayhew's [sic] controversial activities and contacts in both Democratic and Republican circles suggest the possibility that forced embarrassment of O'Brien . . . might well shake loose Republican skeletons from the closet."[7] What kind of skeletons? Could the interest in O'Brien, all the way to the Watergate break-in, have concerned what he might know about Maheu, Rosselli, and the intrigue around "the whole Bay of Pigs thing"?

In February 1971 came another Jack Anderson column about Rosselli.[8] The story was sketchy, but tantalizing. It said: "Confidential FBI files identify him as 'a top Mafia figure' who watched over 'the concealed interests in Las Vegas casinos of the Chicago underworld.'" Also that he'd been recruited by Maheu and "had handled undercover assignments for the CIA." The story concluded: "Rosselli's lawyers are now trying to get clemency for their client, citing our stories about his secret CIA service."

Sure looks like *somebody* was putting out a message through Anderson, doesn't it. Rosselli was facing time, and hinting he might squawk if he got convicted. So what happens next? Nixon's attorney general, John Mitchell, phoned Maheu, who caught the next flight to D.C. and told Mitchell everything he knew about the CIA Mob plots. Mitchell was "shaking" by the time Maheu ended his story, and after that helped Maheu avoid a grand jury.[9]

What happens to Anderson after he does these stories? He's targeted by Nixon's infamous Plumbers Unit, the guys who liked to "plug leaks" by breaking into various places. G. Gordon Liddy and E. Howard Hunt Jr. later admitted during the Watergate hearings that they met with a CIA operative in 1972 to talk about slipping the columnist LSD, or putting poison in his aspirin bottle, or concocting a fatal mugging. The plot was aborted when the Watergate break-in occurred.

Howard Hunt had supposedly retired from the CIA in April 1970, but he'd immediately landed a job with a CIA front outfit called the Mullen Company. They'd been instrumental in setting up the CIA's "Cuban Freedom Committee" that helped disseminate the Castro-did-it rumors after the Kennedy assassination. Their cover specialty was PR, and now they were representing the Hughes Tool Company. "I am sure I need not explain the political implications of having Hughes' affairs handled here in Washington by a close friend," Nixon's hatchet man, Charles Colson, wrote in a memo.

On the tenth anniversary of the Bay of Pigs in 1971, Hunt flew to Miami and got back in touch with two Cuban exiles he'd worked with during the anti-Castro battles of the early Sixties. The exiles knew Hunt as "Eduardo." Their names were Bernard Barker and Eugenio Martinez. Hunt took them along when he did a little "private investigation" visiting a woman who "claimed to have been in the Castro household with one of Fidel's sisters at the time that John Kennedy was assassinated." The woman said the "reaction was one of moroseness because he [JFK] was dead."[10] That may not have been what Hunt wanted to hear, but he said he sent reports to both the CIA and to the White House, although each denied ever getting such. Hunt said that, after he went to work as a White House "consultant" in June 1971 (he also kept his job with the Mullen Company), he kept a copy of his report in his safe there, only to see it destroyed after the Watergate break-in by the FBI. So, I guess we'll never know what was really in it. Meantime, Hunt became chief operative of the Plumbers. As John Ehrlichman later described it, "The Unit as originally conceived was to stimulate the various departments and agencies to do a better job of controlling leaks and the theft or other exposure of national security secrets from within their departments." National security secrets like who killed JFK, maybe?

Early that same summer of '71, columnist Anderson met with Bernard Barker and another of Hunt's recruits, Frank Sturgis, in Miami. Anderson and Sturgis went back to 1960, when they "collaborated on magazine articles about plans to overthrow Fidel Castro." Sturgis also knew a lot of secrets, including the CIA's formation of an assassination squad of Cuban exiles called Operation 40, just before the Bay of Pigs. After the Kennedy assassination, Sturgis had played a key role in spreading the rumors that Castro was behind it. Now Anderson was told the old crew was "back in business" with the legendary "Eduardo," E. Howard Hunt. But for whatever reason, the columnist wrote nothing about it.

Things were happening thick and fast. Daniel Ellsberg leaked the Pentagon Papers to the media, secret policy documents about the Vietnam War build-up, and Nixon went ballistic. That's what first spawned the Plumbers, who mounted a covert "op" to break into the office of Ellsberg's psychiatrist, with assistance from the CIA's Office of Security. Except, it wasn't only the Pentagon Papers that worried the CIA. "Their concern—indeed what seems to have been their panic," focused around Ellsberg's friendship with Frances FitzGerald, "the talented author of *Fire in the Lake* [who] was the daughter of the late Desmond FitzGerald, a former deputy director of the CIA. . . . The CIA saw his liberal daughter's friendship with Ellsberg as a threat, and worried that it might lead to the exposure of operations that the CIA hoped would remain state secrets."[11]

We know today—but it wasn't public knowledge back then—that Desmond FitzGerald, who died of a sudden heart attack on the tennis court in 1967, had ended up in charge of all the anti-Castro plots in 1963. And he'd had his CIA Special Affairs Staff keeping tabs on a fellow named Lee Harvey Oswald.

A few days before the break-in to Ellsberg's psychiatrist's office, the CIA called John Ehrlichman to say that their own assistance to Hunt was being terminated. Ehrlichman says he hadn't realized the CIA was aiding Hunt in the first place. Hunt told Ehrlichman that the latest operation was a failure: the Ellsberg dossier had not been found—even though one of the Cuban exiles involved in that break-in remembered photographing the psychiatrist's notes on Ellsberg. The film taken by the Minox spy camera was passed along to Hunt, who apparently turned it over as part of his regular deliveries to Richard Helms at the CIA. This tells me that Hunt was misleading the White House, at the same time that he was still playing ball with the Agency.

Soon after this, Nixon renewed his pursuit of the CIA's records. He sent an order to Ehrlichman: Tell Helms to fork over "the full file [on the Bay of Pigs] or else." So Ehrlichman went to see Helms, twice within four days. At the second meeting, Helms asked to see Nixon privately once again. A transcript of their tape-recorded session in the Oval Office on October 8, 1971, was released by the National Archives in 2000. Would somebody tell me why a potential bombshell like this had to wait thirty years for us to know about, after all of the participants are dead? Before Helms came into the room, Ehrlichman briefed Nixon on the CIA director's latest excuse for not turning over the documents:

"[Helms] said that his relationship with past presidents had been such that he would not feel comfortable about releasing some of this very, very dirty linen to anyone without first talking it through with you, because he was sure that when you become a former president you would want to feel that whoever was at the agency was protecting your interests in a similar fashion. This is incredibly dirty linen." Ehrlichman then continued: "Helms is scared to death of this guy Hunt that we got working for us because he knows where a lot of the bodies are buried. And Helms is a bureaucrat first and he's protecting that bureau."

When Helms arrived, Nixon pounded his desk and shouted: "The president needs to know everything! The real thing you need to have from me is this assurance: I am not going to embarrass the CIA! Because it's (certainly?) important. Second, I believe in dirty tricks." (Ehrlichman's notes quote Nixon as saying to Helms: "Purpose of request for documents: must be fully advised in order to know what to duck; won't hurt Agency, nor attack predecessor.")

Helms, at least pretending to be contrite, responded: "I regard myself, you know, really, as working entirely for you. And everything I've got is yours." He held up a file folder and continued, "Should I turn this over to John [Ehrlichman]?" Nixon said, "Let me see it."[12] It was a slim report by a Marine colonel who'd been assisting the CIA during the Bay of Pigs planning. In his memoirs, Nixon would complain that what Helms gave him was "incomplete . . . The CIA protects itself, even from presidents."

The day after the meeting with Helms, Ehrlichman sent a staffer to Las Vegas for a four-hour chat with Hank Greenspun. It wasn't long after that when Hunt and his team of Cuban exiles began their discussions about burglarizing Greenspun's safe. The CIA's Office of Security already had 16 agents shadowing columnist Jack Anderson, who then was invited by Helms to a long lunch. Ostensibly Helms wanted to try to dissuade Anderson "from publishing certain sensitive classified material in his forthcoming book." A week after that, Hunt and G. Gordon Liddy started drawing up plans to "neutralize" Anderson. The CIA Office of Security was using another "retired" agent, James McCord, to keep tabs on the columnist. McCord also began working part-time at the White House for the CREEP (Committee to Re-Elect the President). Nixon would be gone when, in 1975, the CIA admitted to Congress its "practice of detailing CIA employees to the White House and various government agencies," including "intimate components of the Office of the President." And we thought double agents only worked against foreign elements!

Hunt and McCord had been acquainted since the mid-Fifties, although Hunt lied under oath that they didn't meet until April 1972. McCord, according to the *New York Times*, was "believed to have played a role in the abortive Bay of Pigs invasion of Cuba in 1961." The CIA denied that, but recently released documents show that in early 1961, "James McCord and David (Atlee) Phillips . . . launched a domestic operation against the FPCC." That's the Fair Play for Cuba Committee, the same organization that Oswald suddenly joined in 1962. And David Phillips was not only involved in the anti-Castro plots, but was also said to have met with Oswald in the summer of '63 in Dallas.[13]

Early in 1972, Hunt's Plumbers and McCord's CREEP security unit had merged into the Gemstone plan, a wide-ranging series of illegal White House–based projects. Then, sometime on the night of May 1–2, FBI Director J. Edgar Hoover died in his sleep. Nixon's attorney general, Richard Kleindienst, immediately ordered Hoover's office sealed. Then the search for Hoover's secret files began. His personal secretary, Helen Gandy, later told Congress she destroyed many files marked "personal" at his home over the next few weeks. At Hunt's urgent request, Bernard Barker brought the Miami crew of Cuban exiles to Washington, where they made plans to break into Hoover's residence. But what happened to Hoover's trove remains unknown to this day.

Around this same time, in a conversation about the shooting that paralyzed Alabama governor George Wallace, Nixon suddenly flashed back to the Kennedy assassination and called the Warren Commission "the greatest hoax that has ever been perpetuated." Somebody might have been able to ask what the president meant by that, except the tape transcript wasn't released by the National Archives until 2002!

Meantime, plans for a break-in to Lawrence O'Brien's office at Democratic National Committee headquarters moved ahead. One of the burglars, Frank Sturgis, said Hunt told him they were looking for "a thick secret memorandum from the Castro government, addressed confidentially to the Democrats . . . a long, detailed listing [of the] various attempts made to assassinate the Castro brothers."[14] The burglars were also coached to look for "anything that had to do with Howard Hughes."

On the night of June 17, five men, all using aliases, were caught red-handed inside the Watergate complex. McCord, the White House's "Security Chief," was booked at the jail along with Sturgis, Barker, Eugenio Martinez, and Virgilio Gonzalez. Hunt's name was in two of the burglars' address books and his link to the operation became known within 24 hours. He quickly left Washington.

In later years, evidence came to light that McCord had likely botched the break-in intentionally. First, he went back and re-taped a garage-level door, which served as a telltale sign to the cops. McCord claimed to have removed the tape from all the doors, but actually several had been taped to stay unlocked. A few days later, all of McCord's papers were destroyed in a fire at his home, while a CIA contract agent stood by.[15] Hunt made a whole series of "mistakes," too, surrounding the Watergate burglary. Nixon, in his *Memoirs*, suggested—referring to the break-in to Ellsberg's psychiatrist's office—that Hunt could have been "a double agent who purposely blew the operation."[16]

There was also the matter of a $25,000 cashier's check that had been deposited into the bank account of a Miami real estate company owned by burglar Barker. This check, laundered through a fund-raiser for the Committee to Re-Elect the President, was the first link connecting the burglars to the CREEP—after Carl Bernstein of the *Washington Post* broke the story about it. Well, it turns out the check wasn't deposited by the CREEP. Liddy had given it to Hunt, who put it in Barker's account. So, money that should have stayed anonymous and untraceable then became an easy "mark" to track.

Three days after the break-in, Nixon called Haldeman, instructing him to "tell Ehrlichman this whole group of Cubans is tied to the Bay of Pigs. . . . Ehrlichman will know what I mean." Six days after the break-in, Hunt sent word through his boss at the Mullen Company that he wanted the White House to find him a lawyer. That same day, June 23, came Nixon's "smoking gun" conversation with Haldeman. When the presidential tape was released two years later, it became proof positive that Nixon had been involved in trying to cover up the burglary—and this led to his resigning before he could be impeached.

"Well, we protected Helms from one hell of a lot of things," Nixon said on the tape, referring to the CIA director. "Of course, this Hunt, that will uncover a lot of things. You open that scab, there's a hell of a lot of things and we just feel that it would be very detrimental to have this thing go any further. This involves these Cubans, Hunt, and a lot of hanky-panky that we have nothing to do with ourselves."[17]

On details of the Watergate burglary, the president seemed confused. Who ordered it? he asked Haldeman. Who was so stupid as to have given a CREEP check for $25,000 to Barker? Then Nixon instructed his aide to tell Helms: "The President's belief is that this is going to open the whole Bay of Pigs thing up again. And, ah because ah these people are playing for, for keeps and that they should call the FBI in and we feel that . . . that we wish for the country, don't go any further into this case, period!"

That afternoon, Helms and his deputy were summoned to the White House, where Haldeman passed on Nixon's message. In his memoirs, Haldeman wrote: "Turmoil in the room, Helms gripping the arms of his chair, leaning forward and shouting, 'The Bay of Pigs has nothing to do with this. I have no concern about the Bay of Pigs.' Silence. I just sat there. I was absolutely shocked by Helms's violent reaction." Haldeman reported back to Nixon that there was "no problem," any leads "that would be harmful to the CIA and harmful to the government" would be ignored.

The White House tape of that conversation trails off cryptically, full of "unintelligible" remarks. "Dulles knew," Nixon said, referring to Allen Dulles, CIA director at the time of the Bay of Pigs who was fired by JFK and later named by LBJ to the Warren Commission. "Dulles told me. I know, I mean [unintelligible] had the telephone call. Remember, I had a call put in—Dulles just blandly said and knew why [unintelligible] covert operation—do anything else [unintelligible]." Those "unintelligibles" might have told us something, wouldn't you guess?

The next day—seven days now since the Watergate burglars' arrest—on the tapes Nixon made some more "unintelligible" remarks about Hale Boggs, the Louisiana congressman who had been another member of the Warren Commission and a dissenter to its conclusion that Oswald acted alone. A few weeks after whatever Nixon said about him, Boggs died in the crash of a light aircraft over Alaska. Some suspected sabotage. The Los Angeles Star (November 22, 1973) reported that "Boggs had startling revelations on Watergate and the assassination of President Kennedy."[18]

The Mullen company's man in Washington, Robert Bennett, met with his CIA case officer, Martin Lukoskie, in a Washington cafeteria. Lukoskie's memo was considered so sensitive that he hand-carried it to Helms, saying Bennett had steered reporters at the *Washington Post* and *Star* away from pursuing a coup d'etat–type scenario that would tie the CIA into a Watergate conspiracy. Bennett later admitted feeding stories to Bob Woodward at the *Post*—"with the understanding that there be no attribution." It's yet another black mark against our media that the *Post* chose not to examine potential CIA complicity to any extent—despite the fact that every one of the Plumbers had a clear-cut CIA connection!

Eleven days after Hunt was arrested, the FBI's acting director, L. Patrick Gray, was summoned to the White house and instructed by Ehrlichman to deep-six the files from Hunt's personal safe. Gray recalled being told that the files were "political dynamite and clearly should not see the light of day." Gray said he took the material home and burned it in his fireplace.[19] Hunt began to threaten the White House with public disclosure of his other secret activities, unless he was paid off.

The House Banking Committee was starting to look into the Watergate break-in, so Nixon brought up the name of congressman Gerald Ford. "Gerry has really got to lead on this," Nixon said. "I think Ehrlichman should talk to him. . . . He's got to know it comes from the top." Not long after that, the banking committee voted against issuing subpoenas concerning the break-in.

Why Ford? Almost a decade earlier, it was Nixon who recommended to President Johnson that Ford be put on the Warren Commission. There, Ford served as the FBI's informant about what the commission was up to. This was confirmed long afterward, in an FBI memo stating: "Ford indicated he would keep me thoroughly advised as to the activities of the commission. He stated that would have to be done on a confidential basis, however, he thought it had to be done."[20]

We also have learned from some handwritten notes of Ford's, produced by the Assassination Records Review Board, that he changed one of the most significant findings in the *Warren Report*. A first draft had said that a bullet had "entered his [JFK's] back at a point slightly below the shoulder to the right of the spine." Woops! That trajectory meant there was no way for that bullet to emerge from Kennedy's neck and then somehow hit Governor Connally. No more "magic bullet"! So Ford urged the commission to change the description and put the wound up higher. Ford wanted it to read: "A bullet had entered the back of his neck slightly to the right of the spine." The commission went with that, except it added two words: "the base of the back of his neck."

So Ford had always been counted on to help out in critical situations. Later, after Spiro Agnew was forced to resign, Nixon named Ford as his vice president and, after Nixon resigned, President Ford proceeded to grant a pardon to Nixon, so he couldn't be pursued by the courts for obstruction of justice and whatever else.

In the fall of 1972, Howard Hunt's wife, Dorothy, paid a call on Cuban exile leader Manuel Artime. He was Hunt's friend dating back to Bay of Pigs days. Mrs. Hunt came to assure Artime that the Cubans imprisoned for the break-in would not endure difficulties in Washington, and that money would be delivered to a legal aid fund. Artime, we know today, was directly connected to the Cuban exiles being used in the anti-Castro plots, and also to mobsters like Trafficante. Not long after that meeting, Dorothy Hunt died in the crash of a United Airlines plane as it made a final approach to Chicago's Midway Airport. More than $10,000 was found on her body; sabotage of the plane was raised, but never proven. A week after the crash, FBI agents combed through Hunt's residence looking for stashed documents, but apparently found nothing.[21] Nixon and Colson met to discuss the possibility of granting clemency to Hunt.

During this same time frame, Helms instructed McCord to send a letter to his friend Jack Caulfield, a New York detective who'd been engaged by the Plumbers—and who, in 1964, had looked into Oswald's possible Cuban connections for the FBI. McCord wrote to Caulfield: "Sorry to have to write you this letter but felt you had to know. If Helms goes, and if the WG [Watergate] operation is laid at the CIA's feet, where it does not belong, every tree in the forest will fall. It will be a scorched desert. The whole matter is at the precipice right now. Just pass the message that if they want it to blow, they are on exactly the right course. I'm sorry that you will get hurt in the fallout."[22]

Nixon had summoned Helms to Camp David—where no taping system existed—and told him to expect to be replaced as CIA director. When Helms then received a request from the Senate to preserve any Watergate-related documents, he set out to destroy all of his private files, some 4,000 to 5,000 pages.[23] Helms also ordered shredded almost the entire record of the CIA's efforts to control human behavior, MK-ULTRA, in the fifties and early sixties. Then he accepted Nixon's offer to become the American ambassador to Iran.

Almost simultaneously with Helms's departure from the CIA, someone broke into the Washington office of the lawyer who'd represented both Maheu and Rosselli, and made off with all *those* files. The lawyer, Edward P. Morgan, said: "Watergate was pernicious, but the biggest cover-up of my lifetime was the assassination of JFK. To the CIA, this was something of life and death—if it could ever be established that their actions against Castro ended up killing Kennedy. The truth of the whole thing is still a helluva long way from being out."[24]

Following the Watergate trail into early 1973 came the bombshell that ignited the Senate hearings: the letter from McCord to Judge John Sirica. McCord wrote: "The Watergate operation was not a CIA operation. The Cubans may have been misled by others into believing that it was a CIA operation. I know for a fact that it was not." Why did McCord feel compelled to state this? Maybe because this was just the latest gambit in his long history of cover-ups on behalf of the CIA? McCord's attorney happened to be Bernard Fensterwald Jr., who had a private Committee to Investigate Assassinations (CTIA) and had once represented James Earl Ray. In exchange for helping McCord post bond, the papers said, "It was understood, however, that McCord agreed to help Fensterwald in some of his research at a later date."[25]

McCord's letter kicked off a chain of events that eventually led to the resignations and indictments of nearly Nixon's entire staff. And the links back to the JFK assassination just kept cropping up. After the infamous "Saturday Night Massacre" in 1973 where Nixon fired Special Prosecutor Archibald Cox, a Houston lawyer named Leon Jaworski was named to replace him. Jaworski had helped the Warren Commission check out a possible connection between Oswald and the CIA. That, in itself, was something of a conflict of interest—since Jaworski was also a board member of a CIA front company, the M.D. Anderson Foundation.[26] When Jack Ruby made his anguished plea that the Warren Commission get him out of Texas and fly him to Washington if it wanted to learn the truth, only three people were present—Earl Warren, Gerald Ford, and Leon Jaworski. They didn't take him up on his offer.

The overlap between the Warren Commission and Watergate legal staffs didn't stop with Jaworski. Arlen Specter, for a time a member of Nixon's defense team, was the originator of the "magic bullet" theory. Albert Jenner, minority counsel during the House impeachment proceedings, had been in charge of looking into conspiracy rumors for the Warren Commission. David Belin, a junior counsel and the commission's staunchest defender through those years, would be President Ford's choice as executive director of the Rockefeller Commission that was assigned to scrutinize the CIA's illegal domestic operations.

General Alexander Haig, who became Nixon's chief of staff through the final days, had been the Pentagon's chief "assistant on all matters pertaining to Cuba" in July 1963. In that capacity, Haig—along with Alexander Butterfield, who revealed the existence of the White House taping system to Senate investigators—had as a primary task the resettlement of the Bay of Pigs prisoners released by Castro, such as Artime. As Charles Colson later told the story, Haig had called him to a meeting in January 1974 and said: "Well, if the President's going to be impeached, better he go down himself than take the whole intelligence apparatus with him."

More than a decade later, I find it remarkable how many of the Watergate players are tied into the Kennedy assassination. They not only escaped justice the first time, but here they are back again. I wonder what else they did in between, what other damage to the country?

In terms of all the burglarizing, you commit crimes because the end justifies the means, I guess. As long as you achieve the goal, the way you do it doesn't matter. One job only leads to the next. In 1974 there occurred six unsolved burglaries into Howard Hughes's offices in only four months: two in Las Vegas, one in an L.A. suburb, one in New York. Another break-in occurred at the Mullen Company's Washington office. In most of these instances, no papers were reported taken. Then someone made off with all of Hughes's handwritten memos, hidden away in a block-long two-story building in Hollywood; a federal judge had just ordered some 500 of these memos to be turned over to Maheu.[27] At the same time, the Watergate Committee staff had just begun looking into the Maheu-CIA-Mob-exile connections from the early sixties.

Soon Nixon was out of there. He'd been cutting deals in politics his whole life, with a closet *full* of skeletons. Over the next couple years, a portion of the CIA's "family jewels" saw the light of day. As they did, Rosselli, Artime, Giancana, Jimmy Hoffa, George de Mohrenschildt and more took whatever they knew about the assassination of JFK to their graves. McCord got out of prison, moved to Colorado, and refused all requests for interviews.

As for Hunt, the man who spooked everybody, he died in January 2007 at the age of 88. His son, Howard St. John Hunt, then came forward with the story that his father had rejected an offer by rogue CIA agents to participate in the Kennedy assassination. Specifically, Hunt had named LBJ as the conspiracy's chief organizer. CIA conspirators supposedly included David Phillips, Cord Meyer, Bill Harvey, David Morales, and fellow Watergate burglar Frank Sturgis. All dead and gone, of course. The younger Hunt remembered his mother informing him on November 22, 1963, that Howard was on a "business trip" to Dallas that day. Before he died, Hunt allegedly told his son there was a "French gunman" firing from the grassy knoll.[28]

So did Howard Hunt come clean with a deathbed confession? Or was he blowing smoke till the end, continuing to spin a web of disinformation that foisted blame onto others? No mention of Helms. Or his pal Artime. Or his Watergate coconspirator, McCord. I'm not one to give E. Howard Hunt the last word. This much I do know: Whatever hidden knowledge he was carrying, it scared the crap out of both Nixon and the CIA.

Who took down whom in the end? I'm placing my bet that Nixon was set up to take the fall, because he was meddling too much in the CIA's business. Nixon's well-known penchant for paranoia may, in this instance, have gotten the better of him. He had shady dealings with so many people, from Howard Hughes to mobsters, it's hard to sort out which particular secrets he was trying to protect. But what I've tried to show, through the chronology of Watergate, is that there was a whole lot more to the story. This chapter exposes the underbelly of "payback" within the government: I've got something on you, so you should know better than to push too far into places I don't want you to go.

In order to climb the ladder of the two political parties in our current system, you have to condone their corruption. I believe most people, when they initially start in politics, are good people. They come into the system wanting to do their job, to change things. But the longer you stay in the system, the more corrupt you become. The two parties to me are today no different than joining the Hell's Angels: Once an Angel, always an Angel. That's what holds true for Democrats or Republicans—unless you separate from them and join a third party movement, knowing that you've broken away and beaten the addiction.

WHAT SHOULD WE DO NOW?

In an open-minded society, alternatives to the accepted version of events need room to be voiced, without being dismissed out-of-hand as fantasy. This is the lesson of Watergate for our time, where President Nixon may have been more a victim than an orchestrator. This story also leaves us to consider that there's more than one way to take down a president, a precedent that surfaced again with the impeachment proceedings against President Clinton.

CHAPTER EIGHT

THE JONESTOWN MASSACRE

THE INCIDENT: At Jonestown in Guyana on November 18, 1978, more than 900 people (most of them Americans) committed mass suicide by drinking a "Kool-Aid" laced with cyanide. This followed the murder of Congressman Leo Ryan, who had come to investigate rumors about Jonestown.

THE OFFICIAL WORD: Cult leader Jim Jones gave the orders, and his "brainwashed" followers did what he asked. Jones then shot himself.

MY TAKE: The first on-scene investigator determined that the majority of the people at Jonestown were murdered. Jones had longstanding ties to the CIA, and may have been involved in mass "mind control" experimentation.

"Research in the manipulation of human behavior is considered by many authorities in medicine and related fields to be professionally unethical, therefore the reputations of professional participants in the MK-ULTRA program are, on occasion, in jeopardy."
—Memorandum from CIA Inspector General Lyman Kirkpatrick to Richard Helms, August 1963[1]

Over the years, it's become a kind of household word aimed at people who join unusual groups: "Oh, you must have taken the Kool-Aid." It's not really all that amusing, in fact the reality is pretty tragic—because the reference is to Jonestown. Deep in the jungles of Guyana, on November 18, 1978, an official total of 913 men, women, and children supposedly came forward to drink Kool-Aid laced with cyanide from paper cups in

aid to be part of the "brainwashed cult" of
People's Temple.

wrestling career at the time. I kept up with the
iority. With Jonestown, I just knew what we
psychotic preacher who had a bunch of nut-
utopia in Guyana, and then things went sour
ngressman, Leo Ryan, had flown in to do an
S. citizens were being abused or held against
he and four others were shot dead by People's
re their plane could leave again. I viewed that
they were killing the congressman as a desperate move, because he was
going to expose them. Then, apparently they felt they would get busted for
it, so Jones and most of his followers supposedly did themselves in first.

When the 30-year anniversary of Jonestown came around, an article
appeared in California's *San Mateo Daily Journal*. The headline was,
"Slain Congressman to be Honored." Representative Ryan's onetime aide,
William Holsinger, spoke out for the first time at the memorial. He'd been
investigating complaints of a Concerned Relatives Group in 1978, and
the night it all happened, he received a message on his phone that "your
meal-ticket just had his brains blown out." Holsinger wore a bulletproof
vest to the congressman's funeral, and then left San Francisco for good. He
said a curious thing in his remarks all these years later: "Whether there was
some broader conspiracy and what it might have consisted of, are matters
I have determined to leave to future generations."[2]

That raised my eyebrows when I read it. Most of what's been said about
Jonestown still sticks with the "brainwashed cult" idea, but I found that
several investigative journalists have come up with leads pointing toward
a "broader conspiracy."[3] By the way, the Temple's assets were estimated at
between $26 million and $2 billion.[4] The Guyanese press for awhile called
it "Templegate," in reference to all the money that the local government
allegedly ran off with from Jonestown.

Before we get into the strange background of Jim Jones, let's start with
some most curious facts about the event itself. It's kind of grisly, but here
goes. Remember the famous color pictures of the bodies lying all over
the compound? Did it strike anybody else as weird that they are all face-
down and looking like they'd been carefully arranged? When they were

first discovered, the body count started out around 200. But it kept going up. The next day's papers reported 363 bodies, 82 of them children, and eventually it escalated to 913. The official word was that immediate identification had been difficult because a lot of the adults had been on top of kids. Hmmm . . . more than 500 bodies hidden under the first 363?[5]

That doesn't quite make sense, but maybe there's a reasonable explanation. But this next one is impossible to explain away: Dr. Leslie Mootoo was Guyana's chief medical examiner and the first forensic specialist on the scene. This man was no fly-by-night doctor down in South America; he was very well-educated, trained in London and Vienna. Dr. Mootoo examined scores of the bodies within the first couple of days, taking specimens. And he thought that in at least 700 of the cases, it wasn't suicide but *homicide*. The doctor observed puncture wounds on the shoulders of a lot of the victims—a bodily location where they couldn't possibly have injected themselves. So were they forcibly held down and injected with poison against their will? He also found the presence of cyanide in bottles that were labeled as Valium, which probably meant that's what some people thought they were taking.[6] A tranquilizer, not a deadly poison.

Dr. Mootoo did find evidence of cyanide in most of the victims' stomachs, and he passed along his samples to a representative of the American Embassy in the Guyanese capital of Georgetown, fully expecting they'd be forwarded on to American forensic pathologists. Except, somehow, they disappeared.[7] A study seven months later published in the *New England Journal of Medicine* found six leading medical examiners describing the handling of the bodies by the U.S. military and others as "inept," "incompetent," "embarrassing," and so on, with only *circumstantial* evidence of "probable cyanide poisoning." The prestigious *Journal* added that only one third of the bodies could be positively identified, and that a medico-legal autopsy should have been performed on each one.[8]

It turns out that only seven autopsies were ever performed—and not until a month after the bodies were embalmed! Some of the pictures from the scene showed victims wearing ID bracelets, but these also vanished somewhere between Jonestown and the U.S. air base where the bodies got shipped. The order to remove the medical tags is said to have come from the National Security Council's staff coordinator for Latin American and Caribbean Affairs, Robert Pastor.[9] (Adding to this macabre story, three bodies actually got lost and turned up years later in storage lockers in Southern California!)[10]

Shortly after the massacre became public, a psychiatrist and anti-cult activist named Dr. Hardhat Sukhdeo came to Georgetown to talk with the survivors. There were 33, most of them having run off into the jungle. Sukhdeo called Jim Jones "a genius of mind control, a master," a statement that was widely quoted in the press and framed the official Jonestown story from then on. Although a native of Guyana, Sukhdeo lived in the U.S. He admitted later that his trip had been paid for by the State Department, and when he returned he met privately with FBI agents. So did Sukhdeo also secretly "debrief" the Jonestown survivors on behalf of the government, trying to find out what they might have seen? Why were Dr. Mootoo's conclusions ignored by the media, while Dr. Sukhdeo's speculation was trumpeted?

It's also curious that "virtually every survivor of the Jonestown massacre was eventually treated" at the Langley-Porter Neuropsychiatric Institute in San Francisco,[11] where Jones himself had once been under psychiatric care. Except, despite attempts to obtain Jones's medical file, it's never been released. A lot of the research done at Langley-Porter happens to be classified, much of it by the Defense Department's Advanced Research Projects Agency (DARPA). It's known, though, that some of this research involves the effect of electromagnetic fields on human beings, and behavior-modification techniques including hypnosis-from-a-distance.[12]

Before he went to Jonestown, Congressman Ryan had already been making a name as a government watchdog. One amendment that he cosponsored required the CIA to get congressional approval before it could undertake any covert activity. Stories about MK-ULTRA had appeared in the press and Ryan wrote a letter to the Agency, "requesting confirmation or denial of the fact of CIA experiments using prisoners at the California medical facility at Vacaville," from which Jones was reportedly getting members of his church as part of a rehab program.[13] Ryan wrote he was especially interested in a former inmate, Donald "Cinque" DeFreeze, who'd ended up leading the Symbionese Liberation Army (SLA) group that kidnapped Patty Hearst. The CIA responded that, yes, it had sponsored tests on some volunteer inmates at Vacaville—but not involving DeFreeze, "in so far as our records reflect the names of the participants."[14] Of course, most MK-

ULTRA records had already been destroyed. A month to the day after this correspondence, Ryan ended up dead on the tarmac in Guyana.

So the central thesis of one investigative writer, Jim Hougan, is that Jones "initiated the Jonestown massacre because he feared that Congressman Leo Ryan's investigation . . . would uncover evidence that the leftist founder of the People's Temple was for many years a witting stooge, or agent, of the FBI and the intelligence community." Also, that the congressman's probe "would embarrass the CIA by linking Jones to some of the Agency's most volatile programs and operations."[15]

That makes a lot of sense to me. But none of that was brought out in the mainstream media. It was almost like they had a cleansed "bio" on Jim Jones. Who was he really? What did he do and who did he work with? When you start following this guy's trail, he's got intelligence community stamped all over him. He's working for the alphabet agencies.

Jones was born in a small town in Indiana in 1931 and, by the age of nineteen, became a faith-healing, anti-communist-spouting preacher. By the late fifties, his charisma drew a congregation of more than 2,000. At the same time, Jones may have been a police or FBI informant gathering "racial intelligence"—as quite a few of his congregation were black and he'd taken to making pilgrimages to the headquarters of Father Divine.[16]

One of Jones's boyhood friends was Dan Mitrione, later an FBI agent and full-time spook operating undercover with the Agency for International Development (AID). Mitrione trained Latin American cops in interrogation techniques that included the use of torture and drugs. In 1970, he was taken hostage and murdered by Uruguay's Tupamaros guerrillas. Jones admitted having stayed friends with Mitrione. He even referred to him several times in taped speeches at Jonestown.[17]

The CIA claimed after Jonestown that its file on "the Rev. Jimmie Jones" was almost empty. Actually, the CIA's Office of Security had opened a 201-file on Jones in the early 1960s, when he took off for Rio de Janeiro. Agency records showed that file stayed open for ten years, only being closed for no explained reason after Mitrione was killed. So it seems pretty likely that Mitrione had recruited Jones into the CIA, using the State Department as his cover.[18]

By the time of his 201-file, Jones had already been to Castro's Cuba in 1960. What was he there to do, preach to them and bring the heathens over to our side? Well, he stayed at the Havana Hilton where the Soviet Union had some Sputnik satellites on display, which the CIA would have been happy to get pictures of. While in Cuba, Jones definitely took photos of some crashed small planes that had carried mercenary pilots. He also encouraged Cubans he met to emigrate to the U.S. Yet somehow, on that trip or another one later, he and his wife had their picture taken with Fidel Castro himself![19]

Also in 1960, Jones got a passport toward making a several-week-long "sightseeing/culture" visit to Poland, Finland, the USSR, and England. That was a very similar journey to the one Lee Oswald made a year earlier, including the USSR part. It raises the question whether both Jones and Oswald were dispatched on some kind of government spy mission. Later the State Department identified this as the first passport Jones ever had. The problem was, a few months earlier he would've needed one to go to Cuba, unless he went there covertly. This again raises cloak-and-dagger type questions.

Jones first visited Guyana in 1961, preaching against Communism. His whereabouts for a six-month period then are unknown. Somebody applied for a new passport in his name, and it looks like Jones was being impersonated on occasion, because he was said to be in Hawaii when he was actually in Guyana. Again, shades of Lee (or Harvey) Oswald! Two passports ended up being issued to Jones, one in Chicago on June 28, 1960, and another in Indianapolis on January 30, 1962.[20]

Brazilian Federal Police records show that Jones and his family arrived in Sao Paolo by plane in April 1962 and traveled on to Belo Horizonte, where his boyhood chum Mitrione was an adviser at the U.S. consulate. People there remembered Jones leaving his house early in the morning and coming back late at night, carrying a big leather briefcase. "Jim Jones was always mysterious and would never talk about his work here in Brazil," according to Sebastian Rocha, an engineer who lived near the Joneses. Rocha assumed he was a spy. Jones socialized regularly with Mitrione during his eight months in Belo Horizonte.[21] Then Mitrione moved to Rio, and Jones ended up in the same neighborhood not far away.[22] In Rio, Jones worked doing commission sales jobs for a "suspected CIA conduit" called Invesco.[23]

Jones "is reported to have been fascinated by the magical rites of Macumba and Umbanda, and to have studied the practices of Brazilian faith-healers... [and] conducted a study of extrasensory perception. These were subjects of interest to the CIA in connection with its MK-ULTRA program. So, also, were the 'mass conversion techniques' at which Jones's Pentecostal training had made him an expert."[24]

Returning to the U.S., Jones became a formally ordained minister and started his People's Temple, first in Indiana and later in Ukiah, California. Espousing socialism, talking against racism, his following grew. The FBI's COINTELPRO and the CIA's OPERATION CHAOS were going strong in the sixties, at the same time that Jones's Temple went out of its way to forge alliances with Huey Newton of the Black Panthers and Angela Davis of the Communist Party.[25] A congressional report showed that various agencies had "target populations" in mind for individual and mass control including blacks and young people.[26]

By 1972, Jones had brought his preaching talents to San Francisco. Four years later—at the same time he started putting Temple funds into Panamanian and Swiss banks—Jones leased some 4,000 acres from the Guyanese government. Forbes Burnham, the prime minister who'd come to power with help from the CIA, approved the deal. Weirdly, the location in Guyana's Northwest district was virtually the same place where, back in 1845, a Reverend Smith had brought together the native population to tell them that the end of time was at hand. When this didn't happen, 400 of Smith's followers committed mass suicide, supposedly believing they'd be resurrected as white people.[27] Whether Jones was aware of this, nobody knows. It was a place of either bad karma or heavy voodoo, I'm not sure which.

Jones became a fairly prominent figure, even getting appointed to San Francisco's Human Rights Commission, with a testimonial dinner in his honor. At the same time, though, there were rumors of heavy-handed cult tactics being employed. He didn't head for Guyana with his nearly one thousand followers until July 1977, when *New West* magazine was putting together an exposé of the People's Temple. Things soon got mighty strange in the jungle compound. Jones set up loudspeakers all over and would do long readings and speeches. A State Department officer who paid a visit reported that members seemed "drugged and robot-like in their reactions to questions and, generally, in their behavior towards us visitors."[28]

Congressman Ryan first heard rumblings about abuses of Americans in Jonestown from Deborah Layton, who'd been in charge of the finances in Jones's inner circle before she "defected." She was the daughter of Dr. Laurence Layton, former chief of the army's Chemical Warfare Division.[29] When Ryan decided to have a personal look, at first the State Department stonewalled him. After he arrived along with a national news crew, he was met by Richard Dwyer, Deputy Chief of Mission at the U.S. Embassy. Dwyer accompanied Ryan to the compound for a two-day visit, and was present when the congressman and his party were later ambushed at the airport—also at the massacre itself. Jones, in the "Last Tape" transcribed by the FBI, can be heard amid wailing and screams exhorting his followers to take their lives and also saying: "Get Dwyer out of here before something happens to him!" [30]

For a long time, Dwyer was assumed to be the CIA's station chief in Guyana. But this was really a man named James Adkins—who turns up later approving CIA pilots to resupply the Nicaraguan Contras, against U.S. law. It was Adkins who, monitoring radio transmissions in the middle of the night, was the first outsider to hear about what one Jonestown escapee called the "suicides *and murders*."[31] As for Dwyer, he may still have been keeping tabs on Jonestown for the State Department; in a later court proceeding, Justice Department attorneys kept him from being questioned.

Before Congressman Ryan left the Jonestown compound, he was attacked by a fellow wielding a knife. A death squad was then waiting for him back at the airstrip. Witnesses described the killers as walking mechanically and emotionless, "like zombies" and "looking through you, not at you."[32] Larry Layton, Deborah Layton's brother, was one of Ryan's executioners. He ended up the only individual ever prosecuted and sent to prison.

Within hours of the airstrip killings came the mass deaths at Jonestown. Later, an autopsy on Jones's body concluded he didn't take poison, but had killed himself with a self-inflicted gunshot to the head. The pistol, however, was found about 200 feet away from his body. Other researchers think the body identified as Jones couldn't have been him, because it didn't mesh with his essential physical characteristics.[33] One raised these questions: "Photos of his body do not show identifying tattoos on his chest. The body and face are not clearly recognizable due to bloating and discoloration. The FBI reportedly checked his finger prints twice, a seemingly futile gesture since it is a precise operation. A more logical route would have been to check dental records."[34] None of the survivors were around to witness what actually happened.

And here is what Congressman Ryan's friend, Joe Holsinger (the father of William, who raised the "broader conspiracy" idea), once wrote: "The more I investigate the mysteries of Jonestown, the more I am convinced there is something sinister behind it all. There is no doubt in my mind that Jones had very close CIA connections. At the time of the tragedy, the Temple had three boats in the water off Brazil. The boats disappeared shortly afterwards. Remember, Brazil is a country that Jones is very familiar with. He is supposed to have money there. And it is not too far from Guyana. My own feeling is that Jones was ambushed by CIA agents who then disappeared in the boats. But the whole story is so mind-boggling that I'm willing to concede he escaped with them."[35]

Holsinger is deceased now, so there's no way to pursue what he based his conjecture on. But almost three years after Jonestown, some of the survivors filed a $63 million lawsuit against Stansfield Turner, CIA director when the massacre occurred, and Secretary of State Cyrus Vance. The lawsuit alleged there had been a conspiracy to "enhance the economic and political powers of James Warren Jones" in conducting "mind control and drug experimentation." The suit was dismissed for "failure to prosecute timely," and all requests for an appeal were turned down.[36] The surviving children of Congressman Ryan also sued the government, charging the State Department with knowing of the dangers ahead of time but failing to warn him; also, that Jonestown was a CIA mind-control experiment and the community was heavily armed and infiltrated by the CIA. The lawsuit was later dropped, for reasons that never got explained.[37]

"Bo" Gritz trained a special forces team that went into Jonestown afterwards, which he says was needed "after it had reached a point where they had to destroy the evidence." Gritz believed Jonestown "was an extension of MK-ULTRA from the CIA and there are probably other experiments going on."[38]

Will we ever know what actually happened at Jonestown? At this point, I doubt it. Since this was the time MK-ULTRA was coming to light and there could possibly be investigations into it, maybe Jonestown was "collateral damage." By that I mean, if they had a camp going that was part of mind-control experimentation and you needed to destroy the evidence of that, what better way to do it than the "mass suicide" of a brainwashed cult?

After studying Jonestown, I think sometimes of the large, hand-lettered sign that was found in front of all those bodies. It said: "Those who fail to learn from history are condemned to repeat it."[39] Whether that was a reference to MK-ULTRA is impossible to know, but it wouldn't surprise me one bit.

WHAT SHOULD WE DO NOW?

The government should release all its files on Jim Jones and how he may have been tied into the spy network or even the mind-control program of the CIA. The Jonestown story should also give us pause, when it comes to the standard thinking that any group with a strong leader is necessarily a "brainwashed cult." Would we say the same thing about the founder of Christianity?

CHAPTER NINE

"OCTOBER SURPRISE": THE FIRST STOLEN ELECTION

THE INCIDENT: On the same day that Ronald Reagan was inaugurated as president, January 20, 1981, Iran released the American hostages it had been holding in our embassy there for 444 days.

THE OFFICIAL WORD: The timing was coincidental.

MY TAKE: Reagan's people had cut a deal with Iran to keep the hostages beyond the presidential election, to ensure that President Carter's negotiations with Iran failed and that he lost to Reagan.

"Concentrated power has always been the enemy of liberty."
—Ronald Reagan

"How can a president not be an actor?"
—Ronald Reagan

If you're like me, maybe you wondered a little about the timing. Within an hour after Ronald Reagan was inaugurated as president on January 20, 1981, the government of Iran released all but one of the 52 American hostages they'd been holding for 444 days. The American people rejoiced. The long ordeal that began when militant Muslims took over the American Embassy in Tehran was over.

But what if those hostages could actually have gained their freedom months earlier? And if Jimmy Carter had been successful in his negotiations, what if he'd been reelected to a second term? What if the Reagan-Bush team cut a secret deal with Iran to hold on to their American prisoners until after the November election? Would anybody call that treason?

Even at the time, as busy on the wrestling circuit as I was, I thought—whaaaat?! This stinks. It reeked of a behind-the-scenes deal. Here's the thing everybody forgets: Even though Reagan ended up swamping Carter in the election, as late as the middle of October Reagan's own poll-taker had Carter ahead by two percentage points. If Carter had managed to free the hostages before the election, good chance he'd have won. Instead, we had what Gary Sick, both Ford and Carter's Middle East expert on the National Security Council, called "a political coup" in his book *October Surprise*.

Most of us remember Operation Desert One, a hostage-rescue attempt by our military early in 1980 that ended up dead-in-the-desert, got eight Americans killed, and resulted in a major embarrassment for Carter. During negotiations after that, Iran was demanding of the Carter people that we exchange $150 million in American military equipment that they'd already ordered and paid for, before the Shah was overthrown and the Ayatollah Khomeini took power. Carter said he wouldn't deal with arms merchants, but otherwise thought this seemed fair enough. Meantime, the Reagan campaign was busy monitoring Carter's every move on this.

As early as March 1980, William Casey—who was then managing Reagan's election campaign and later was named his CIA director—approached two Iranian wheeler-dealers in Washington. The Hashemi brothers, Jamshid and Cyrus, were asked if they'd set up a meeting with some representatives of the government.[1] The thing was, Cyrus Hashemi, who'd done some work for the CIA, was also an important intermediary for the Carter White House in the talks.[2] Anyway, what was basically a bidding war proceeded from there.

Casey went to Spain in July and worked out arrangements to get arms to the Iranians from several locations in Europe, by way of Israel, once the hostages were freed.[3] The equipment was worth billions and involved arms dealers, not to mention $40 million in bribes going to various individuals.[4] Abol Bani-Sadr, president of Iran at the time, later wrote about the "secret deal" in two books.[5] One of Khomeini's nephews was supposed to present Iran with a proposal from Carter, but he instead returned home with one "from the Reagan camp." Bani-Sadr was told that if he didn't accept it, the Republicans would make the same offer to his radical rivals. "Lastly,

he told me my refusal of their offer would result in my elimination."
Bani-Sadr said he first resisted and tried to get the hostages released right
away—there had already been an official agreement with Carter done in
Algeria—but, not surprisingly, Ayatollah Khomeini was working both
sides of the street.[6]

A secret plan by the Carter administration for a second hostage rescue
mission went operational in September. But it was leaked to Richard V.
Allen, soon to be Reagan's national security adviser. "Shortly thereafter,
the Reagan-Bush campaign launched a major publicity effort warning
that President Carter might be planning an 'October surprise' to obtain
the release of the hostages prior to the election."[7]

That fall, Cyrus Hashemi received a $3 million deposit arranged by
a Houston lawyer who was associated with vice-presidential candidate
Bush.[8] Around that time came a meeting in Paris that involved Bush
himself—although the U.S. government, and most of the media, would
do their best to pretend it never happened. (Bush called it "that ugly little
word-of-mouth rumor.")

Playing their cards close to the vest, Iran's leadership was saying it
wanted either Reagan or Bush to personally put their John Hancock on a
final agreement. On September 22, Iraq invaded Iran, which made Iran's
need for war equipment all the more urgent. A series of meetings ensued
over five days at different hotels in Paris. Bush and Casey are said to have
arrived at the Paris Hilton for a 90-minute discussion to cut the final deal
on October 19. Secret Service spokesmen later claimed that Bush was in
Washington that weekend, but their logs showed a missing 21 hours in his
itinerary. There's nothing from the time of a speech he gave on a Saturday
night, until another speech that he arrived late for the next night, and
other Secret Service documents show that he flew into National Airport at
7:35 PM on that Sunday. [9] He left for Paris on a BAC-111 owned by one
of the Saudi royal family, and returned on a fast SR-71 aircraft that the
CIA loaned him.[10]

"At least five of the sources who say they were in Paris in connection with
these meetings insist that George Bush was present for at least one meeting. Three of the sources say that they saw him there."[11] Ari Ben-Menashe,
an ex-member of Mossad Israeli intelligence, said he'd been part of an
advance team working with the French in arranging the meetings.[12]

CIA contract agent Richard Brenneke testified under oath that he'd seen Bush, along with NSC official Donald Gregg, in the French capitol that weekend.[13]

There was also an investigation overseen by Sergey V. Stepashin, who later became Russia's prime minister. On January 11, 1993, he had a six-page report translated by the American Embassy in Moscow and forwarded to Congress. At the Paris meeting, the Russians independently learned, "R[obert] Gates, at the time a staffer of the National Security Council in the administration of Jimmy Carter, and former CIA director George Bush also took part."[14]

Robert Gates, eh? Well, that brings us right up to the present. Gates came in to replace Donald Rumsfeld as defense secretary under Bush-II, late in 2006, and Obama decided to keep him there. If truth be known, Gates has a shady history as a career intel guy. In 1991, there were accusations he brushed aside that he'd had a secret role in arming both sides in the Iran-Iraq War. Witnesses in the Middle East said this had included Saddam Hussein getting hold of cluster bombs and material for chemical weapons. Later, a sworn affidavit by one of Reagan's National Security Council guys said that when Iran was gaining the upper hand in the spring of 1982: "The CIA, including both CIA Director Casey and Deputy Director Gates, knew of, approved of, and assisted in the sale of non-U.S. origin military weapons, ammunition and vehicles to Iraq."[15] It was also 1982 when the U.S. kindly removed Iraq from its list of terrorist states.

Kinda makes you wonder about who our "enemies" really are, doesn't it? There the Republicans were, sending weapons first to Iran to make sure Reagan got elected, then turning around and arming Saddam Hussein—right down to getting him stuff for chemical weapons that would justify W's invasion of Iraq twenty years later! And now today, it's all about demonizing another recipient of our generosity—Iran! Who's the real demon here? We are, behind the scenes, because we're the ones giving these countries weapons that they can turn around and use on us. It's utter craziness, and so frustrating to watch our leaders operate with so little regard for human life.

I'm a believer that If Congress and the media had been doing their jobs right when the October Surprise story began coming out in the late eighties and early nineties, we'd never have gone to war in Iraq. In fact, there would—or at least should—have been impeachment proceedings against George Bush Sr., and that would have been it for the family in politics. No two-term presidency for Junior.

Of course, it was Poppa Bush who set the family precedent for stealing elections. Keep in mind that he'd been director of the CIA in 1976. "Bush had also protected wayward or hot-triggered Agency operatives—veterans of everything from Chilean assassinations to Vietnam's Phoenix program and improper domestic surveillance—from indictment by President Ford's Justice Department."[16] Then Carter came along and replaced Bush with Stansfield Turner. The CIA's good-old-boy network hated Carter, because Turner proceeded to clean house and dismiss many of the longtime covert operatives.

But I digress. Let's pick up the 1980 story with the fact that, right after the Paris meeting with Bush and Gates in attendance, Iran suddenly told the Carter administration it had no further interest in receiving military equipment.[17] Then, over the next several days, Israel quietly shipped F-4 fighter-aircraft tires to the Iranians, in violation of the U.S. arms embargo,[18] while Iran started dispersing the hostages to several different locations.

So, Carter lost the election and then came the timed release (like a good sleeping pill) on Reagan's inauguration day. Banker Ernest Backes from Clearstream in Luxembourg later said he'd been in charge of a transfer of $7 million from Chase Manhattan and Citibank on January 16, 1980, to help pay for the hostages' liberation.[19] According to Bani-Sadr of Iran: "We have published documents which show that US arms were shipped, via Israel, in March, about 2 months after Reagan became president."[20]

Call me naïve, but I just find it amazing how powerful people can do illegal things and so easily cover their tracks. If George Bush went over and used the hostages for pawns in a political game, shouldn't he and his cronies go to jail for that? I mean, let's make a comparison. Say some people were being held hostage in a bank, and you found out that a lieutenant on the police force delayed getting them freed simply to advance his own personal agenda, wouldn't you be appalled enough to think that officer should be fired or even stand trial for doing this? The hostages in Iran had been there for months! But ultimately, the Bush-Casey types figure, it's fine because we'll win the presidency and all will be better off. You sacrifice the few for the many, not really knowing whether the many are going to profit or not. It's like saying, if somebody had killed Charles Manson a year before the Sharon Tate murders, none of those people would have died.

Anyway, they'll violate all the laws of human decency to make sure Ronald Reagan gets elected. I've always believed you'll govern like you campaign. If you lie and cheat during the campaign, it's not going to end there. And, of course, it didn't. Before long we had the Iran-Contra scandal, which we'll look at in the next chapter. I angrily look at the American people and wonder how they can possibly accept this. We just throw our hands up in the air and say, "Oh, well, that's government, that's what they do." No, we need to understand, government is us!

The whole seamy saga surrounding the hostages started to unravel in 1987, when the *Miami Herald* published an article quoting some statements from a CIA agent, Alfonso Chardy, about the secret October meetings. Also that year, Bani-Sadr wrote a book that was published in Europe and got into some of what he knew. *Playboy* and *Esquire* followed up with articles. In 1989, Barbara Honegger came out with her book *October Surprise*; she'd been a loyal Reagan staffer until she left out of disillusionment with some of the practices she'd observed. Honegger said she was present on inauguration day when she heard Reagan say to "tell the Iranians that the deal is off if that [last] hostage is not freed."[21] Reagan had left office by the time of Honegger's book, and Poppa Bush was just beginning his first term.

In early November 1989, Ari Ben-Menashe was arrested in L.A. The Mossad agent was charged with having violated the U.S. Arms Export Control Act, by attempting to sell Iran three C-130 transport planes with a false-end-user certificate. Apparently our left hand didn't know what the right hand was doing. Israeli master spy Rafi Eitan was worried that Ben-Menashe "was in a position to blow wide open the U.S./Israeli arms-to-Iran network whose tentacles had extended everywhere: down to Central and South America, through London, into Australia, across to Africa, deep into Europe."[22]

Sure enough, Ben-Menashe was soon squawking to reporters. He implicated Bush and Gates in the October Surprise. He talked of a secret American policy to send weapons through Chile to the Iraqis. (We're playing both ends against the middle again). The government of Israel tried to discredit Ben-Menashe as a fabricator, but *Associated Press* journalist Robert Parry uncovered internal Israeli documents proving he'd worked for an arm of their military intelligence for a decade (1977–1987). So the Israelis had some egg on their face, but meantime both they and the White House were seeking out more friendly reporters. One of these was Steven Emerson, who wrote that he'd seen derogatory records on the "delusional" Ben-Menashe. But corroboration for what Ben-Menashe had to say did surface over time, including the Iraq weapons deal.[23] A federal jury acquitted him of the charges at the end of 1990.

Also in 1990, PBS's *Frontline* aired a program on the October Surprise that included a sound bite of Reagan playing golf with Bush in Palm Springs and saying he'd "tried some things the other way" to free the hostages but that the details were "classified." Oops, open mouth and insert foot, Mr. Former President. By now, there was enough outside pressure for the House of Representatives to form an October Surprise Task Force in February 1992. The fellow who chaired the committee was Lee Hamilton, a "bipartisan" Democrat who from then on always seemed to end up in charge of these types of investigations. Next time would be the Iran-Contra hearings that made Oliver North a household name. Then Hamilton would be vice chair of the 9/11 Commission, whose shoddy work we'll look at later. Now he's retired after serving 34 years in the House, but he's still on Obama's Homeland Security Advisory Council. I guess they need expertise in cover-ups—Freudian slip, I mean clandestine-ops.

The chief counsel for the House's October Surprise Task Force was a fella named Barcella, fresh from Larry's having been lead attorney for the Bank of Credit and Commerce International, or BCCI for short. BCCI had paid his firm more than $2 million to keep it shielded from investigations by the press or government agencies.[24] When a reporter asked Barcella if he saw any conflict of interest, since BCCI had helped finance arms deals to Iran in 1983, Barcella accused the man of McCarthy-like behavior. Well, you won't find BCCI mentioned once in the Task Force's report. Even though, within days after William Casey became head of Reagan's CIA, BCCI officials along with Iranian banker Cyrus Hashemi set up two Hong Kong–based banks that were underwritten by $20 million in Iranian assets from the Shah's royal family.[25] As for Barcella, he was "apparently quite sensitive to the interests of the U.S. intelligence community during his days as a federal prosecutor."[26]

Given who was in charge, we shouldn't be too surprised at the task force's conclusions. In 1993, the House report found "no credible evidence supporting any attempt by the Reagan presidential campaign—or persons associated with the campaign—to delay the release of the American hostages in Iran." Lee Hamilton noted that the vast majority of sources for the allegation were "wholesale fabricators or were impeached by documentary evidence."[27] *Washington Post* columnist David Broder lauded Hamilton as the "conscience of Congress" for repudiating the accusations.

The Senate Foreign Relations Committee also conducted a small-scale investigation. They'd imposed travel restrictions on checking out leads in Europe, denied subpoena power, and claimed a shortage of funds. The Secret Service wouldn't allow any questioning of agents who might have gone with Bush to Paris. The Senate's report, issued on November 19, 1992, said the "vast weight of all available evidence" was that Bush never made that trip to cut a deal with Iran.

William Casey was dead by now, and his family decided not to supply any of his records. Donald Gregg, a member of Bush's NSC staff after working more than 30 years for the CIA, failed a lie-detector test on the matter, but the Senate committee would only say "that Gregg's response was lacking in candor."[28] The House found "credible" French intelligence sources about the Paris meetings, but still concluded somehow that it was all "baseless."[29]

As for that report by the Russians, which ended up in Hamilton's hands two days before he was to announce the Task Force's conclusions, he instead took at face value a cable from an American Embassy official in Moscow that the report might be "based largely on material that has previously appeared in the Western media." (Not the *Times* or the *Post*, I'll bet!) The Russians continued to insist that the intel was their own and reliable; they considered the report "a bomb" and "couldn't believe it was ignored."[30]

There's one journalistic hero in all this, and it's Robert Parry. He just kept plugging away and, in 1984 after he uncovered Oliver North's role in the Iran-Contra story for *Newsweek*, he was awarded the George Polk Award for National Reporting. Pretty soon, though, he was persona non grata with the establishment media, so he started *Consortium News* as an online magazine dedicated to investigative reporting. He's also written several books, and he's still out there pitching for truth.

Most other journalists stayed the course with Lee Hamilton. *Newsweek* did a piece headlined: "The October Surprise Charge: Treason; Myth." *The New Republic* called it "The Conspiracy That Wasn't." The author of that piece was Steven Emerson, who is today considered one of our top authorities on Islamic extremists, their financing and operations. Since 9/11, he's given many briefings to Congress on Al Qaeda, Hamas, Hezbollah, and other networks. To say the least, he's a well-connected journalist.[31]

I can't let this chapter go without talking a little about Bill Clinton's reaction to it all, after he defeated Bush to become president in 1992. Twice emissaries from Iran told members of his cabinet about those Republican contacts with Islamic radicals close to Khomeini. But Clinton turned away, or at least his team did, not wanting to open themselves to charges of playing politics. The Germans, as well, are said to have offered the Clinton Administration information from their Stasi intel files. But whatever they turned over, Clinton kept secret.[32]

I sometimes get a strange sense of déjà vu, when I think of how the Obama Administration now wants to put all of Bush-II's torture policies behind us.

WHAT SHOULD WE DO NOW?

We need to realize that the precedent-setter for one political party to steal a presidential election from another happened with Ronald Reagan, a man some would like to see join our greatest presidents on Mount Rushmore. Like the political assassinations earlier, this was a continuation of an ends-justify-the-means mentality that will ultimately destroy our democracy altogether if we allow this attitude to continue. Also, let's consider how our "friends" so quickly become our "enemies." Is it all about what suits certain people in power? Who's really benefiting from the overthrow of Saddam Hussein and the demonization of Iran?

CHAPTER TEN

YOUR GOVERNMENT DEALING DRUGS

THE INCIDENT: The Iran-Contra scandal of 1986–88 involved members of the Reagan administration breaking an arms embargo and selling weapons to Iran, in order to secure the release of six U.S. hostages and to fund the Nicaraguan Contras.

THE OFFICIAL WORD: Fourteen administration officials were charged with crimes, and eleven were convicted. Reagan eventually admitted "trading arms for hostages."

MY TAKE: Congress covered up the fact that illegal drug deals were at the heart of the Iran-Contra story, just as the CIA has been deeply involved in drug trafficking for decades. It's a situation that continues today in Mexico and Afghanistan, and the reality is that our economy is secretly deeply embedded in the global drug trade.

"But what's important in this whole thing is that our policy has always been consistent . . ."
—Oliver North, interviewed on *Frontline: The Drug Wars*, PBS

One of the reasons I'm writing this book is because our country has such a short-term memory. How many of us recall that, as far back as 1972, a report of the National Commission on Marihuana and Drug Abuse recommended that possession of pot for personal use be decriminalized? And that was when Nixon was president! Later on, Jimmy Carter called for getting rid of penalties for small-time possession, but Congress stonewalled him. Since then, we've had another president (Clinton) who claimed he didn't inhale and our latest (Obama) admitting he took some tokes back in the day. Federal law still considers marijuana a dangerous illegal drug, although fourteen states have now enacted laws allowing for some use for medical purposes.

Let me cite a few statistics that I find mind-boggling. According to NORML, an advocacy group for legalizing marijuana, more than 700,000 of America's estimated 20 million pot-smokers got arrested in 2008. About *half* of the 200,000 inmates in our federal prisons are in there for drug-related offenses. Between 1970 and 2007, we saw a 547 percent increase in our prison population, mainly because of our drug policies. Of course, that's just fine with the new prison-industrial complex, where corporations are now running the show. We as taxpayers shell out $68 billion every year for prisons, and a lot of that ends up going into private contractors' pockets![1]

Of course, they're not the only ones getting rich. Well-documented reports by Congress and the Treasury Department lead to the conclusion that American banks are "collectively the world's largest financial beneficiary of the drug trade." Not including real estate transfers, there's an estimated inflow of $250 billion a year coming into the country's banks—which I suppose is welcomed by some as offsetting our $300-billion trade deficit.[2]

We'll talk more about banks several times in this chapter, but I want to start with some history on our government's involvement with drug traffic. You want to talk hypocrisy? This sordid saga takes the cake. We started using drug lords like Lucky Luciano to help fight the Communists back during World War II. The OSS, predecessor to the CIA, had the Sicilian Mafia and the Corsican gangsters in Marseilles working with them, which enabled their "key role in the growth of Europe's post war heroin traffic . . . which provided most of the heroin smuggled into the United States over the next two decades."[3]

The heroin epidemic that ravaged our cities during the fifties and sixties basically originated with the CIA out of Southeast Asia. Almost from the moment of their founding in 1947, the CIA was giving covert support to organized drug traffickers in Europe and the Far East, and eventually the Middle East and Latin America. During the Vietnam War—hold onto your hats!—heroin was being smuggled into this country in the bodies of soldiers being flown home, coded ahead of time so they could be identified at various Air Force bases and the drugs removed.[4]

Toward the end of American involvement over there in 1975, a former Green Beret named Michael Hand arranged a 500-pound shipment of heroin from Southeast Asia's "Golden Triangle" to the U.S. by way of Australia. That's where Hand had set up shop as vice chair of the Nugan Hand Bank, which was linked by the Australian Narcotics Bureau to a drug smuggling network that "exported some $3 billion [Aust.] worth of heroin from Bangkok prior to June 1976." Several CIA guys who later came up in the Iran-Contra affair (Ted Shackley, Ray Clines, and Edwin Wilson) used the Nugan Hand bank to channel funds for covert operations. By 1979, the bank had 22 branches in 13 countries and $1 billion in annual business. The next year, chairman Frank Nugan was found shot dead in his Mercedes, a hundred miles from Sydney, and the bank soon collapsed.[5] Two official investigations by Australia uncovered its financing of major drug dealers and the laundering of their profits, while collecting an impressive list of "ex"–CIA officers.

After the CIA's involvement with the Southeast Asian drug trade had been partly disclosed in the mid-1970s, and the U.S. left Vietnam to its fate, the Agency started distancing itself from its "assets." But that only left the door open to go elsewhere. Which the Reagan Administration did big-time, to fund its secret war in Nicaragua. The 1979 Sandinista revolution that overthrew Anastasio Somoza, one of our favorite Latin dictators, was not looked upon fondly by Ronnie and his friends. He called the counterrevolutionary Contras "freedom fighters," and compared them to America's founding fathers. In his attempt to get Congress to approve aid for the Contras, Reagan accused the Sandinista government of drug trafficking. Of course, Nancy Reagan had launched her "Just say no" campaign at the time, but I guess she hadn't given the word to her husband. After his administration tried to mine the Nicaraguan harbors and got a hand-slap from Congress, it turned to secretly selling missiles to Iran and using the payments—along with profits from running drugs—to keep right on funding the Contras. Fifty thousand lost lives later, the World Court would order the U.S. to "cease and to refrain" from unlawful use of force against Nicaragua and pay reparations.[6] (We refused to comply.)

The fact is, with most of the cocaine that flooded the country in the Eighties, almost every major drug network was using the Contra operation in some fashion. Colombia's Medellin cartel began quietly collaborating with the Contras soon after Reagan took office. Then, in 1982, CIA Director Casey negotiated a little Memorandum of Understanding with the attorney general, William French Smith. Basically what this did was give the CIA legal clearance to work with known drug traffickers without being required to report it, so long as they weren't official employees but only "assets."[7] This didn't come out until 1998, when CIA Inspector General Frederick Hitz issued a report that implicated more than 50 Contra and related entities in the drug trade. And the CIA knew all about it. The trafficking and money laundering tracked right into the National Security Council, where Oliver North was overseeing the Contras' war.[8]

Here's what was going on behind the scenes: In the mid-1980s, North got together with four companies that were owned and operated by drug dealers, and arranged payments from the State Department for shipping supplies to the Contras. Michael Levine, an undercover agent for the DEA (Drug Enforcement Administration), later said that "running a covert operation in collaboration with a drug cartel . . . [is] what I call treason." The top DEA agent in El Salvador, Celerino Castillo III, said he saw "very large quantities of cocaine and millions of dollars" being run out of hangars at Ilopango air base, which was controlled by North and CIA operative Felix Rodriguez (he'd been placed in El Salvador by Vice President Bush's office, as a direct overseer of North's operations). The cocaine was being trans shipped from Costa Rica through El Salvador and on into the U.S. But when Castillo tried to raise this with his superiors, he ran into nothing but obstacles.[9]

Early in 1985, two *Associated Press* reporters started hearing from officials in D.C. about all this. A year later, after a lot of stonewalling by the editors, the AP did run Robert Parry and Brian Barger's story on an FBI probe into cocaine trafficking by the Contras. This led the Reagan Administration to put out a three-page report admitting that there'd been some such shenanigans when the Contras were "particularly hard pressed for financial support" after Congress voted to cut off American aid. There was "evidence of a limited number of incidents."[10] Uh huh. It would be awhile yet before an Oliver North note surfaced from July 12, 1985, about a Contra arms warehouse in Honduras: "Fourteen million to finance came from drugs."[11]

Also in 1986, an FBI informant inside the Medellin cartel, Wanda Palacio, testified that she'd seen the organization run by Jorge Ochoa loading cocaine onto aircraft that belonged to Southern Air Transport, a company that used to be owned by the CIA and was flying supplies to the Contras. There was strong corroboration for her story, but somehow the Justice Department rejected it as inconclusive.[12] Senator John Kerry started looking into all this and said at one closed-door committee meeting: "It is clear that there is a network of drug trafficking through the Contras. . . . We can produce specific law enforcement officials who will tell you that they have been called off drug trafficking investigations because the CIA is involved or because it would threaten national security."[13]

All this, remember, while we're spending millions supposedly fighting the "war on drugs," a phrase first coined by Nixon in 1969. If you want the ultimate double standard, here's what was happening simultaneously in '86. After Len Bias, a basketball star at the University of Maryland, died of a supposed cocaine overdose (even though the coroner found no link between his sniffing some coke and the heart failure), Congress proceeded to pass the Anti-Drug Abuse Act. Up until this time, through the entire history of America, there had been only 56 mandatory minimum sentences established. Now, overnight, there were 29 more. Even for minor possession cases, you couldn't get parole. They established a 100-to-1 sentencing ratio for cheap crack cocaine (used more by African-Americans) over the powder variety (favored by Hollywood types).[14] This was at the same time we were *knowingly* allowing crack to be run into this country as part of financing the Contras—but we'll get to that in a moment.

What became known as the Iran-Contra affair came to light in November 1986. We were selling arms to Iran, breaking an arms embargo, in order to fund the contras. Fourteen Reagan Administration officials got charged with crimes and eleven were convicted, including Secretary of Defense Caspar Weinberger. Of course, Poppa Bush pardoned them all after he got elected president. And do you think a word about drug-running came up in the televised House committee hearings that made Ollie North a household name? Fuhgedaboutit.

The thousand-page report issued by Senator Kerry about his committee's findings did discuss how the State Department had paid more than

$800,000 to known traffickers to take "humanitarian assistance" to the Contras.[15] The *New York Times* then set out to trash Kerry in a three-part series, including belittling him for relying on the testimony of imprisoned (drug-running) pilots.[16] The *Washington Post* published a short article heavy on criticisms against Kerry by the Republicans. *Newsweek* called him "a randy conspiracy buff." (Wonder what they were snorting.)

But are we surprised? In 1987, the House Narcotics Committee had concluded there should be more investigation into the Contra-drug allegations. What was the *Washington Post's* headline?: "Hill Panel Finds No Evidence Linking Contras to Drug Smuggling." The paper wouldn't even run Chairman Charles Rangel's letter of correction! That same year, a *Time* correspondent had an article on this subject blocked and a senior editor privately tell him: "*Time* is institutionally behind the Contras. If this story were about the Sandinistas and drugs, you'd have no trouble getting it in the magazine."[17]

The list of government skullduggery goes on, and it's mind-boggling. Remember when Poppa Bush ordered our military to invade Panama back in 1990? The stated reason was that its leader, Colonel Manuel Noriega, had been violating our laws by permitting drugs to be run through his country. In fact, Noriega had been "one of ours" for a long time. After Noriega was brought to the U.S. and convicted by a federal jury in Miami and sentenced to 40 years, filmmaker Oliver Stone went to see him in prison. There Noriega talked freely about having spied on Castro for the U.S., giving covert aid to the Contras, and visiting with Oliver North.[18] Noriega and Bush Sr. went way back, to when Bush headed the CIA in 1976. The brief prepared by Noriega's defense team was heavily censored, but it did reveal significant contact with Bush over a 15-year period. In fact, Bush had headed up a special anti-drug effort as vice president called the South Florida Task Force, which happened to coincide with when quite a few cargoes of cocaine and marijuana came through Florida as part of the Contra-support network. So why did we finally go after Noriega? Some said it's because he knew too much and was demanding too big a cut for his role in the Agency's drug-dealing.[19]

I can't exempt Bill Clinton from possible knowledge about some of this. A little airport in Mena, Arkansas, happened to have been a center for international drug smuggling between 1981 and 1985. That's when Clinton was governor of the state. Barry Seal, who had ties to the CIA and was an undercover informant for the DEA, kept his plane at Mena and "smuggled between $3 billion and $5 billion of drugs into the U.S."[20] Seal was also part of the Reagan administration's effort to implicate the Sandinistas in the drug traffic, though he was actually smuggling weapons to the Contras. He ended up brutally murdered by his former employers with Colombia's Medellin cartel, in Baton Rouge, on February 19, 1986. Among the articles found in Seal's car were then–Vice President Bush's private phone number.

Clinton said he learned about Mena after that, in April 1988, even though the state police had been investigating the goings-on there for several years. In September 1991, he spoke publicly about "all kinds of questions about whether he [Seal] had any links to the C.I.A . . . and if that backed into the Iran-Contra deal." But Seal's contraband in Mena generated hundreds of millions that needed to be money-laundered, and his papers show that he dealt with at least one big Little Rock bank. Several inquiries into Mena were stifled, and IRS agent Bill Duncan told Congress in 1992—during the Clinton presidential campaign—that his superiors directed him to "withhold information from Congress and perjure myself."[21] Looks like Clinton may have been tainted by the Iran-Contra madness himself.

Okay, the Reagan-Bush gang is gone, and Clinton is now president. It's 1996 when the *San Jose Mercury News* comes out with a remarkable 20,000-word series by reporter Gary Webb that he'd been researching for more than a year. It described a pipeline between Colombian cartels, middlemen, and street gangs in South Central L.A. that involved tons of crack cocaine. Webb's article featured Oscar Danilo Blandón, a drug importer and informant who'd testified in federal court that "whatever we were running in L.A., the profit was going to the Contra revolution." Blandón also said that Colonel Enrique Bermudez, the CIA asset leading the Contra army against the Sandinista government, was aware that these funds came from drug running. Except the CIA had squelched a federal investigation into Blandón in the name of "national security." The crack was being funneled to a young new-millionaire named "Freeway" Ricky Donnell Ross, who supplied it to the Crips and Bloods and beyond. When Ross got nailed and went to trial in 1996, the prosecutors obtained a court order to prevent the defense from questioning Blandón about his

CIA connections. All of which raised a huge question: how involved was the CIA in the crack epidemic then raging across our country?[22]

Well, you'd think Gary Webb should have gotten a Pulitzer. Instead, he got torn apart by the big media. In page-one articles, the *Washington Post*, *New York Times*, and *L.A. Times* insisted that Contra-cocaine smuggling was minor, and that Webb was blowing it all out of proportion. They made it look like Webb was targeting the poor CIA, when he'd never said that the CIA, *per se*, was arranging the drug deals, only that it was protecting the Contra dealers.

In 2009, a new book came out that makes my blood boil. It's called *This Is Your Country on Drugs*, and among other revelations, it tells of how the *Washington Post* "had facts at its disposal demonstrating that the [Webb] story was accurate," except they ended up on the editing-room floor. That's because National Security correspondent Walter Pincus made sure they would. Pincus, it turns out, had "flirted with joining the CIA and is routinely accused of having been an undercover asset in the '50s," a charge the journalist once called "overblown."[23]

Here's another example of the media's role in the cover-up: the *L.A. Times*, two years earlier, had profiled "Freeway" Ricky as South Central's first millionaire crack dealer. But, two months after Webb's series tied Ross into the Contra network, the *Times* turned to a whole new slant. Ross, the paper said, was but one of a number of "interchangeable characters."[24]

So Gary Webb was basically drummed out of journalism by his "brethren" at the larger papers. Who gives our media these mandates to arbitrarily destroy someone's credibility, blackball them because they've written something controversial? I guess people forget the simplicity of the First Amendment—it's there to protect *unpopular* speech. Because popular speech doesn't need protecting.

In 2004, Gary Webb's body was found and it was ruled a suicide. I call this a tragedy that should weigh heavily on the consciences of those who intentionally destroyed his reputation. Or maybe it was actually murder: Webb was shot *twice* in the head with a vintage revolver—meaning he would have had to have cocked the hammer of the revolver back after being shot in the head at point-blank range with a .38.

It's a proven fact that the CIA's into drugs, we even know why. It's because they can get money to operate with, and not have to account to

Congress for what they're doing. All this is justified because of the "big picture." But doesn't it really beg for a massive investigation and trials and a whole lot of people going to jail? This includes the big banks that allow the dirty money to be laundered through them.

Let's take a longer look at the Bank of Credit and Commerce International—or, as our current defense secretary Robert Gates once called BCCI, the Bank of Crooks and Criminals.[25] As CIA deputy director twenty years ago, Gates was in position to know. But when US Customs Commissioner William von Raab was getting ready to arrest some folks involved with drug money laundering at a BCCI subsidiary in Florida, "Gates failed to disclose the CIA's own use of BCCI to channel payments for covert operations, which the customs chief learned about only later— and thanks to documents supplied to him by British customs agents in London."[26]

At one time BCCI had more than 400 branches in 78 countries and assets of over $20 billion. Most everywhere, "BCCI systematically relied on relationships with, and as necessary, payments to, prominent political figures," as a Senate report put it. The bank had started out in Pakistan in 1972, with much of the start-up funding being provided by the CIA and the Bank of America. By the early 1980s, the National Security Council's man charged with tracking terrorist financing, Norman Bailey, said "we were aware that BCCI was involved in drug-money transactions," but the NSC took no action. Probably because CIA Director Casey was relying on BCCI to distribute American assistance to the Afghan mujahideen who were fighting the Russians at the time. Except most of the aid went to the faction controlled by Gulbuddin Hekmatyar, who was probably the leading heroin trafficker in the world. Pakistani president Muhammad Zia in 1983 let local traffickers put their drug profits into BCCI.[27] John Kerry's committee came across the bank's role in drugs and started to investigate, but received basically zero "information or cooperation provided by other government agencies."[28]

BCCI was the seventh biggest bank on the planet when it collapsed, shortly after the Soviets withdrew their troops from Afghanistan. The mainstream media had started reporting on BCCI's activities early in 1991—"The World's Sleaziest Bank" was the headline on *Time* magazine's cover story. Soon the Bank of England pulled the plug and regulators started shutting down BCCI's offices in dozens of countries. It was also the largest Islamic bank, and one fellow said to have lost a lot of invested money when BCCI fell apart was Osama bin Laden.[29] After that, to make up for his missing revenue, bin Laden started cooperating with Gulbuddin Hekmatyar, the Afghan warlord who was taking profits from drugs and putting them into Islamic terrorist movements.[30]

This brings us up to the present, and what's going on today in Afghanistan and Mexico. I'm going to rely first on a recent article by Peter Dale Scott, called "Afghanistan: Heroin-Ravaged State."[31] He says that's how we should think of Afghanistan, rather than as a "failed state." One statistic he cites is that in 2007, according to our State Department, Afghanistan was supplying 93 percent of the world's opium, the illicit production of poppies bringing in $4 billion—more than half the country's total economy of $7.5 billion.

But even though 90 percent of the world's heroin is originating in Afghanistan, their share of the proceeds in dollar terms is only about 10 percent of that. It's estimated that more than 80 percent of the profits actually get reaped in the countries where the heroin is consumed, like the U.S. According to the U.N., "money made in illicit drug trade has been used to keep banks afloat in the global financial crisis."

So who's making out like bandits? It's a familiar story. Drug trafficking is tolerated in exchange for intelligence, simple as that. Here's what Dennis Dayle, a former top DEA agent in the Middle East, said at an anti-drug conference a couple years back: "In my 30-year history in the Drug Enforcement Administration and related agencies, the major targets of my investigations almost invariably turned out to be working for the CIA."

After 9/11, when the U.S. sent troops to Afghanistan that fall of 2001, "the Pentagon had a list of twenty-five or more drug labs and warehouses in Afghanistan but refused to bomb them because some belonged to the CIA's new NA [Northern Alliance] allies."[32] The CIA mounted its anti-Taliban coalition by recruiting and sometimes even importing drug dealers, many of them being old assets from the 1980s. Friends, family, and allies of Afghan president Hamid Karzai are heavily involved. It recently came out that Karzai's brother is not only involved with the drug trade, but has been receiving regular payments from the CIA for the last eight years![33]

Another of the traffickers, Marshal Muhammad Qasim Fahim, was the country's defense secretary and may be its next vice president. He was a general when the U.S. swept into Afghanistan after 9/11, worked closely with the CIA, and got rewarded with millions in cash. Except by 2002, the CIA was well aware that Marshal Fahim was into the heroin trade—long before the invasion, and after becoming defense minister. "He now had a Soviet-made cargo plane at his disposal that was making flights north to transport heroin through Russia, returning laden with cash." So what was the Bush Administration's response? "American military trainers would be directed to deal only with subordinates to Marshal Fahim."[34] Gee, I'll bet *they* were clean! As clean as Karzai's brother anyway.

Pakistan's ISI intelligence service, which we'll be talking about again in terms of financing the 9/11 terrorists, is another big player. One expert says there is an ISI-backed Islamist drug route of al Qaeda allies that stretches across all of North Central Asia.[35] Richard Holbrooke, who is now Obama's special representative to Afghanistan and Pakistan, wrote in an op-ed in 2008 that "breaking the narco-state in Afghanistan is essential, or all else will fail." Holbrooke also said that it's a complete waste of money to aerial-spray the poppy fields, which costs about a billion dollars a year, as this only serves to strengthen the Taliban and al Qaeda with the local people.

Of course, Donald Rumsfeld and the Pentagon under Bush-II "fiercely resisted efforts to draw the United States military into supporting counter-narcotics efforts" because they feared this "would only antagonize corrupt regional warlords whose support they needed." Now, under Obama, supposedly "fifty suspected Afghan drug traffickers believed to have ties to the Taliban have been placed on a Pentagon target list to be captured or killed."[36] But at the same time, the CIA and the DIA now say that the Taliban are getting much *less* money from the drug trade than was previously thought, and "that American officials did not believe that Afghan drug money was fueling Al Qaeda." The question this raises in my mind is: then who's making off with the profits? Karzai's brother, Marshal Fahim, the Pakistani government, and some people in the CIA maybe?

The heroin trade took a dive at the beginning of this century because the Taliban put them out of business. When that poppy supply was put on hold for awhile, isn't it ironic that some of the big banks tumbled?

Is it because that dirty money wasn't getting laundered through their establishments? But apparently, we think it's better to be in bed with the heroin producers than work with the Taliban.

Now let's turn our attention closer to home, and our neighbor Mexico. "Even in the last decade, when it has become more fashionable to write about Mexico as a 'narco-democracy,' few, if any, authors address the American share of responsibility for the staggering corruption that has afflicted Mexican politics."[37] Drug trafficking in Mexico actually dates back to the Harrison Anti-Narcotics Act of 1914 that made it illegal here at home, coupled with Mexico's revolution making its northern section pretty much ungovernable.

The same year the CIA was formed in 1947, the U.S. helped create Mexico's intelligence service called the DFS. Colonel Carlos Serrano, the brains behind that, was already connected to the drug traffic. Mexico soon became the main way station for smuggling heroin into the U.S. and Canada. Over time, the collusion only increased. Just as in Afghanistan, the CIA "was consciously drawing on Mexican drug-traffickers and their protectors as off-the-books assets." When Miguel Nazar Haro got busted in San Diego in 1981, the FBI and CIA both intervened because he was "an essential repeat essential contact for CIA station in Mexico City."[38] When DEA agent Enrique Camarena was murdered, the CIA got busy protecting the top traffickers behind it. During the eighties, CIA Director Casey helped keep drug lord Miguel Felix Gallardo safe, because he was passing funds along to the Contras. Gallardo's Honduran supplier was estimated to supply "perhaps one-third of all the cocaine consumed in the United States."[39]

Not surprisingly, narco-corruption in Mexico quickly spread to other agencies of law enforcement. By the time Carlos Salinas became president in the nineties, his attorney general's office was "as much as 95 percent . . . under narco-control." DFS agents were regularly escorting narcotics shipments through Mexico, and selling drugs they seized to organizations they favored. The DFS was carrying out high-level busts with the assistance of even higher-level traffickers. Operation Condor, carried out with the CIA's help, did the Guadalajara cartel "a great service by winnowing out the competition."[40]

A new class of oligarchs—known as the "twelve billionaires"—sprang up under Salinas's policy of "directed" deregulation. Some of the privatized businesses got "snapped up by traffickers in order to launder and invest the profits from their drug operations." Citibank helped the president's brother, Raul Salinas, hide his fortune in safe places, and Citibank's role would later be described as "willfully blind" drug money laundering. Now-defunct Lehman Brothers was right in there too, helping Mexico's regional governor Mario Villanueva Madrid go into hiding after he got targeted in a drug-and-racketeering investigation.[41]

Beginning in the nineties, drug dealers in Mexico were taking charge of half of Colombia's drug trade into the U.S. While Mexico used to be just the trans shipping point from South America, now it was a major producer and distributor. Numerous new cartels came into existence— Sinaloa, Los Zetas, La Familia Michoacana, and more—with its gangs even taking control of cocaine networks in many American cities and clandestinely growing marijuana on our public lands. Today, authorities figure that between $19 billion and $39 billion in proceeds from drugs heads back south every year from the U.S.[42]

Of course, the death toll figures on what's happening in Mexico's drug war are astounding. Between December 2006 and the spring of 2009, more than 10,780 people were killed.[43] And most of the guns fueling the violence are coming from the U.S. About 87 percent of the firearms that Mexican authorities have seized over the last five years can be traced to here, many of them from gun shops and gun shows in the Southwestern border states.[44] And these are no longer simply handguns, but now military-grade weaponry and very serious ordnance. How come the manufacturers are not being held accountable for selling these weapons over the border? My wife and I have driven across the border three times and nobody's even stopped us—I could have had a Hummer-full of automatic weapons.

Since Bush-II and Mexican president Felipe Calderon announced their $6 billion Plan Mexico in 2007—with the bulk of the money going to military training and hardware—the production of Colombian cocaine seems to have actually increased.[45] To his credit, Obama stepped things up on the drugs-and-guns front, threatening to prosecute any Americans doing business with three of the most violent cartels and looking to seize billions of dollars in the cartels' assets.[46]

I give Obama praise for renouncing the "war on drugs" phrase, on grounds that it promotes incarceration and not treatment. Before the election, Obama said: "I think it's time we take a hard look at the wisdom of locking up some first time nonviolent drug users for decades. . . . Let's reform this system."[47] I'm waiting for him to follow through on that promise. To his credit, the Justice Department has released new guidelines that reverse a Bush Administration policy. Now federal officers are instructed not to go after marijuana users or suppliers who are in compliance with states' laws on medical usage.

But isn't it high time for complete reform of our drug policy? We've got a shadow economy happening, friends. One hundred million Americans have sampled marijuana, and that includes almost half of all the seniors in high school. More than 35 million Americans have tried cocaine at some point, and almost as many have taken LSD or other hallucinogenic drugs.[48] Meantime, we've got "grows" or "gardens" of pot springing up all across our western states on public lands—and that includes almost 40 percent of national forests. About 3.1 million marijuana plants were confiscated in national forests over a one-year period, September '07 to September '08, carrying a street value calculated at $12.4 billion.[49]

I mean, how stupid are we? Go back to Chicago and Prohibition, when Al Capone became more powerful than the government because we'd outlawed the selling of liquor. Legalize marijuana, and you put the cartels out of business! Instead, we're going to further militarize our border and go shoot it out with them? And if a few thousand poor Mexicans get killed in the crossfire, too bad. I don't get that mentality. I don't understand how this is the proper way, the adult answer, when they could do it another way. Eventually, after thousands more people get killed, they'll probably arrive at the same answer: legalization. Because there's nothing else that will work.

And legalization would go a long way toward giving us a more legitimate government, too—a government that doesn't have to shield drug dealers who happen to be doing its dirty work. There are clearly people in government making money off drugs. Far more people, statistically, die from prescription drugs than illegal drugs. But the powers that be don't want you to be able to use a drug that you don't have to pay for, such as marijuana. Thirteen states now have voted to allow use of medical marijuana. Thank goodness Barack Obama just came out with a new policy stating that the feds are not going to interfere as long as people are following state law. That's a great step toward legalization.

You can't legislate stupidity, is an old saying I used in governing. Just because you make something illegal doesn't mean it's going away, it just means it'll now be run by criminals. But is using an illegal drug a criminal offense, or a medical one? I tend to believe medical, because that's customarily how addictions are treated, we don't throw you in jail for them. In a free society, that's an oxymoron—going to jail for committing a crime against yourself.

The government is telling people what's good for them and what's not, but that should be a choice made by us, not those in power. Look at the consequences when it's the other way around.

WHAT SHOULD WE DO NOW?

The hypocrisy of our federal drug policy has to be seen for what it is. When millions of dollars from illegal drug sales are being used to fund government agencies like the CIA and being laundered through our leading banks, isn't it time to rethink this situation? The fact is, the "war on drugs" is killing and imprisoning our citizens, way out of proportion to how it's helping anyone. Revamping a criminal justice system that incarcerates thousands of people for using "illicit substances" is a necessity. Legalizing marijuana, and putting a tax on its purchase like we do with cigarettes and alcohol, would be a start toward truly dealing with our "drug problem."

CHAPTER ELEVEN

THE STOLEN ELECTIONS OF 2000, 2004 (AND ALMOST 2008)

THE INCIDENT: In 2000 and again in 2004, George W. Bush won closely contested presidential elections against Democratic contenders Al Gore and John Kerry.

THE OFFICIAL WORD: The Supreme Court stopped a recount in Florida in 2000, giving Bush an Electoral College victory on December 12. In 2004, Bush took the deciding state of Ohio by a 100,000-vote margin and gained a second term.

MY TAKE: Both elections were stolen by Republican operatives, above all through manipulation of the electronic voting machines in deciding states, where votes were shifted from one candidate to the other. A guy who might have blown the whistle was killed in a plane crash right after the 2008 election.

"If this were a dictatorship, it'd be a heck of a lot easier, just so long as I'm the dictator."
—George W. Bush, CNN, December 18, 2000

We all know what happened back in 2000, when the Supreme Court handed George W. Bush the presidency by ordering the vote recount stopped in Florida. Al Gore had won the popular vote nationwide by about a half million votes, but couldn't get a majority in the Electoral College without Florida. A lot of us also suspect that John Kerry actually won the presidency in 2004, except for Ohio's Republican secretary of state manipulating the vote totals there in Bush's favor.

Would it surprise you to learn that massive conspiracies were involved in both those elections—and that the Republicans were on the verge of trying to steal it again in 2008? The main reason they didn't was because their key vote-stealer got forced into a court deposition the day before the election—only to die in the crash of his private plane a little more than a month later. His name was Michael Connell. He was Karl Rove's IT (Information Technology) guy, whose computer handiwork helped swing Florida in 2000 and Ohio in 2004 for Bush. We'll get to Connell's story later in the chapter, including some new information that's never been published before.

But let's start with a look back at what happened in 2000. It was around 2:15 AM Eastern time when Fox News led the networks' charge in projecting Bush the winner. The fellow who started this was John Ellis. He headed up Fox's decision team and just happened to be the cousin of W and Jeb, who just happened to be the governor of Florida. "Jebbie says we got it! Jebbie says we got it!" Ellis was heard shouting as he got off the phone with his Florida cousin, and it didn't take more than a couple of minutes before Fox called it that way.[1] And within the four minutes after that, like bleating sheep, NBC, CBS, ABC, and CNN followed suit. That was when Gore made his phone call to Bush conceding the election, although he reconsidered as the Florida results suddenly tightened up.

Obviously there was nepotism involved in Fox News's decision. CBS later said that a "critical" factor in its own call for Bush was the vote count in Florida's Volusia County, where it turned out that more than 16,000 votes had been subtracted from Gore's total by the electronic voting machines. One of Gore's campaign staff got suspicious and found out he was actually ahead in Volusia by 13,000 votes. That's when Gore took back his concession. Later on, the "mistake" was tracked to a company called Global Election Systems. Two months after the election, an internal memo from their master programmer, Talbot Iredale, blamed the problem on a memory card that had been uploaded improperly—and unnecessarily. Iredale said: "There is always the possibility that the 'second memory card' or 'second upload' came from an unauthorized source."[2]

That phrase "unauthorized source" kinda raises a red flag, doesn't it. This "faulty memory card" was pretty much forgotten once everybody started talking about hanging chads and butterfly ballots. Now I myself am pretty much computer illiterate, but my wife is not. She's not a person that swears often, but every day when she's on the computer, I'm listening to her cuss. That speaks volumes to me on a basic level; it tells me that computers often screw up. Because, let's face it, they're still made by humans, and we're going to make mistakes. So they can be manipulated. When you see all the identity fraud that goes on today, how easy would it be to create voter fraud? It's ripe.

I believe all votes should still be paper ballots and hand-counted. I'm proud to say Minnesota is still that way, and I hope this never changes. Look at it like this: Would you use an ATM machine that didn't give you a receipt? Well, these electronic voting machines don't do that. There's no way to keep a record of whom you voted for, so there can't be a valid recount. When computers can be used to change votes, it challenges the legality of our system. The only way to change that is to go back and make it as primitive as you can, one person one vote.

Changing the vote electronically was far from the only scam going down in Florida in 2000. Journalist Greg Palast was reporting soon after the election about how Katharine Harris and Jeb Bush set out to do some "ethnic cleansing" on the voter rolls ahead of time. You see, Florida has a state law that convicted felons aren't allowed to vote. So they hired a private contractor called Database Technologies (DBT), a division of ChoicePoint, whose board was studded with Republican bigwigs, to look for any crooks who were also registered voters. The database eventually listed 57,700 Florida citizens, and local election supervisors were told to purge them.

Except, more than 90 percent of those people never committed any felonies! More than half of them were either black or Hispanic, and likely to have voted for a Democrat. Early in 2001, when the U.S. Civil Rights Commission became the only agency to look into how Florida handled the disputed election, it concluded there had been a possible conspiracy by Katharine Harris and others. Besides denying the so-called "felons" their voting rights, Jeb Bush had ordered state troopers near the polling sites to delay people for hours while they searched their cars. Two photo IDs were required at some precincts, even though Florida law only required one. In certain black precincts, ballot boxes disappeared or ended up found later in strange places, never having been collected.[3]

This story ran big in the media—but only across the Atlantic in England. Palast tried to get it into the American media in the weeks when the recount was still happening. CBS told him it didn't seem to hold up. Why? Well, because they'd called Jeb Bush's office to ask.[4] The *Washington Post* did run a Page One story, but not until June of 2001—even though they'd had the story seven months earlier, when it might have made a difference.[5] Our media should be ashamed of their part in undermining American democracy. You had newsmen like Tim Russert saying, the day after the election, that it was probably time for Gore to "play statesman and concede."[6] Did you ever hear of any media suggesting that Bush call it a day? Not a one!

The dirty tricks just kept on happening. Remember how both sides fought about the counting of absentee ballots from overseas? One Republican operative says there was a long conference call after the election where Bush's boys talked about having some people near overseas military bases organize a little get-out-the-vote drive. They'd be registered voters, of course, but just happened to have forgotten to cast their ballot on election day. So what if it was a few days later? As of November 13, a total of 446 military absentee ballots had arrived; by the 17th, the number had soared to 3,733. Raise any eyebrows that maybe somebody should've been charged with a felony?[7]

I get a sense of déjà vu when I see what's happened more recently with the disrupters of the Obama Administration's Town Hall meetings on health care. There was a manual recount underway in Miami-Dade County when dozens of screaming GOP demonstrators—shipped in from Washington—started banging on doors and a picture window at the election headquarters. Several people got "trampled, punched or kicked." Gore had already received a net gain of 168 votes when the canvassing board panicked and stopped the recount. Most of the mob ended up receiving nice rewards within the Republican Party.[8]

So, on December 12, just when a Florida District Court judge was about to order a complete statewide hand recount, the Supreme Court rendered its decision. Justice Anthony Scalia said he thought that to keep on counting would "threaten irreparable harm to the petitioner [Bush] and to the country, by casting a cloud upon what he claims to be the legality of his decision."[9] What legality? I have never understood what precedents the Supreme Court used in doing this. You had a branch of federal government stepping in and interfering with what should be completely a states' rights issue. The feds should have no dog in the fight. I agree with Vince Bugliosi, who wrote that the justices who did this should be put in jail for overstepping their bounds!

After it was too late, the *Washington Post* published a piece about how if all the votes had been recounted in all 67 counties, Gore would probably have been in the White House. A study cited by CBS and AP, conducted by the University of Chicago, reported: "Under any standard that tabulated all disputed votes statewide, Gore erased Bush's advantage" and won by a narrow margin.[10] Ho-hum, I guess, the deal was already done.

Of course, Gore won the national popular vote from the get-go. How can you get a half million more votes than the other guy and lose? The presidential is the only election where we allow that to happen. We should have gotten rid of the Electoral College long ago. It was fine back in the days when everybody was still on horseback. We now have cars and airplanes, and it's time to leave an antiquated system behind. Who's profiting from keeping it going? As a third-party guy, I was hoping 2004 would bring the opposite result: Bush would win the popular vote and Kerry would take the Electoral. Maybe that would have brought them to the table to abolish the whole thing.

But 2004, it turned out, was even more blatant election theft than in 2000. The exit polls were predicting a huge victory for Kerry. But, by late that night, somehow Bush had taken a decisive lead and Kerry conceded on the day after. "There is no evidence of vote theft or errors on a large scale," the *New York Times* "informed" us. The *Washington Post* called any talk of vote fraud "conspiracy theories."[11]

Bull-crap. For starters here's what Robert F. Kennedy Jr. later documented: "Nearly half of the 6 million American voters living abroad never received their ballots—or received them too late to vote—after the Pentagon unaccountably shut down a state-of-the-art Web site used to file overseas registrations. A consulting firm called Sproul & Associates, which was hired by the Republican National Committee to register voters in six battleground states, was discovered shredding Democratic registrations. In New Mexico, which was decided by 5,988 votes, malfunctioning machines mysteriously failed to properly register a presidential vote on more than 20,000 ballots. Nationwide, according to the federal commission charged with implementing election reforms, as many as 1 million ballots were spoiled by faulty voting equipment—roughly one for every 100 cast."[12]

The electronic voting machines played an even bigger role in the 2004 election, with 36 million votes being cast on the touch-screen systems owned by four private companies that use their own proprietary software. Three of those companies had close ties to the Republican Party. One of them, Diebold (including employees and their families) had contributed at least $300,000 to GOP candidates and party funds since 1998. The company's CEO, Walden O'Dell, had gone so far in a fund-raising e-mail as to promise to deliver Ohio to Bush in '04![13] With enemies like that, Kerry could have used a few friends demanding a return to paper ballots.

Ohio was where Bush's "victory" put him over the top in the electoral college. From 12:20 in the morning until around 2 AM, the flow of information in Ohio mysteriously stopped while the vote count switched dramatically to Bush's side.[14] A comfortable 118,000-vote-plus official margin in Ohio then gave him a second term as president. But what really went down? "Officials there purged tens of thousands of eligible voters from the rolls, neglected to process registration cards generated by Democratic voter drives, shortchanged Democratic precincts when they allocated voting machines, and illegally derailed a recount that could have given Kerry the presidency."[15] Lou Harris, who basically invented modern political polling, said: "Ohio was as dirty an election as America has ever seen."[16]

The fellow in charge of the vote-counting was Ohio secretary of state J. Kenneth Blackwell, who also happened to be the co-chair of Bush's reelection committee there. And nobody seemed concerned about a conflict of interest? Back in 2000, Blackwell had been Bush's "principal electoral system adviser" during the Florida recount, where I guess he took some lessons from Katharine Harris. When Congressman John Conyers looked into what took place in Ohio, his report in January 2005 set forth "massive and unprecedented voter irregularities and anomalies in Ohio. . . . caused by intentional misconduct and illegal behavior, much of it involving Secretary of State J. Kenneth Blackwell." Conyers told RFK Jr. that Blackwell "made Katharine Harris look like a cupcake."[17]

Playing devil's advocate for a minute, I heard from a Democratic friend who worked Ohio that they just didn't get the people out to vote like they should have. And I think the Democratic Party blew the 2004 election, to the point where it shouldn't have come down to Ohio. Why did they allow the Republicans to twist things around and make George Bush a war hero, when he was actually a draft-dodger? And then turn Kerry, who fought valiantly in Vietnam, into a coward? I would never have handled it that way. Let's pull the military records and compare them, find out who was the real guy serving his country. I can't understand why the Democrats allowed this to take place. But maybe Kerry had played too many games of compromise over his years in politics. He told my collaborator, Dick Russell, in 2008, and I quote: "I know I won the election. But by the time my lawyers could come up with a smoking gun in Ohio, it was too late." My question is, how come Kerry has never come out publicly and talked about that. Doesn't he think he has a responsibility to try and stop history from repeating again?

The story of what went on behind the scenes in Ohio really started to surface as we approached the next presidential election in 2008. That's where things get interesting. To set the stage, we need to go back to a lawsuit brought by a group of citizens against Ohio officials in August of 2006. At the time, Blackwell was still secretary of state and was running for governor on the Republican ticket. A well-known voting rights attorney named Cliff Anebeck set out to charge Blackwell and his cronies with "election fraud, vote dilution, vote suppression, recount fraud and other violations."[18] The judge in the case followed up with a court order that all ballot evidence relating to the 2004 election be preserved for another year (beyond the legally required 22 months, which was about to expire).

After Democrats swept into the major Ohio offices in 2006, the judge ordered everything turned over to the new secretary of state, a woman named Jennifer Brunner. Well, guess what? The board of elections in 56 of Ohio's 88 counties had either lost, shredded, or dumped nearly 1.6 million ballots and other election records. The reasons? Oh, various things. Spilled coffee, a flooded storage area, some miscommunication with "greenies" there to pick up recyclables. All accidental, sorry about that.[19]

There were a lot of discussions after that between lawyer Cliff Arnebeck and government officials. They talked about a settlement, or a grand jury investigation, or Congress getting involved. Secretary of State Brunner wanted to focus on assuring the integrity of the next election, rather than be distracted by the past. So Arnebeck agreed to narrow things to taking the deposition of one man, Michael Connell, who was Karl Rove's computer expert and lived in Akron, Ohio.[20]

A friend of Connell's named Stephen Spoonamore had already decided to go public. Arnebeck says Spoonamore is "the best expert witness I've ever worked with, courageous and willing to take complex facts and circumstances and give you highly qualified, credible judgments."[21] His friends call him "Spoon," and he's an expert in electronic data security and what's called "digital network architecture." He'd designed or consulted on computer systems for MasterCard, American Express, the State Department and many more companies and government agencies. A registered Republican, Spoonamore was a staunch believer in the democratic process. Knowing plenty about how thieves could hack information, he'd been concerned about the prospects for fraud with electronic voting machines since the late 1990s.[22]

Spoonamore also happened to live in Ohio, and on election night 2004, was doing some monitoring when he began noticing trends in a number of Ohio counties where Kerry started out ahead but then radically different totals ended up favoring Bush. Spoonamore started thinking about the possibility of a "kingpin attack," where a computer inserted into the communications flow has the ability to change information at both ends of an IT system. It's Greek to me, but for you geeks out there, it's also known as the "man in the middle" plan. Based on the Internet Protocol (IP) addresses that were registering, Spoonamore figured out that the same server form was used by the GOP for most of their hosting, and that tracked back to a company in Chattanooga, Tennessee, called SMARTech.

Here's an excerpt from the Chattanooga daily paper, from March 2004: "Along the information superhighway, the road to another term in the White House for George Bush begins in Chattanooga. From a second story suite in the Pioneer Bank Building on Broad Street, millions of Internet connections and e-mail blasts by the president's reelection campaign are regularly broadcast by SMARTech Inc." The company was run by Jeff Averbeck, an "Internet entrepreneur who first began working as a consultant for the Republican National Committee in 2000."[23]

Lawyers made a Freedom of Information Act request that confirms what Spoonamore uncovered. In November 2003, Blackwell's office had enlisted a company called GovTech Solutions, owned by Mike Connell, to establish a duplicate control center for election day '04. The results would be sent directly to subcontractor SMARTech and its backup server out in Tennessee. The contract specified that there would be "a hardware VPN device [that] will allow access to a private network connecting the servers for database replication services as well as remote admin[istration]." Meaning, I'm told, that anybody could get into the network and make whatever adjustments they wanted. The election results could be observed and changed, using remote access through high-speed Internet from any location.[24] The primary control was SMARTech headquarters. "We have no idea what was set up in Chattanooga," Spoonamore says. "There could have been 20 Republican operatives, and from that point they could have made a direct hop to the White House. They could have been running this from the War Room!"[25]

Early on Election Day, George W. Bush and Karl Rove flew into Columbus, Ohio, to meet with Blackwell.[26] Connell managed the setup that enabled Blackwell to study maps of the precincts and voter turnout in order to figure out how many votes they needed.[27] A third company that Connell brought into the scheme was Triad, a major donor to Bush's campaign. They were run by some far-right Christians, the Rapp family. Triad supplied the network computers that stored all the voter registration information, and hosted the county board of elections results on its Web server.[28]

Connell admitted making Govtech, SMARTech, and Triad look like a single unit for the Ohio election returns.[29] Congressman Conyers had written to Triad in December 2004, asking about their ability to access the vote-counting computers remotely.[30] Triad, it seems, had changed the hard drive in the tabulator computer before the recount. The only reason to do that, Spoonamore says, would be to erase and destroy evidence of a software manipulation of that tabulator.

Out of the blue, Connell called Spoonamore late in 2005. They'd never met before, but Connell had heard of the systems Spoonamore developed to protect democracy advocates from being hacked in hostile overseas environments. In one such location, Connell was helping out some Christian advocacy groups. Unbeknownst to Connell, Spoonamore already knew a fair bit about him from his research into election activities and the voting machines. Connell had created Web sites for Jeb Bush's run for governor, and for George W. in 2000. Connell's company got the first private contract to build and manage congressional e-mail servers and firewalls. This gave him the ability and means to read documents and e-mails, copy data, and set up "back doors."[31] Then he did the Web site for Blackwell's office in Ohio; another client of Connell's was Swift Boat Veterans for Truth, the group that went after Kerry on his service record!

Spoonamore told us, "Mike was a front-end guy, who built Web sites and really sophisticated databases to track voters. The way computers actually function and talk to each other, he didn't have the expertise and would have to work with others, like the guys at SMARTech."[32] When he and Connell first met in Washington, Spoonamore didn't reveal his own interest in the electronic voting world. The two hit it off, and started working together on a couple of unrelated overseas projects. Then, when they happened to be at the same conference in London, somebody pulled Connell aside to warn him that Spoonamore was "an insane guy who opposes voting machines." Connell told Spoon, "You have some people who are really nervous about you."

As they became friends, Spoonamore sensed that Connell was having second thoughts about what he'd been doing for the Republicans. Maybe you've followed some of the flap about all of those e-mails of Karl Rove's that somehow disappeared over time. Well, it was Connell who set up the site used by Rove for 95 percent of his e-mail communication, known as GWB43.com. At the end of a private meeting in 2006, Connell asked Spoonamore what he knew about "the complexity of trying to erase e-mail." Spoon explained that, in most cases, it can't be done. Connell pointed in the direction of the White House a few blocks away, saying that he'd "kinda been asked to look at a challenge, whether you could recover or get back e-mails." Spoonamore recalls: "He was fishing around for what the steps might be. I said, 'Mike, I'm involved in a lot of stuff to protect people's privacy and bank accounts, but I don't use those skills to destroy information. And I would encourage you to tell people to walk away from this because, one, it doesn't work and, two, the cover-up is always worse than the crime, Mike.'"

With the 2008 election year coming up, Spoonamore decided to "stop opposing things in the background and go very public." He approached Arnebeck's legal team in Ohio and offered himself as an expert witness. He also went to Connell. "I basically said, 'Mike, there's a lot of people you work with—and frankly, some of them I've worked with as well, and with some I still do—who treat democracy as a game, where if their side wins it doesn't matter if you cheat. Mike, I don't think you're in that camp but I do think you've worked very closely with some of the people who are. I intend to spend some of my time and resources and reputation on making their lives uncomfortable. And I'm giving you a heads-up about it.' Well, Mike didn't react the way I expected. He reacted by taking my hands and asking to pray, and he said, 'I don't think you know how far over your head you're gonna get.'"

At that point, Spoonamore didn't know how involved Connell had been in the Florida 2000 situation. A guy named Roy Cales had been Connell's top computer expert for a long time. In the summer of 2000, Jeb Bush had appointed Cales as Florida's first Chief Information Officer, or tech czar, and gave him the authority to take over all of Florida's government computer systems, which included "unrestricted access" to all election reporting and tabulating computers used by Secretary of State Katharine Harris.[33] Cales resigned in early September 2001, after being charged with grand theft in connection with a 1996 forgery.[34]

Learning more about this, Spoonamore invited Connell to breakfast. It went on for five hours. Spoonamore revealed he was "going forward with attorneys, and I have no question it's going to end up in discovery on your desk. I hope we continue with our friendship, but there's a period of time when this is gonna get ugly." Spoonamore described whom he believed the guilty parties were, starting with Rove. "You're really good at this," he remembers Connell saying. Then Connell admitted he'd gone too far, and there were things he was ready to get off his chest.

A meeting was arranged with Congressman Conyers's office. The memo prepared for the House Judiciary Committee said: "Well before the 2000 election, one of Connell's employees created a 'Trojan Horse' software application which, when installed on one computer, allows its remote control by another computer. Prior to the 2004 election in Ohio, Connell administered and developed important parts of the Secretary of State's computer network including the election results reporting server systems. . . . During the 2004 (and 2006) elections, Connell routed the election results from the OH SOS office through SMARTech servers in Chattanooga, Tennessee."[35]

Then, at the last minute, Spoon says Conyers's office "dropped the ball. Mike was going to come forward and talk about everything he'd seen and been asked to do, in regard to voting machines. I even had a senior priest who he really respected, and who he'd never lie in front of, agree to come with him. I have no idea what happened."

In July 2008, attorney Arnebeck asked U.S. Attorney General Michael Mukasey to hold onto all of Rove's e-mails. Rove was identified in the lawsuit as the "principal perpetrator of a pattern of corrupt activity" under the Ohio Corrupt Practices Act. "We have been confidentially informed by a source we believe to be credible that Karl Rove has threatened Michael Connell . . . that if he does not agree to 'take the fall' for election fraud in Ohio, his wife Heather will be prosecuted for supposed law lobby violations."

Then, in September, Connell got issued a subpoena. His attorney, Bill Todd, who happened to also have been legal counsel for Bush/Cheney '04, said that Connell couldn't be deposed before the election because he was too busy working for the John McCain campaign.[36] Shortly before the November election, Connell appeared with a trio of lawyers before an Ohio judge, who ordered him to give a deposition. With the election one day away, Connell denied any role in recommending the Chattanooga SMARTech company to Ohio officials in 2004, but he did admit for the record that his company had subcontracted with SMARTech.

This might have shaken up Rove and company. In mid-October, Rove had an article in the *Wall Street Journal* headlined "Obama Hasn't Closed the Sale." The latest Gallup tracking poll showed nearly twice as many undecided voters than in the 2004 election, Rove said, so Obama's 7.3% lead didn't necessarily mean that much. McCain, entering the final weekend of the race, predicted a come-from-behind victory, based on how things were looking in battleground states like Ohio. But then suddenly, on Monday night, after Connell gave his deposition, it all changed. The new Rove electoral map predicted a 338-to-200 electoral vote margin in favor of Obama. Rove had basically done a 180-degree turn.[37]

Spoonamore told us: "I have had conversations with knowledgeable people who say that there were significant discussions as to whether or not, if they manipulated the election, they'd get caught this time. Their biggest fear, and frankly it was rightfully so, was that there were a number of us who were working to hack into the systems to watch for their hacking."[38]

Personally, I don't think they dared fix the election, because the people knew overwhelmingly that Obama was going to win. If it would all of a sudden have come back McCain, I think there would have been an outcry in the streets that would have gotten the Bilderberg types upset—if you know what I mean.

So then, on December 19, 2008, Michael Connell, 45 years old, father of four, went down in the fiery crash of his Piper Saratoga II single-engine plane. He was flying back alone from a meeting in Maryland and only two and a half miles from the Akron airport. The airplane's right wing clipped a flagpole in the front yard of an empty house before it broke up and set fire to the garage. Connell was thrown out of the burning plane and died instantly. He was an accomplished pilot, flying in decent weather.[39] A friend told a reporter that twice over the past two months, Connell had canceled flights due to suspicious problems with his plane.[40]

"A number of people with expertise are of the opinion that this was a hit," Ohio attorney Arnebeck told us. "There is a method called electromagnetic pulse technology, where you can disrupt the electronics in an airplane and it's very hard to detect, particularly after the fact. The motive would be that Connell was an extraordinary individual in terms of his knowledge and expertise in a fairly vast racketeering kind of conspiracy, in that it involved Karl Rove, business groups, multiple elections, and a fairly broad geography."[41]

Spoonamore says this: "I found out something about the system that Mike had on board, where he fundamentally had a system without mechanical controls that was computer operated. Eyewitnesses on the ground say all the plane's lights turned off, the engine stalled. At that point, he would have regained manual control by wire, he flattens it out and tries to fix the problem. But when he turns the engine back on, the plane guns itself and dives into the ground. So what happened? Simple. You program a chip. They changed the chip that runs the plane. Despite the fact that FAA rules require you leave the site alone until daylight, completely document and photograph it, instead they pick up the entire plane and haul it to a Lockheed-Martin hangar. Trust me, by the time the FAA started pulling it apart, the right chip was back in the computer."

To say what happened to Connell was weird timing is an understatement. Here's a guy getting ready to be a whistle-blower on the biggest series of election frauds in our history. Whether it was an accident or by design, he was silenced. Gee, what bad luck this guy had. Hmmmm. . . .

Spoonamore, for one, is scared that if we continue with electronic voting, stolen elections are going to happen again. He says most of these companies are run by far-right evangelical Christians. "A tiny group of people who call themselves Christians, but who clearly do not believe in Christ's message or our democracy, seem to repeatedly be behind every questionable voting outcome. They aren't Christians. They are fascists. Fascists who don't have the balls to go public, round people up, and kill them, except on very rare occasions—like Mike Connell."

WHAT SHOULD WE DO NOW?

It's obvious that, to avoid the specter of vote fraud always hanging over our elections, we've got to outlaw the electronic voting machines and return to a system where there's a "paper trail." How can we not see the blatant conflict of interest that currently exists, with the computer companies and the vote-counters being dominated by the Republican Party? Give the Democrats enough years in power, and you can bet they'd follow the same pattern. While we're after real reform, let's finally abolish the antiquated Electoral College and allow the popular vote to prevail. And let's open the ballot and the debates to legitimate third-party candidates, and break the stranglehold that big money has on the two-party system.

CHAPTER TWELVE

WHAT REALLY HAPPENED ON SEPTEMBER 11?

THE INCIDENT: On September 11, 2001, four airplanes were hijacked on American soil and crashed into the Twin Towers, the Pentagon, and a field in Pennsylvania.

THE OFFICIAL WORD: The 19 hijackers were all fanatic Muslim terrorists linked to al-Qaeda and its ringleader, Osama bin Laden.

MY TAKE: Our government engaged in a massive cover-up of what really happened, including its own ties to the hijackers. Unanswered questions remain about how the towers were brought down, and whether a plane really struck the Pentagon. The Bush Administration either knew about the plan and allowed it to proceed, or they had a hand in it themselves.

"The truth is incontrovertible. Malice may attack it; ignorance may deride it. But in the end—There it is. . . ."

—Winston Churchill

I was in my third year as Minnesota's governor on September 11, 2001. After the devastation of the Pentagon being hit and the Twin Towers falling, I put the National Guard on alert and secured some of our public buildings. The following Sunday morning, we were the first state to hold a memorial for the nearly 3,000 victims. More than 40,000 people showed up on the front lawn of the State Capitol, while a steady rain fell. I'll never forget Native American shamans beating drums alongside honor guards who represented the police and firefighters and military. It still chokes me up to think about it. Looking out on hundreds of flags fluttering in the breeze, I remember saying at the end of two hours: "We will promote good against evil. And finally, we will together restore our sense of freedom by conquering this enemy!"

I never wanted to believe anything different than what our government told us about that tragic day. But here is what John Farmer, a Senior Counsel for the 9/11 Commission who drafted the original report, has to say in a new book: "At some level of the government, at some point in time . . . there was an agreement not to tell the truth about what happened."[1] What more do we need? Are we willing to live with another lie to go with the Warren Report, the Iran-Contra cover-up, and many other "official" stories?

I certainly never expected to think that elements of the Bush Administration were complicit with the enemy. Today, though, I am convinced that some people inside our government knew the attack was going to happen and allowed it to come to pass—because it furthered their political agenda. I don't necessarily believe that they orchestrated it themselves, although the door is definitely open to that. I say this after expending many hours researching things about the official story that don't add up, and interviewing a number of witnesses with firsthand knowledge that contradicts what we were told. As a patriotic American, I say this with a heavy heart—and with an outrage that really knows no words. But it's something we, as a nation, must come to terms with. Otherwise, it could happen again.

From day one, there was something that puzzled me. You had four airplanes being hijacked on the same morning. Maybe the first one snuck by the radar—but the next three? I'd been inside air traffic control, where you've got a dozen people watching every plane in their sector. They know what direction all the aircraft are supposed to be going, and here were four planes going directly opposite of their normal flight path. But we're supposed to believe that no alarm bells went off anywhere, so no fighter jets got scrambled to intercept the planes. Was everybody asleep at the switch? How could the FAA and our air defenses experience such a miserable failure?

I want to tell you a short story about a guy named Charles Lewis, who my writing colleague Dick Russell interviewed recently in Southern California. Until two months before September 11, Lewis had worked at

LAX as the Quality Control Manager for Kiewit Pacific Construction on its Taxiway "C" project. A large part of his duties involved security in the Airport Operations Area, or AOA. There he got to know employees of various agencies—the LA World Airport Police, the LAPD, California Highway Patrol, the FBI, U.S. Customs, and others.

When the 9/11 attacks occurred, Lewis was a deputy inspector for the city of LA during a seismic retrofit of the LA Hilton Towers Hotel, only a few minutes from the airport by car. After making sure the hotel construction crew went home, Lewis rushed over to LAX's Guard Post 2, because he was one of very few people who knew how to fix certain parts of the new security systems in case any problems developed.

Lewis estimates he arrived at about 6:35 AM (PT—9:35 AM Eastern), not long after the second plane struck the World Trade Center. As on other days, there was "chatter" on LAX Security walkie-talkies and he could easily hear what they were saying, sometimes both sides of the conversation. Lewis remembers: "The first thing I noticed was that the guards—and that day they were the LA World Airport Police and the FBI—were very upset and agitated because apparently no one [from FAA] had notified NORAD [North American Aerospace Defense Command]. They were making calls and demanding to know why not. Eventually word came back that NORAD had indeed been notified, but they had been ordered to stand down. Then LAX Security wanted to know who could have made that order. And word came back that it was from the highest level of the White House. Later on, watching television, I knew the order didn't come from Bush because he was reading 'My Pet Goat' to the school kids in Florida, so the only other person it could be was Dick Cheney."[2]

It turns out there were some "war games" taking place that morning. September 11 was the second day of Vigilant Guardian, an exercise of the Joint Chiefs and NORAD that simulated planes being hijacked in the Northeastern United States. Another drill, called Northern Vigilance, had shifted some fighter jets to Canada and Alaska to monitor Russian MIGs flying training missions. This one put "phantoms" on military radar screens that would look real to the participants in the exercise. "We fought many phantoms that day," Richard Myers of the Joint Chiefs later testified to Congress.

But could the attack have been scheduled intentionally to coincide with those war games? If so, this raises a couple of questions. Either there was a major intelligence leak, whereby the terrorists realized the war games would be a good cover for their operation. Or else some people in the administration knew of the attack ahead of time and let it proceed simultaneously, knowing the confusion this would cause.

Between September 2000 and June 2001, on 67 different occasions fighter jets were sent to intercept aircraft that had lost radio contact or their transponder signal or were flying off course, usually within ten minutes of any sign of a problem.[3] (Contrary to what some people think, presidential approval wasn't needed to intercept or even shoot down an aircraft.) Then, on June 1, 2001, the existing hijacking response procedures were changed to require approval by the secretary of defense before responding to a situation with lethal force.[4] And when the call came into the Pentagon on 9/11, nobody answered the phone!

The stand-down order that Charles Lewis heard about was confirmed by none other than Norman Mineta, transportation secretary at the time. According to the 9/11 Commission, Cheney didn't arrive underground at the PEOC (Presidential Emergency Operations Center) until almost 10 AM. Mineta, however, said the Vice President was already down there when he arrived at about 9:20 AM. Richard Clarke and Cheney's photographer indicated the same thing. That was before the Pentagon had been hit, and Mineta recalled a young man coming into the PEOC three times to tell Cheney how far out the plane was from Washington. After the third report, according to Mineta, the young fellow asked, "Do the orders still stand?" and Cheney responded, "Of course the orders still stand. Have you heard anything to the contrary?" The 9/11 Commission chose to ignore Mineta's testimony and went so far as to remove it from the video archive. Instead, they had Cheney ordering, almost 45 minutes later than Mineta said, the inbound aircraft be shot down. Except, by then, all four planes had already gone down.[5]

That was cover-up number one by the 9/11 Commission. Now let's look at whether it was actually those two planes that were responsible for the falling towers. I was amazed, watching the 2007 version of the documentary *Loose Change* (which I urge everyone to see), at the many firefighters and other eyewitnesses who talked about a whole series of explosions before and during the collapse of the buildings. All of this was reported on the news at the time. Before the South Tower collapsed, video footage clearly shows sizable amounts of white smoke starting to pour out of the base. There was described a "giant rolling ball of flame" that came up from street level; an elevator that exploded on the 65th floor as some-one stood beside it; a woman on the 49th floor seeing people with burns and broken arms in the stairwells. "For every window in the lobby to be exploding . . . it wasn't from the jet fuel, no way," according to one of the witnesses. And a whole lot more that did not jive with any plane striking the building. Barry Jennings, the city's emergency coordinator, was at the scene before and after the building collapses. Jennings puts it out there plainly: "I know what I heard. I heard explosions."[6]

For my TV show, I interviewed a witness named William Rodriguez, a janitor who happened to have a master key and rescued many people and got honored at the White House as a national hero. He says that shortly before American Airlines Flight 11 struck the North Tower at 8:46 AM, an explosion simultaneously rocked the building so hard "it pushed us up." Rodriguez later testified behind closed doors to the 9/11 Commission, but his name was never mentioned in the report. Rodriguez also gave the com-mission and the FBI a list of fourteen people who'd been with him, but not a single one was ever contacted. He produced his boss for us, who looked me right in the eye and in essence told me the same story. What's happened to Rodriguez today? He's on the no-fly list. A guy who went back in to save people, with no regard for his own life! When he goes somewhere, he's pulled out of the line, interrogated, harassed. All because, I guess, he didn't give the "proper testimony" they wanted.

Some people have argued that the twin towers went down, within a half hour of one another, because of the way they were constructed. Well, those 425,000 cubic yards of concrete and 200,000 tons of steel were designed to hold up against a Boeing 707, the largest plane built at the time the towers were completed in 1973. Analysis had shown that a 707 traveling at 600 miles an hour (and those had four engines) would not cause major damage. The twin-engine Boeing 757s that hit on 9/11 were going 440 and 550 miles an hour.[7]

Still, we are told that a molten, highly intense fuel mixture from the planes brought down these two steel-framed skyscrapers. Keep in mind that no other such skyscraper in history had ever been known to collapse completely due to fire damage. So could it actually have been the result of a controlled demolition from inside the buildings? I don't claim expertise about this, but I did work four years as part of the navy's underwater demolition teams, where we were trained to blow things to hell and high water. And my staff talked at some length with a prominent physicist, Steven E. Jones, who says that a "gravity driven collapse" without demolition charges defies the laws of physics. These buildings fell, at nearly the rate of free-fall, straight down into their own footprint, in approximately ten seconds. An object dropped from the roof of the 110-story-tall towers would reach the ground in about 9.2 seconds. Then there's the fact that steel beams that weighed as much as 200,000 pounds got tossed laterally as far as 500 feet.

The National Institute of Standards and Technology (NIST) started its investigation on August 21, 2002. When their 10,000-page-long report came out three years later, the spokesman said there was no evidence to suggest a controlled demolition. But Steven E. Jones also says that molten metal found underground weeks later is proof that jet fuel couldn't have been all that was responsible. I visited the site about three weeks after 9/11, with Governor Pataki and my wife, Terry. It didn't mean anything to me at the time, but they had to suspend digging that day because they were running into heat pockets of huge temperatures. These fires kept burning for more than three months, the longest-burning structure blaze ever. And this was all due to jet fuel? We're talking molten metal more than 2,000 degrees Fahrenheit.[8]

Probably the most conclusive evidence about a controlled demolition is a research paper (two years, nine authors) published in the peer-reviewed *Open Chemical Physics Journal*, in April 2009. In studying dust samples from the site, these scientists found chips of nano-thermite, which is a high-tech incendiary/explosive. Here's what the paper's lead author, Dr. Niels Harrit of the University of Copenhagen's chemistry department, had to say about the explosive that he's convinced brought down the Twin Towers and the nearby Building 7:

"Thermite itself dates back to 1893. It is a mixture of aluminum and rust-powder, which react to create intense heat. The reaction produces iron, heated to 2500 degrees Centigrade. This can be used to do welding. It can also be used to melt other iron. So in nano-thermite, this powder from 1893 is reduced to tiny particles, perfectly mixed. When these react, the intense heat develops much more quickly. Nano-thermite can be mixed with additives to give off intense heat, or serve as a very effective explosive. It contains more energy than dynamite, and can be used as rocket fuel."[9]

Richard Gage is one of hundreds of credentialed architects and structural engineers who have put their careers on the line to point out the detailed anomalies and many implications of controlled demolition in the building collapses. As he puts it bluntly: "Once you get to the science, it's indisputable."[10]

So what happened to the steel debris from the World Trade Center that might have backed this up? Well, for the most part it was shipped overseas. The removal by four companies contracted by the city was carefully controlled and monitored. The building assessment performance team wasn't allowed to take samples.[11] One firefighter I spoke with, who got dug out of the rubble on 9/11, said: "The one thing that always troubled me is, why were they in such a hurry to remove all the evidence? Why did they take away everything from the site as fast and expediently as possible?"

I tried to talk to someone from the 9/11 Commission, but got turned down multiple times. They simply said, we stand by our report. I also tried to speak with Mayor Giuliani, but he refused also. We recently learned, through the D.A. of Manhattan's testimony in a court case, that the city of New York did nothing to investigate 9/11. That tells me Giuliani was nothing but a straw man. Why is he paraded around as this big hero when he really had nothing to do with it, other than be a figurehead? Again, I ask what happened to state and local laws. Homicides are supposed to be investigated by the jurisdiction where they happen. Who has the power to suspend all those laws and make them irrelevant, turning it into an investigation completely controlled by the feds? Seems that they feel they're above us. We work now for the government, not the other way around. That's not the way this country was founded. I think we have a right to know who ran that investigation, so we can properly critique it.

I wanted to ask Mayor Giuliani specifically about the collapse of Building 7, late on the afternoon of the attacks. If all these buildings are falling as a result of fires, shouldn't we be changing the way we build them? In this case, you had Building 7 that wasn't struck by anything. I went to the BBC and got the footage where a reporter is standing in front of it, incongruously saying that it's already come down—almost a half-hour before it did! I tried to talk to the reporter, but the BBC turned me down, explaining that that day was extremely hectic and they're not part of any conspiracy.

A few hours before the attack, for some reason Building 7's alarm system went on test status. The power was shut off and all tenants evacuated after the second plane hit. People were reporting major fires on the east, north, and west faces that covered about six of the floors. One witness, Michael Hess, reported a major explosion on the sixth floor and being trapped for 90 minutes two floors above that, until he was rescued by the fire department.

Well, just like the Twin Towers, the 47-story Building 7 fell symmetrically into its own footprint (in 6.5 seconds), sending the same type of pyro-plastic cloud down the surrounding streets that demolition is known to cause. Keep in mind that other nearby buildings with much worse damage never collapsed. Not Building 3, which was split in half by the South Tower's debris. Not Building 4, otherwise almost completely destroyed. Not Buildings 5 or 6, which suffered severe fires and structure damage. And they were much smaller than Building 7, where 81 columns all had to collapse at the same time due to fires on just a few floors. So why did Building 7 come down as it did? What's being covered up?

I've got questions about the attack on the Pentagon also. Getting back to Charles Lewis and what he heard that morning on the walkie-talkies out at LAX: The security guards referred to a "missile" having hit the Pentagon. "I was kinda puzzled," Lewis says, "because by the time the airport had been evacuated and I got home, the missile that had hit the Pentagon had mysteriously changed to being another plane. I couldn't figure that out, because I didn't take the FBI or the LA World Airport Police to be putting on a pageant for me."[12]

Of course, officially it was American Airlines Flight 77 that crashed into the ground floor at 9:37 AM. Only a section of the Pentagon that had been reinforced to withstand a terrorist attack was hit. Anywhere else, the damage and the casualties would have been much worse.[13] Left behind by a plane 100-some feet wide was a hole 16 feet deep, but no evidence to accompany it, which is something that former air force fighter pilot Russ Wittenberg says he'd never seen happen. Captain Wittenberg also says that jet engines do not leave a trail of white smoke, as was seen at the Pentagon. "We don't know what it was, but you can tell what it wasn't," according to Wittenberg. And he believes it wasn't a 757 aircraft.[14]

Another doubter is Major General Albert Stubblebine, retired Commanding General of the U.S. Army Intelligence and Security Command, who was responsible for the army's strategic intelligence sources worldwide. "I have had a lot of experience looking at photographs," Stubblebine says. "I don't know exactly what hit it [the Pentagon], but I do know from the photographs I have analyzed, it was not an airplane. For one thing, if you look at the hole that was made in the Pentagon, the nose penetrated far enough so that there should have been wing marks on the side [of the building]. One person counteracted my theory and said, 'Oh, you've got it all wrong, the airplane came across, one wing hit the ground and broke off.' Which is possible, but if I understand airplanes correctly, most of them have two wings. So there should have been a mark for the second one."[15] Stubblebine also believes the Twin Towers were brought down by a controlled demolition.

"How could a Boeing 757, with its engines extending beneath its wings, have struck the Pentagon so low without damaging the lawn and destroying the large cable spools on the ground in front of the damaged area?" asks 9/11 expert David Ray Griffin, a California professor and the author of eight books exploring the contradictions of the official 9/11 story. Griffin also cites the observation of Karen Kwiatkowski, then an air force lieutenant colonel employed at the Pentagon, who saw "no airplane metal or cargo debris."[16]

Here's what troubled me: the law was immediately and completely broken there. They had military personnel out on the lawn cleaning everything up, before an investigator ever arrived. Those hasty cleanups now seem to be Standard Operating Procedure when it comes to assassinations and events like 9/11, don't they. Whenever there's a plane crash, things are strewn about. So where are the seats, the luggage? The wings, vertical stabilizers, and engines were never fully recovered. A number of parts to a 757 are pretty much indestructible, but not a single piece has ever been positively identified as originating with Flight 77. The Department of Justice has admitted to having 85 videos, but they've refused a Freedom of Information Act request to release them.

Another expert we communicated with is Colonel George Nelson, who during 30 years of commissioned service in the air force served as an aircraft accident investigation board member. Colonel Nelson says: "With all the evidence readily available at the Pentagon crash site, any unbiased rational investigator could only conclude that a Boeing 757 did not fly into the Pentagon as alleged. . . . In all my years of direct and indirect participation, I never witnessed nor even heard of an aircraft loss, where the wreckage was accessible, that prevented investigators from finding enough hard evidence to positively identify the make, model, and specific registration number of the aircraft—and in most cases the precise cause of the accident."[17]

Then there's the background on the pilot. His name was Charles "Chic" Burlingame, and he was not only well-schooled in martial arts, but a retired Top Gun pilot, the best of the best. All his friends said there's no way he'd give up his plane, it wasn't in the man's makeup. Unless the hijackers got to him and killed him—but with box cutters? Supposedly, a hijacker named Hanjour got control of the plane. Except, later, his flight instructor described Hanjour as barely being able to handle a single-engine Cessna a month earlier. And Flight 77 is said to have made a complicated 330-degree turn, dropping 7,000 feet, executing a maneuver that experienced pilots say is nearly impossible.[18]

The section of the Pentagon that was struck happened to be the headquarters for naval operations and intelligence, as well as housing quite a few accountants and budget analysts. Important Pentagon financial information disappeared in the aftermath of the attack.[19] So it's quite a coincidence that, just the day before, Defense Secretary Rumsfeld had announced publicly: "According to some estimates, we cannot track $2.3 trillion in transactions."[20] That's right, not million, not even billion, that was trillion.

Flight 77 disappeared from the FAA radar screen at 8:56 AM, when it made an unauthorized turn to the south somewhere near the Kentucky–Ohio border. The only evidence that the plane was still flying and headed toward Washington were two phone calls that Ted Olson said he received from his wife Barbara onboard, not long before the Pentagon strike. Ted Olson was a longtime Republican operative who spearheaded the legal effort for Bush in Florida after the disputed 2000 election, and then went to work in the Justice Department as Solicitor General. His wife was the only person who's reported to have mentioned box cutters. According to Olson, she said that "all passengers and flight personnel, including the pilots, were herded to the back of the plane by armed hijackers." Yup, 60-some people (including a weightlifter pilot), being held off by a few short, slender guys holding knives and boxcutters.

At first, Olson said the calls were made from Barbara's cell phone. Except, high-altitude cell phone calls were pretty much impossible in 2001. Olson then changed his story to claim she'd used an onboard phone to make a collect call. Except, American Airlines didn't have such phones on the Boeing 757s. Here's what the FBI reported in 2006, at the trial of Zacarias Moussaoui (the so-called twentieth hijacker): Barbara Olson made only one call, an "unconnected call" that lasted "0 seconds."[21]

So what's going on? Captain Wittenberg has said that, if Flight 77 was actually off the radar screen for 36 minutes, then it was no longer airborne.[22] Did it land in some remote field, while something else—maybe the missile Charles Lewis heard about at LAX—hit the Pentagon's financial records area?

This probably sounds far-fetched, if not crazy, until you consider that elements of our military had an eerily similar plan ready to roll back in the early 1960s. It was called Operation Northwoods, first described in a book published in 2001, *Body of Secrets* by James Bamford. Operation Northwoods was approved by the Joint Chiefs of Staff for action against Castro's Cuba—"what may be the most corrupt plan ever created by the U.S. government," as Bamford put it. The Kennedy brothers seemed to be going soft on Castro, so the generals came up with a number of "terrorist" schemes to launch a war.

Bamford tells us: "Among the most elaborate schemes was to 'create an incident which will demonstrate convincingly that a Cuban aircraft has attacked and shot down a chartered civil airliner.' . . . An aircraft at Eglin AFB would be painted and numbered as an exact duplicate for a civil registered aircraft. . . . At a designated time the duplicate would be substituted for the actual civil aircraft and would be loaded with the selected passengers, all boarded under carefully prepared aliases. The actual registered aircraft would be converted to a drone [a remotely controlled unmanned aircraft]. Take off times of the drone aircraft and the actual aircraft will be scheduled to allow a rendezvous south of Florida.

"From the rendezvous point the passenger-carrying aircraft will descend to minimum altitude and go directly into an auxiliary field at Eglin AFB where arrangements will have been made to evacuate the passengers and return the aircraft to its original status. The drone aircraft meanwhile will continue to fly the filed flight plan. When over Cuba the drone will be transmitting on the internal distress frequency a 'May Day' message stating he is under attack by Cuban MiG aircraft. The transmission will be interrupted by destruction of the aircraft, which will be triggered by radio signal."[23] If you're interested, you can read the whole plan on the Web site of the National Security Archive.

Now let's examine the anomalies around the last plane, United Airlines Flight 93 that crashed in Shanksville, Pennsylvania, reportedly at 10:03 AM and 20 minutes away from Washington. The official story made me proud to be an American: The passengers overcame the hijackers and sacrificed their lives, so that others might be spared. Back to Charles Lewis again at LAX that morning: "They said fighter jets had been scrambled from two different military bases, and that they had shot down the plane over Pennsylvania. And that was way before we got the hero story."[24]

The first news reports expressed surprise at how little debris was visible at the crash site. The Pennsylvania state Web site even said it was hard to believe that a 757 plunged into the ground with such force that it literally disintegrated and created a still-smoldering crater in the ground. Then, five days later, CNN News reported "apparently another debris site" that had been cordoned off six to eight miles away. This, the commentator said, "raises a number of questions, why . . . could it have blown that far away?"[25]

The FBI immediately took over the investigation, and for a long time wouldn't honor family members' requests, asking if they could listen to the cockpit voice recorder. This was finally allowed on April 18, 2002, provided they'd agree not to reveal anything about what they heard. And, for some reason, the last three minutes weren't on there. Barry Lichty, the mayor of the nearby town of Indian Lake, says he heard what sounded like a missile fire that morning. The military did admit, some years later, that it was tracking Flight 93 and a Colonel Robert Marr recalled hearing that "we will take lives in the air to preserve lives on the ground." He then ordered the air controllers to have fighter jets intercept the plane. But supposedly, the commercial flight crashed before that could happen. "Of course we never fired upon the plane," said Dick Cheney, "we just witnessed an act of heroism."[26]

The official story is that, for the first time in history, the black boxes were not recovered. Not from any of the four planes. For the TV pilot I did about 9/11 on truTV, we spoke to a guy who knew about the existence of three black boxes. He physically saw one, and his partner saw two more. He says they were taken away in a black government van. Another thing I find very interesting: Also for the first time in history, no attempt was made to reconstruct the planes with whatever parts they could find. They even did this with TWA Flight 800 that went down in 1996 in the Atlantic, and for that they had to dive down 1,200 feet.

After Pearl Harbor, General Martin Short and some admirals were fired because of their alleged negligence. After 9/11, not a single employee at the FAA or NORAD got punished. In fact, all the major military men involved received promotions. They included General Richard Myers, who was named Chairman of the Joint Chiefs on October 1.

The way I see it, with all the advance warnings about a terrorist attack, a fair number of Bush's team should have gotten the axe. Except, right up to the president himself, it was all about denial. Here was Bush in 2004: "Had I had any inkling whatsoever that the people were going to fly airplanes into buildings, we would have moved heaven and earth to save the country." Here was Rumsfeld, testifying before the 9/11 Commission: "I knew of no intelligence during the six-plus months leading up to September 11 to indicate terrorists would hijack commercial airlines, use them as missiles to fly into the Pentagon or the World Trade Center towers." And here was Condoleezza Rice: "This kind of analysis about the use of airplanes as weapons actually was never briefed to us."[27]

Oh really? What about the intelligence briefing Bush received on August 6, 2001, that was headed "Bin Laden Determined to Strike in U.S." and even mentioned possible hijackings.[28] Or Condi Rice being warned about al-Qaeda's plotting by then–CIA Director George Tenet on July 10, 2001, but brushing him off.[29] The 9/11 Commission was aware of this, but decided to leave it out of their report. The CIA's counterintelligence chief, J. Cofer Black, later "felt there were things the commission wanted to know about and things they didn't want to know about."[30] Rice responded: "What I am quite certain of is that I would remember if I was told, as this account apparently says, that there was about to be an attack in the United States, and the idea that I would somehow have ignored that I find incomprehensible."[31] Seems she stammered over her words a little.

These were far from the only warnings. Israel sent two senior agents of the Mossad to Washington in August 2001 to "alert the CIA and FBI to the existence of a cell of as many as 200 terrorists said to be preparing a big operation."[32] Eight months before the attacks, French intelligence warned the U.S. in nine different reports about "Airplane Hijacking Plans by Radical Islamists" connected to bin Laden and the Taliban.[33] FBI agents working out of the Minneapolis and Phoenix offices tried to alert their superiors. Dr. Parke Godfrey, an associate professor of computer science at Toronto's York University, said under oath in a New York courtroom that a longtime associate of his, Susan Lindauer, warned him several times and as late as August 2001 "that we expected a major attack on the southern part of Manhattan, and that the attack would encompass the World Trade Center," an attack "that would involve airplanes and possibly a nuclear weapon." Lindauer, who says she was a CIA asset, claimed to have made an attempt to inform John Ashcroft at the Justice Department, who referred her to the Office of Counter-Terrorism.[34]

Which brings us to the whole question of the 19 alleged hijackers. Did you ever wonder how our government came up with their identities so fast? Even before the last plane crashed, the FBI was telling counter-terrorism official Richard Clarke they had a list of the names.[35] It took two years to get indictments on the Lockerbie bombing, but not this time! Except, on September 16, one of the supposed hijackers walked into the consulate in Saudi Arabia—he was actually a pilot for Saudi Airlines. On September 22, one of the Flight 11 hijackers announced he was alive and well. Two more Saudi pilots did the same thing the next day. On September 27, CBS found hijacker Hamzi (Flight 77) working for an oil refinery in

Saudi Arabia. No matter. All these guys are still on the list today as being among the perpetrators.[36]

What evidence do we have then? Two days after the attacks, our government said it was clear-cut that Osama bin Laden was the man behind it all, and that the Taliban in Afghanistan would soon be handing over its proof. Ten more days went by, at which time Colin Powell said he'd soon show us the documentation. Meantime, in three separate statements, bin Laden denied any involvement. On December 13, the State Department released a video purporting to show him describing the attacks, but before long a lot of people were questioning whether it was authentic. On the day after Christmas, a Taliban official said he'd attended Osama's funeral! But on the 27th of December came a bin Laden video praising al-Qaeda's successful hit on us. Another couple years went by before a third tape surfaced—October 29, 2004, a few days before the presidential election (think "heightened terror alert!")—with a blatant taking of full responsibility. However, as of June 6, 2006, the FBI said it had "no hard evidence connecting bin Laden to 9/11." He's been charged with several crimes related to terrorist attacks, but not with 9/11.[37] I find that very odd. Not one shred of evidence produced in a courtroom that leads to the conclusion bin Laden spearheaded these attacks. The justice system that works for anything else is suddenly suspended over terrorism.

We're led to believe that a hijacker's passport flew out of his pocket when his plane hit the tower, made it safely through 9,000 gallons of jet fuel, and landed to be found on a sidewalk a thousand feet below. Another hijacker's ID supposedly turned up in the Pentagon wreckage, one of a few pieces that survived. Meantime, awaiting discovery in rental cars left behind at Boston Logan and Washington Dulles airports, was enough evidence to convict had they lived: an Arabic flight manual, a check made out to a Phoenix flight school, maps of Washington and New York, and more.[38] Does this remind anyone else of Oswald leaving behind a paper trail to his purchase of the rifle, or James Earl Ray depositing his bundle full of incriminating evidence near the scene of the crime? Alleged hijacker Mohamed Atta was first said to have left a rented Mitsubishi at Boston Logan, but that story was later changed into a blue or silver Nissan left in Portland, Maine. Didn't seem to matter which vehicle, because both were said to be filled with box cutters and other incriminating items.

These guys were all made out to be fanatic, Koran-toting Muslims ready to die for Allah in a Holy War against America. Except, in their final days, according to people who knew them, they were drinking, visiting strip clubs, soliciting prostitutes, and watching porno on the tube. Atta's girl-friend said he liked to snort cocaine. Atta seemed to be all over the place before 9/11: doing coke in Hollywood, Florida; living in Venice, Florida, near the NSA; and in Hamburg, Germany.[39]

Who some of the hijackers were really working for, at least once upon a time, first came out in media tidbits. From *Newsweek* (September 15, 2001): "U.S. military sources have given the FBI information that suggests five of the alleged hijackers of the planes that were used in the terror attacks received training at secure U.S. military installations in the 1990s." Same day, *New York Times*: "The Defense Department said Mr. Atta had gone to the International Officers School at Maxwell Air Force Base in Alabama; Mr. al-Omari to the Aerospace Medical School at Brooks Air Force Base in Texas; and Mr. al-Ghamdi to the Defense Language Institute at the Presidio in Monterey, Calif."

Well, our military's School of the Americas once helped train the Central American death squads, so our providing lethal skills to terrorists—excuse me, I mean "freedom fighters"—shouldn't come as a huge surprise. But it gets stranger still. Two of the alleged hijackers rented an apartment from and actually lived with FBI informants. The CIA had operational interest in two of them, Nawaz al-Hazmi and Khalid al-Mihdhar. FBI agents believed "that the agency was protecting Midhar and Hazmi because it hoped to recruit them," or alternatively that "the CIA was running a joint venture with Saudi intelligence" using them.[40]

The CIA goes way back with these guys. They were recruited into the secret war against the Soviets in Afghanistan, back in the late 1980s. In fact, the term al-Qaeda is said to have been invented by the CIA to designate a database of recruits into the Mujahideen. Michael Springman was head of the visa section at our embassy in Jeddah from 1987 to 1989, and he remembers granting visas to "terrorists" who'd been recruited by CIA and sent for training to America. Some of them fought in Bosnia during the '92 to '95 period. Springman can be seen in the documentary *Zero* saying that many of the hijackers he read about in the *L.A. Times* were once on his visa list in Jeddah. He called the FBI a number of times, who Springman says responded: "We'll get back to you. Six years later I'm still waiting."[41]

Osama bin Laden himself started out helping the CIA in Afghanistan. In 2009, a former FBI translator named Sibel Edmonds dropped a bombshell.[42] The U.S., she said, had kept up "intimate relations" with bin Laden "all the way until that day of September 11"—using him sometimes for ops in central Asia, including Xinjiang, China. The process Edmonds outlined involved the use of Turkey (with assistance of "actors from Pakistan, and Afghanistan and Saudi Arabia") as proxies, with those folks in turn employing bin Laden and the Taliban. The goals? Control of the huge energy supplies in Central Asia, for one. Maybe the real reason we invaded Afghanistan? Sibel Edmonds testified for three and a half hours to the 9/11 Commission, but it ended up being classified.[43]

Bin Laden, like 15 of the 19 alleged hijackers, came from Saudi Arabia. Back in October 2003, an article in *Vanity Fair* had questioned the FBI's letting six planes of Middle Eastern nationals—most of them members of the Saudi royal family—fly out of the U.S. soon after 9/11. The 9/11 Commission concluded that, after the Saudi government requested this out of fear for their safety, the FBI had "conducted a satisfactory screening of Saudi nationals who left the United States." But one of those planes stopped four times at different locations around the U.S. on September 19, picking up half-siblings and other bin Laden relatives who supposedly had no connection to him. Finally, in 2007, a heavily censored FBI report said: "The plane was chartered either by the Saudi Arabian Royal Family or Osama bin Laden."[44] Osama? You mean to tell me the ringleader of the 9/11 attacks might have been chartering a plane on our soil eight days after this happened?

It just gets curiouser and curiouser, in the words of Lewis Carroll from *Alice in Wonderland*. FBI Director Robert Mueller testified about how the terrorists managed to finance themselves, saying that they'd had all their money wired in small amounts to avoid being detected. Except, it came out that General Mahmoud Ahmad, the head of Pakistan's ISI intelligence service, had ordered one of his agents to wire transfer $100,000 to Mohamed Atta. The ISI and the CIA's relationship dates back to the 1980s when the

Mujahideen got set up. Ahmad, as it happened, had come to Washington a week before the attacks for a meeting with CIA chief George Tenet and some people from Bush's National Security Council.[45,46] When the story came out about the wire transfer to Atta, Ahmad abruptly retired from the ISI.

The families of many 9/11 victims have gone to court seeking evidence of the Saudi royal family's bankrolling of al-Qaeda. Senator Bob Graham wrote a book that discussed the 28-page section about Saudi Arabia that the CIA, FBI, and NSA had blacked out of his committee's report. In the book, Graham noted ties between the hijackers and the Saudis and flatly stated that "the White House was directing the cover-up" to protect "America's relationship with the Kingdom of Saudi Arabia."[47]

Ever heard of an army project called Able Danger? It was established in 1999 as part of the Defense Department's Special Operations Command (SOCOM). According to Colonel Anthony Shaffer, a leading member of the team with the Defense Intelligence Agency (DIA): "Able Danger was an offensive counter-terrorism project which was designed to take and kill—the military term is reduce—senior al-Qaeda leadership."[48] It wasn't long before the Able Danger squad uncovered al-Qaeda cells in the New York City area, one of whose members was Mohamed Atta. At least six witnesses later recalled seeing Atta's picture on a chart they'd drawn up back in January 2000. Turns out three more of the alleged hijackers had been ID'ed by Able Danger before 9/11, as well.[49]

Colonel Shaffer worked closely with navy captain Scott Phillpott, and says he attempted to set up a meeting between Phillpott's superior officer and FBI counterterrorism agents in D.C., so they could work together on following these cells. But three times the SOCOM lawyers kept a meeting from happening. Soon after that, Shaffer got transferred to a DIA project in Latin America.[50]

Then, after 9/11, he and Phillpott tried to bring the story forward to Congress and the 9/11 Commission. In June 2005, a reporter for a small-town Pennsylvania paper wrote a piece that opened with: "Two years before the Sept. 11, 2001, attacks, US intelligence officials linked Mohamed Atta to al-Qaida, and discovered he and two others were in Brooklyn." You might think the national media would have jumped all over that, but they didn't. Eventually, the *New York Times* did a few stories. But when the 9/11 Commission came up with reasons for leaving Able

Danger out of its report, the media nodded off again. Chairman Thomas Kean went so far as to say that "the recollections of the intelligence officers cannot be verified by any document." Hence, it didn't happen. And the Pentagon wouldn't let Shaffer or anyone else testify before the Senate Judiciary Committee.[51]

We talked to Shaffer while putting together this chapter. In his opinion, both the Clinton and Bush administrations were covering up their incompetence. "The Department of Defense does not want to get blamed for making bad decisions, which resulted in information not being passed to the FBI, and therefore being a material factor in why 9/11 happened," he told us. "That's why you had DOD coming after me because I blew the whistle. DOD has admitted there are 10,000-plus Able Danger documents, but they won't release a single one. To me that's bizarre, because most of the targeting information was done on the open Internet and completely unclassified. It does cause you to wonder."

9/11 expert David Ray Griffin concluded that the commission and the Pentagon were "covering up dangerous information—information that suggested Atta was being protected. When we combine this observation with other things we have learned about the alleged hijackers—including the money reportedly sent to Atta by the CIA-created [Pakistani] ISI— the Able Danger evidence provides additional reason to suspect that the 'hijackers' were really paid assets."[52]

A think tank called The Project for the New American Century, composed mainly of right-wing ideologues, wrote a report pre-9/11 titled *Rebuilding America's Defenses*. The document contains this line: "The process of transformation, even if it brings revolutionary change, is likely to be a long one, absent some catastrophic and catalyzing event—like a new Pearl Harbor."

We all know the results of 9/11: two unending wars, in Afghanistan and Iraq. Remember the Gulf of Tonkin incident in 1964? We were told that two American ships were attacked by the North Vietnamese. Now we know that the incident was manufactured by the Pentagon in order to gain support for escalating the Vietnam War. If the United States government was prepared to stage such a gargantuan event in leading our nation to war then, why would they refrain from doing so again today? Might we look at this as a trend, going into these wars under false pretenses?

Richard A. Clarke, national coordinator for security and counterterrorism at the time, wrote in 2009 that Iraq was "a move that many senior Bush officials had wanted to make before 9/11. . . . While the Pentagon was still burning, Secretary of Defense Don Rumsfeld was in the White House suggesting an attack against Baghdad. . . . Despite being repeatedly told that Iraq was not involved in 9/11, some, like Cheney could not abandon the idea."[53]

The 9/11 Commission Report states that "the Bush Administration had repeatedly tied the Iraq War to September 11th. . . . The panel finds no al-Qaeda-Iraq tie." Bush then did some backpedaling, saying: "This administration never said that the 9/11 attacks were orchestrated between Saddam [Hussein] and al-Qaeda. We did say there were numerous contacts. . . ." Meetings, it turned out, between bin Laden and Iraqi Intelligence that took place in Sudan back in the mid-1990s! But one prisoner, Ibn al-Sheikh al-Libi, was tortured in 2002 until he'd agree to say that al-Qaeda was linked to Saddam (he died suddenly after being transferred from Egypt to another prison in Libya).

The 9/11 Commission was a whitewash from the front, after Bush and Cheney had stonewalled an investigation for more than a year. The fellow named as the first commission chairman was none other than Henry Kissinger, who said no thank you on December 13, 2002, when told that he'd have to disclose his list of private business clients (Kissinger was also busy advising the Bush Administration on how best to go into Iraq). The commission's executive director ended up being Philip Zelikow, who got a jump on the game by putting together a detailed outline of the final report just as they were starting to investigate! The outline was kept secret from others on the 80 member staff.[54] Zelikow decided everything. After all, back in 1998 he'd co-written an essay on "catastrophic terrorism," which he foresaw "would be a watershed event in American history. . . . Like Pearl Harbor, this event would divide our past and future into a before and after. The United States might respond with draconian measures, scaling back civil liberties, allowing wider surveillance of citizens, detention of suspects, and use of deadly force."[55] Sound familiar?

Zelikow had also been principal author of a paper aimed at justifying a preemptive strike on Iraq. And he tried, without success, to insert a sentence into the report suggesting repeated communication between al-Qaeda and Iraq.[56] Zelikow happened to leave off his resumé the fact that, at Condi Rice's request, he'd been part of the Bush transition team. But then, he'd coauthored a book with Rice, too. Zelikow engaged in "surreptitious" communications with Karl Rove in the course of the investigation.[57] With Zelikow running the show, "there was no hope that the commission would carry out an impartial investigation."[58] It recently came out that there were "minders" from Bush's team sitting there with the witnesses, answering questions for them and positioning themselves physically in an intimidating manner.[59]

The 9/11 Commission politely informs us that "conspiracy theories play a peculiar role in American discourse. Whenever there is a particularly surprising, traumatic, and influential moment in our history, people are left with unsettling questions." As an example, they go on to cite "conspiracy theorists [who] propagate outrageous notions that Kennedy was assassinated by the CIA or some shadowy secret society of the rich and powerful."

Outrageous notions? I find it outrageous that yet another government-appointed commission allows itself to become part of the cover-up. Especially when they knew damned well that's what they were doing. "The 10-member commission, in a secret meeting at the end of its tenure in summer 2004, debated referring the matter to the Justice Department for criminal investigation, according to several commission sources. Staff members and some commissioners thought that e-mails and other evidence provided enough probable cause to believe that military and aviation officials violated the law by making false statements to Congress and to the commission."[60]

The 9/11 Commission's Chairman Thomas Kean, and Vice Chair Lee Hamilton, have since come out and said: " . . . the recent revelations that the C.I.A. destroyed videotape interrogations of Qaeda operatives leads us to conclude that the agency failed to respond to our lawful requests for information about the 9/11 plot. Those who knew about those videotapes—and did not tell us about them—obstructed our investigation."[61] Now we know from the new book by senior counsel John Farmer that almost every person involved in the official version of 9/11 lied about the events of that day.

Our country has changed since 9/11. We've been frightened into half the people saying torture's okay now, if it prevents terrorism. Americans are marching in the streets to try to stop someone who's sick from going to the doctor, but where is the outcry now that it's been proven that the whole Iraq War was trumped up? Maybe something stopped in us all on 9/11, and we're stuck back there collectively and can't truly move forward until we have a new, independent investigation to get to the bottom of what really happened.

The 9/11 Truth Movement has a growing number of groups—Political Leaders, Architects and Engineers, Firefighters, Lawyers, Medical Professionals, Pilots, Religious Leaders, Scholars, Scientists, Journalists and Other Media, and Veterans. Check them out online, get involved as I have. But if you challenge the status quo, be prepared for retaliation. That's what seems to have happened to Charles Lewis, the man with whom we began this chapter's revelations. After he noticed another lapse at LAX as a Quality Control Manager—this time observing a Saudi Airlines 747 disembark a host of passengers into the cargo area—his security clearance got revoked. He's currently unemployed.

WHAT SHOULD WE DO NOW?

When enough people came to question the Warren Commission, the door was opened for Congress to do a further investigation and come to a different conclusion about the Kennedy assassination. That should be precedent enough, now that it's become clear the 9/11 Commission was a whitewash, for Americans to call for a new and honest investigation into the greatest attack ever perpetrated on our soil. Was our own government asleep at the switch, or might it even have played a role in what happened? It's time to demand an answer, as independent truth-seeking groups from many walks of life are already calling for.

CHAPTER THIRTEEN

THE WALL STREET CONSPIRACY

THE INCIDENT: America's worst economic crisis since the Great Depression occurred in the fall of 2008, brought on originally by the collapse of a housing bubble that damaged financial institutions and caused the stock market to plummet.

THE OFFICIAL WORD: Huge corporations like AIG and Goldman Sachs were considered "too big to fail," and received multibillion-dollar bailouts from the federal government in order to prevent economic collapse.

MYTAKE: The government has conspired to keep the "fat cats" in business, while the American taxpayers are left holding the bag. CEOs that should be going to jail for scams beyond belief are instead reaping the biggest bonuses ever. Corporations basically run the government, and the same players that made the mess still have a stranglehold on our future.

"Too much cannot be said against the men of wealth who sacrifice everything to getting wealth. There is not in the world a more ignoble character than the mere money-getting American, insensible to every duty, regardless of every principle, bent only on amassing a fortune, and putting his fortune only to the basest uses."

—Theodore Roosevelt, 1895[1]

If you're surprised to find what's been happening to our economy in a book on American conspiracies, you shouldn't be. This may be the grand-daddy of all plots, one that's been going on for almost a century (although

I'm not one who blames all our national woes on the Trilateral-Bilderberg-Bohemian-Grove crowd). Before diving into what I've been learning about the big financial institutions and their cronies in government and at the Federal Reserve, let me suggest you quickly review the earlier chapter about the Wall Street plot to overthrow FDR and the insights of Professor Carroll Quigley.

The economy, and how it got into its current mess, is a complicated, tangled tale, and I certainly don't claim to be an expert about it. But you can learn a great deal from some thoughtful reading. Let's face it, capitalism isn't always fair. So if you're looking to bring fairness to life, you have to take steps more toward socialism. Which then causes a conflict of interest, because socialism means you're going to be even more controlled in your decision-making by the Establishment. Then again, is that what's required to keep an equal balance? Do you have to go that way to ensure that the middle class survives? What I really see leaving is the American Dream. The destruction of the middle class means you're no longer going to have that dream, which is that a young person can achieve anything if you put your mind to it because the opportunities are there. Now are they still? Yes. But are they more difficult? Yes. I see many more obstacles in the way of the American Dream today, and a great deal of it is caused by greed. It's understood that a certain amount of wealthy people are going to control the majority of the money, but when it's moving so drastically that you've got 5 percent of the people having 90 percent of the money, that can't be healthy.

Deregulated "free market" capitalism sure hasn't benefited the American people. We've had a revolving door between Wall Street and Washington, which led to a Wild West mentality on "the Street." For awhile the whole casino seemed to be doing just fine, but really the financial sector was completely out of control—"running on a perverse set of incentives that made it incredibly profitable to essentially throw caution to the wind and take on incomprehensible amounts of risk."[2] Don't let them fool you into thinking it was reckless borrowers and subprime loans that built the house of cards. In this chapter, I'm going to particularly zero in on the greed and excesses of two companies—banking giant Goldman Sachs and insurance behemoth American International Group, better known as AIG. They're atop the pyramid of the "too big to let fail" crowd, and their execs are still getting richer while the home foreclosures increase and the unemployment numbers keep rising.

Until it received the largest government subsidy that any corporation ever has (about $170 billion in bailouts, the tab being picked up by us the taxpayers), AIG was the biggest private insurance company in the world. It had more than 100,000 employees globally and $1 trillion in assets.[3] Their history is worth looking into. AIG started out selling insurance to the Chinese in 1919, based in Shanghai where it was then called American Asiatic Underwriters. The company was founded by Cornelius Vander Starr, the uncle of Ken Starr, future special prosecutor of Bill Clinton. Starr moved his headquarters to New York twenty years later, but kept his Asian branch going. Soon after World War II began, General "Wild Bill" Donovan of the OSS started using his contacts to create a deep-cover intel network over there. Files were finally declassified in 2000, showing how the OSS set up an ultra-secret insurance unit through Starr, which perused records on the Japanese to find blueprints of possible targets. As victory against the Nazis approached, U.S. intelligence began examining "ways the Nazis would try to use insurance to hide and launder their assets so they could be used to rebuild the war machine. . . . Starr sent insurance agents into Asia and Europe even before the bombs stopped falling and built what eventually became AIG, which today has its world headquarters in the same downtown New York building where the tiny OSS unit toiled in the deepest secrecy."[4]

After the CIA was founded in 1947, AIG was tied into figures like Paul Helliwell, who ran air transport companies with connections to the drug trade. Helliwell was legal counsel for Starr's insurance interests.[5] Drugs come up again forty years later, when in 1987, AIG made a deal with Goldman Sachs and the Arkansas Development Financial Authority (ADFA) to found an offshore reinsurer in Barbados called Coral Re. The ADFA allegedly helped launder drug money for Barry Seal, the Contras, and the Medellin cartel out of Mena, Arkansas.[6] In 2000, AIG's annual report announced its fleet of 494 full-sized jets was "the world's most modern fleet of aircraft," including leasing still more planes "to a number of established customers" in Latin America.[7] It helps to have friends in high places with deep pockets.

"Hank" Greenberg had been appointed as director of AIG's North American operations in 1962. After Starr died six years later, Greenberg became chairman of AIG, C.V. Starr & Company, and today's Starr

International, which is an offshore company, incorporated in Panama with a Bermuda headquarters, and still the biggest shareholder in AIG.[8] Seems rather incestuous, but that's the way it is. AIG became the biggest foreign insurance company in Japan, and more than one third of its $40 billion in revenues in 1999 "came from the Far East Theatre Starr helped carpet bomb and liberate."[9] Greenberg let AIG be used by the CIA for placing many of its Asian officers, and continued to keep tabs for "the company" on places like China, Japan, Korea, Singapore, Hong Kong, and Taiwan. The company's massive database in San Francisco was also made available to the CIA. In 1995, Greenberg was one of the candidates to become the next CIA director.[10]

It's a small, tight-knit world, and they don't call AIG's favorite trading partner "Government Sachs" for nothing. Treasury secretaries under the two previous presidents—Robert Rubin with Clinton and Hank Paulson with Bush-II—went from running Goldman Sachs into the most powerful financial position in the administrations. That's just for openers. The company pretty much had a lock on high-level jobs at the treasury. Neel Kashkari—pronounced Cash-Carry—started out as a low-level Goldman investment banker, and now runs the bailout under the government Office of Financial Stability. Are we surprised that AIG and Goldman became the biggest beneficiaries in the bailout?

Goldman Sachs's history has some intrigue in it, too. This company was founded back in 1869 by Marcus Goldman, a German immigrant who slowly built it up with his son-in-law, Samuel Sachs. They made a killing off the 1929 stock market crash, and applied that knowledge later to the dot-com and housing booms. The formula of the most influential investment bank on the planet has been described like this: "Goldman positions itself in the middle of a speculative bubble, selling investments they know are crap. Then they hoover up vast sums from the middle and lower floors of society with the aid of a crippled and corrupt state that allows it to rewrite the rules in exchange for the relative pennies the bank throws at political patronage. Finally, when it all goes bust, leaving millions of ordinary citizens broke and starving, they begin the entire process over again, riding in to rescue us all by lending us back our own money at interest, selling themselves as men above greed, just a bunch of really smart guys keeping the wheels greased."[11]

To get a grasp on what's lately been going on, we also need to take a look at our central bank, otherwise known as the Federal Reserve. The Fed controls our monetary policy. By changing the supply of dollars in circulation, they have influence over interest rates, mortgage payments, whether the financial markets boom or collapse, and basically whether our economy expands or stumbles. But the Fed is only partly an institution of government. The stockholders in a dozen different Federal Reserve banks in different regions of the country are the big private banks.

The Federal Reserve was created by Congress in 1913, after a financial panic that led to a secret meeting at banker J.P. Morgan's private resort, off the coast of Georgia at a place called Jekyll Island. (I'm not sure if Hyde was present). "Those who attended represented the great financial institutions of Wall Street, and, indirectly, Europe as well. The reason for secrecy was simple. Had it been known that rival factions of the banking community had joined together, the public would have been alerted to the possibility that the bankers were plotting an agreement in restraint of trade—which, of course, is exactly what they were doing. What emerged was a cartel agreement with five objectives: stop the growing competition from the nation's newer banks; obtain a franchise to create money out of nothing for the purpose of lending; get control of the reserves of all banks so that the more reckless ones would not be exposed to currency drains and bank runs; get the taxpayer to pick up the cartel's inevitable losses; and convince Congress that the purpose was to protect the public. It was realized that the bankers would have to become partners with the politicians and that the structure of the cartel would have to be a central bank."[12]

These are some of the same players who wanted to take down FDR during the Great Depression. During his last year in office, JFK made an attempt to strip the Federal Reserve of its power to loan money to the government at interest. Executive Order No. 11110 gave the treasury back the power to issue currency, and not have to go through the Federal Reserve. Kennedy put nearly $4.3 billion into circulation of U.S. notes backed by silver certificates, whereas the Federal Reserve's notes aren't backed by anything. The handwriting was on the wall: They could be soon out of business. But guess what? After JFK was assassinated only five months later, there weren't any more silver certificates issued. The Executive Order has never been repealed, but not a single president since has chosen to utilize it.[13]

Dare I say it—Will my life be at risk?—I'd like to see us back on some type of standard where our money truly has value. My big problem with the Federal Reserve is, why does the government allow this monopoly that's in bed with the banking industry to make basically all of our country's financial decisions? Those people aren't elected. We form these other entities that are permitted to make policy, when in reality they're unconstitutional. The public has to be involved in the process, our Constitution says. Here, whoever controls the money has the power. So the Federal Reserve is really more powerful than the government—and we don't elect them.

Once Reagan and the free-market ideologues came to power in 1980, FDR's and JFK's legacies were like a distant memory. Alan Greenspan, named as Fed chairman by Reagan, backed up my previous point, writing: "The Federal Reserve is an independent agency, and that means basically that there is no other agency of government which can overrule actions that we take."[14] Does that sound like democracy or something else?

The new era of deregulation resulted in a boom time for the rich getting richer. Reagan opened wide the door for companies to gamble with taxpayers' money—or loot it outright, as in the savings-and-loan scandal and bailout. The New Deal restrictions on mortgage lending went by the boards, which eventually led to the foreclosure crisis.[15] In 1999, the Glass-Steagall Act was repealed by a "bipartisan" Congress during Clinton's last year, and a real free-for-all began. You might not know how important this legislation was. It was passed in 1933 to keep separate the low-risk commercial banks where we put our deposits, and the brokerage banks that engage in high-risk speculative investments. This worked just fine for more than 50 years. During the Reagan years, the lobbyists for the finance, insurance, and real estate outfits started pushing to dump the law. Rubin and Greenspan got behind them. When this law got wiped off the books, the rules of the game changed totally. Mergers and commercial/investment partnerships skyrocketed. Now commercial banks like Citigroup could start taking multiple home mortgage loans and turning them into securities to trade on Wall Street. They could all gamble like crazy with billions raised from predatory lending practices, and with very little regulation.[16]

How insane was it to destroy one of the main protection devices created out of the pain of the Great Depression, and let Wall Street gamble with what had been Main Street's money? But Congress wasn't done yet. In 2000, after getting some heat from a regulator named Brooksley Born about the need to regulate commodities trading, legislation was slipped into an 11,000-page spending bill to exempt derivatives from any oversight, on the very last day of the session. Wonder how many Congresspeople read that one? Probably about as many as read the Patriot Act, I suspect.

Enter George W. Bush with a rousing mandate of "Free-dom! Free-dom!," as Richie Havens once sang at Woodstock. You'd think something might have been learned from the scandals that sank Enron and WorldCom soon after Bush took office. Instead, "this administration made decisions that allowed the free market to operate as a barroom brawl."[17] Bank regulators took a chainsaw to thousands of pages of troublesome things that Wall Street objected to. States that tried to do something about predatory lending were blocked by the federal comptroller of the currency. Back in 2003, the Office of Federal Housing Enterprise Oversight warned that Fannie Mae and Freddie Mac—the icons that held trillions in mortgages—were in deep doo-doo. But the White House set out to deep-six Armando Falcon's report and replaced him with a Bush buddy from their prep school days together. To W, home ownership was at an all-time peak and that was what America was all about, forgetting that thousands of those people couldn't really afford the loan payments. When the house of cards collapsed, W commented that "Wall Street got drunk." I guess it takes one to know one.[18]

The Securities and Exchange Commission was another legacy of the New Deal, a watchdog agency created after Wall Street had pushed our economy over the cliff. Bush sliced its budget, and his first SEC chairman promised a "kinder, gentler agency." It sure was, when it came to looking the other way. They did six investigations into Bernie Madoff, and knew back in 2005 that he was running a Ponzi scheme—taking bucks from new victims and using it to reimburse some of the old ones. Madoff said in a jailhouse interview that nobody was more surprised than he was, when he didn't get busted long ago. But, like Bernie once said, "In today's regulatory environment, it's virtually impossible to violate rules . . . and this is something the public really doesn't know." So he was able to scam folks out of at least $50 billion. Once he couldn't come up with any more "investors" and people started asking for their money back, they found out that Bernie had none left. It had all gone toward financing his yachts and a number of mansions. Eventually, SEC Chairman Christopher Cox admitted they'd failed to check out "multiple credible and specific allegations regarding Mr. Madoff's financial wrong-doing." In fact, the agency had been missing numerous "red flags" since at least 1992.[19] It took one in-house expert all of 20 minutes to figure out that Madoff's claims were bogus—but somehow, that analysis didn't make it to the SEC's investigative team.[20]

After Bush's second SEC chairman wanted to regulate high rollers playing fast-and-loose with their hedge funds, he got dumped fast. There was even a hotline for Wall Street companies to ring up SEC brass to "stop an investigation or slow it down."[21] Then again, "For many SEC attorneys, especially those atop the enforcement division, their time at the agency is a stop on their way to seven-figure jobs representing Wall Street elite."[22]

Through most of the eight Bush years, insurance giant AIG was having a grand old party at the bottomless money pit. Eliot Spitzer, as attorney General of New York, had begun investigating AIG, especially its shady affiliates like the Coral Re outfit in Barbados. CEO Greenberg was forced to resign during an accounting scandal in 2005. It looked like the jig might be up. But it wasn't too long after that when Spitzer, by then governor of New York, was forced to resign when his involvement with a prostitution ring suddenly became public.[23] And now that our own government holds 80 percent of AIG's stock as part of the $85 billion "bridge loan" bailout, don't bet on much scrutiny from outsiders anymore. The day after that deal was made, AIG's top execs took a nose-thumbing retreat at a luxury spa, costing $443,000 of what was now taxpayer money.[24]

Before he resigned, Greenberg had appointed a guy named Joseph Cassano to run AIG's Financial Products Unit (FPU) and given him all the rein he wanted. Cassano had gotten his start at Drexel Burnham Lambert under "junk bond king" Michael Milliken, who ended up going to prison. A number of Drexel's employees, Cassano included, just moved over to the FPU, where they started dealing in securities called "credit default swaps." Same scam, same players, simply a different name for leveraging worthless paper to sell to clueless investors. These swaps, like collateralized-debt obli-gations or CDOs, are so complicated that even a lot of CEOs can't make heads or tails of them. Cassano established dozens of companies, many offshore, to keep all the transactions off AIG's books and out of sight of regulators here and at the "London casino." Nobody inside the company apparently noticed things on the accounting books like "Lichtenstein Subsidiary Profit, $10 billion."[25] The government's Office of Thrift Supervision was supposed to be keeping an eye on the FPU, but it thought the swaps were "fairly benign products"—because that's what AIG told them. Meantime, the FPU was transforming these into the world's biggest bet on the housing boom, and until the bottom fell out of the sub-prime mortgage scam, they made a ton of money doing it.[26]

Hank Paulson was still Goldman's CEO in 2004, when he went to the SEC and petitioned to have lending restrictions relaxed for the five leading investment banks.[27] Then Goldman went "berserk with lending lust. By the peak of the housing boom in 2006, Goldman was underwriting $76.5 billion worth of mortgage-backed securities—a third of which were subprime—much of it to institutional investors like pensions and insurance companies. And in those massive issues of real estate were vast swamps of crap."[28] Crap that permitted Goldman to pay each employee roughly $350,000 a year. Moving on to become treasury secretary, Paulson declared in 2007 that the American economy was the "strongest in decades."[29]

When our gas prices spiked to $4-and-up a gallon in the summer of 2008, resulting in all the outcry about needing to drill for more oil offshore, the reality was that Goldman Sachs—the biggest trader in the energy derivatives market—had led the way by issuing high analyst predictions for the price of oil (a Goldman guy in 2008 talked up $200-a-barrel) and buying up oil futures. They could move the markets by stimulating other investors to jump in, and then selling oil back to them at the higher price. "By 2008, a barrel of oil was traded 27 times, on average, before it was actually delivered and consumed." Once again, a Depression-era law had been lifted (thanks to Goldman) that previously kept commodities markets in check. "Between 2003 and 2008, the amount of speculative money in commodities grew from $13 billion to $317 billion, an increase of 2,300 percent."[30] There was no oil shortage, except when it was convenient for Goldman and its cronies.

There was only one rub to it all: Early in 2008, Cassano got fired after the huge losses of his arm of AIG became known. Black September wasn't far away. This crisis wasn't about the little guy. It was a bailout of these financial giants unprecedented in our history, because they were "too big to fail." "For the money spent on subsidizing the industry, the government could have bought out every single outstanding mortgage in the country. Plus, every student loan and everyone's health insurance. And on top of that, still have trillions of dollars left over."[31] That's what a former managing director at Goldman Sachs, Nomi Prins, is laying out in her muckraking book, titled *It Takes a Pillage*.

The behind-the-scenes story of the taxpayer-funded bailout is still emerging. I'd like to have been a fly on the wall when Hank Paulson called the "big nine" kleptocrats into his office at the treasury for an emergency chat in September 2008. Remember how Lehman Brothers, the heaviest competitor to Goldman Sachs, was allowed to go broke? Well, that's because Paulson's crew wouldn't let them become a bank holding company and thus qualify for federal bucks. That's exactly the deal Goldman got—remember, it's Paulson's former company—which was worth a quick $10 billion. Goldman had kept right on selling questionable mortgage derivatives to unsuspecting buyers, even while playing smart and divesting its own. This looks to me like a clear case of fraud that ought to land some people in prison.

I can't help but believe there was method to this madness, that it was all designed. I learned in Minnesota that it should not be government's place to pick winners and losers, but to make policy that all have to follow. The disturbing thing is how this was utterly manipulated by the government. Paulson also gave billions to Bank of America so it could pay an inflated price to rescue Merrill Lynch, whose CEO John Thain had once headed Goldman's mortgage desk and then was CEO of the New York Stock Exchange. While Merrill Lynch was going belly-up, Thain was busy buying an $87,000 area rug for his office and a $35,000 toilet bowl. Some might call him a four-flusher, since he'd lost about $15 billion in just three months at Merrill Lynch, and Bank of America then decided to fire Thain when he demanded a $30 million bonus.[32] Oh, by the way, Thain was a mentor of Timothy Geithner, who's now treasury secretary under Obama.

Then came the bailout of AIG. We were told that, if AIG collapsed, every large American financial institution and a lot of foreign ones would have gone under with them. Guess who sat in on the closed-door meeting where Paulson and Geithner—who then headed the New York Fed—made the decision to rescue them? Goldman's CEO, Lloyd Blankfein, who'd have been in major trouble if they didn't. That week, Paulson's calendars show he spoke to Blankfein two dozen times, far more than to any other Wall Street exec.[33] Birds of a feather and all that. "The government then wrote Goldman a $12.9 billion check to cover its losses to AIG, which were predicated on contractual arrangements that would have been worthless had AIG gone bankrupt."[34] Other AIG trading partners who bought subprime insurance got "saved," too, like Bank of America, JP Morgan Chase, and Citigroup. Hallelujah! The way Eliot Spitzer sees it, "The appearance that this was all an inside job is overwhelming. AIG was nothing more than a conduit for huge capital flows to the same old suspects, with no reason or explanation."[35]

What did AIG do with $181 billion altogether in taxpayer-funded bailouts? Do Americans realize that our money went to pay off foreign debt owed by private enterprise in the U.S.? When rescued, AIG had at least $40 billion in credit default swaps outstanding.[36] $11.9 billion went to pay its debt to France's Societe Generale, and $11.8 billion more went to Deutsche Bank of Germany, and $8.5 billion to Barclays Bank in Britain.[37] During the last three months of 2008, AIG was losing more than $27 million an hour or $465,000 every minute. With numbers like that, Bernie Madoff comes off as chump change.[38] But they were still giving bonuses totaling around $450 million to everybody in the Financial Products Unit—the very same people who'd bankrupted the company![39] Until Congress did an intervention, Joe Cassano continued to pull down a million-dollar-a-month salary.[40]

This whole bailout business stinks. And we've been left holding the bag. That original $700 billion bailout figure has mushroomed into a commitment that includes about $1.1 trillion in taxpayer money. Total financial support from the Fed, Treasury, and FDIC is actually around $3 trillion, with potential support authorized of $23.7 trillion![41] One economist says government officials "see all this as a Three Card Monte, moving everything around really quickly so the public won't understand that this really is an elaborate way to subsidize the banks" and "won't realize we gave money away to some of the richest people."[42]

Wasn't the expectation that, once it got rescued, Wall Street would then be good sports and send money into creating jobs and initiating a major recovery? But the big banks didn't start lending again, instead they hoarded the cash and paid out huge bonuses to their execs. The behemoths got even more beastly. Today JPMorgan Chase holds more than one out of every ten dollars on deposit in America. Bank of America and Wells Fargo are close behind. Those three, plus Citigroup, now issue one half of all mortgages and about two thirds of our credit cards. The big guys can borrow more cheaply because creditors assume they're at no risk for failing.[43] "Incredibly, despite the events of last fall, nearly every one of Wall Street's proprietary trading desks can still take huge risks and then, if they get into trouble, head to the Federal Reserve for short-term rescue financing."[44]

Presiding over the money pit is "Gentle Ben" Bernanke, whom Obama reappointed to head the Federal Reserve. Even though they were a major contributor to the disaster that millions have suffered, we're now supposed to cheer their heroic attempt to clean up their own mess. Regional and smaller banks are still crumbling, while the Street gangs are on government life-support. Do you ever wonder where the Fed gets the money? Well, basically they print it out of thin air. Check out Article 1, Section 8 of the Constitution: Only Congress is granted the power "to coin money" and "regulate the value thereof." No separate agency or concession like the Federal Reserve is given the power. But today, they aren't even required to send a budget to Congress. The Federal Reserve can enter into agreements with foreign banks and governments that we can't find out about. The dozen regional Federal Reserves around the country have bankers on their boards who tell them what they should be thinking about. And the Fed basically owns the economics profession. Their Board of Governors has 220 PhD economists on its payroll, not to mention scores more with the regional banks, plus all the research and support staff.[45]

Ron Paul, a congressman I admire, has introduced the Federal Reserve Transparency Act, calling for "more effective oversight and auditing of the Fed." Paul points out that, since the Fed was created almost a hundred years ago, the dollar has lost more than 95 percent of its purchasing power. "Only big-spending politicians and politically favored bankers benefit from inflation," Paul says.[46] Bernanke has said that an audit would mean "a takeover of monetary policy by the Congress," perish the thought. The reality is that the road we're currently on "leads to the corporate state—a fusion of private and public power, a privileged club that dominates everything else from the top down."[47] Mussolini once had a term for that: he called it fascism.

Almost 700 execs who participated in running our economy into the ground have received more than a million bucks apiece in bonuses.[48] Goldman Sachs had a spectacularly profitable first half of 2009—due to less competition (go figure why), and a revenue surge from trading foreign currency and bonds. Goldman's 30,000 employees will each earn an average of $700,000 this year.[49] Good old Warren Buffett, who thought smart and bought $5 billion in Goldman shares in January, had already scored a billion on that investment.[50] Edward Liddy, the dollar-a-year guy who was installed by our government as AIG's new CEO, happens to still own a significant stake in Goldman, so I guess he's doing all right.[51]

The banking lobby in Congress "frankly own the place," Illinois senator Dick Durbin has said.[52] Over the last decade, the financial sector spent over $5 billion on lobbying and federal campaign contributions.[53] Nearly half the members of the Senate Banking Committee (which happens to oversee the bailout bucks) had holdings in the same financial institutions that gained funds from the Troubled Asset Relief Program (TARP).[54] "If TARP had been a credit card, it would have been called Carte Blanche."[55] In April 2009, the Treasury Department's Special Inspector General came out with a report describing TARP as mismanaged and ripe for fraud. There's no accountability. Hedge funds, which are still completely unregulated, have been brought into the program as key players.[56] A few months before Neel Kashkari got appointed to run TARP, he'd told a group of bankers that "there is no problem here" with the subprime-mortgage crisis.[57] A real forward-thinking fellow.

"There wasn't even anyone within the TARP office to keep track of the money as it was being disbursed. TARP gave that job—along with a $20 million fee—to a private contractor, Bank of New York Mellon, which also happened to be one of the Big 9. So here was a case of a beneficiary helping to oversee a process in which it was a direct participant. . . . There was enormous potential for conflicts of interest, and no procedure to deal with them."[58]

Another example of a company that came in under the TARP, so to speak: GE Capital. We all think of General Electric in terms of light bulbs and home appliances (along with ownership of NBC), but its finance wing is GE Capital, which lends out money for real estate ventures and Wal-Mart credit cards and the like. They'd be the seventh largest bank in the U.S., if they were classified that way. But since GE Capital is an arm of an industrial corporation, they can put forth handsome finance arrangements for those who purchase their products. And when the bailout happened, they ended up somehow qualifying for a government-guaranteed program allowing them to raise almost $75 billion by the close of the first quarter in '09. The debt comes due when FDIC guarantees run out in 2012. In the banking realm, that's called "the cliff."[59] Seems like there's quite a few of those pinnacles to climb and fall down.

President Obama's largest private campaign donor was Goldman Sachs, whose employees coughed up $981,000 to him during the presidential campaign.[60] I would have a hard time sleeping at night if I was running for public office and knew Goldman Sachs was my top contributor. But that's what makes me different from a Democrat or a Republican. To them, it's all about winning. Altogether, Obama got $9.9 million from Wall Street bankers and investment and security firms.[61] No matter how nice we think the president is, and what a brilliant speaker he is, he's still beholden to these power brokers. I don't hold out much hope for the new Financial Crisis Inquiry Commission to be any different than the Warren Commission or the 9/11 Commission when it comes to exposing the truth.

Look who Obama named as his chief economic adviser: Lawrence Summers, the ex–Harvard president who made $5.2 million for a one-day-a-week job with a hedge fund (D.E. Shaw) in 2008 and simultaneously earned $2.7 million in speaking fees from folks like Goldman and Citigroup.[62] In a "past lifetime," Summers joined with Rubin and Greenspan in the bankers' crusade to stop the government from regulating the same financial derivatives market that ended up causing the economic meltdown.[63]

Then there's Obama's treasury secretary, Timothy Geithner. He's the fellow who, while president of the New York Fed, suggested to Paulson and other economic bigwigs in June 2008 that the president should be given "broad power to guarantee all debt in the banking system." Considered politically unfeasible at the time, as it potentially put taxpayers on the hook for trillions, the government has since come to largely embrace "his

blue-sky prescription."[64] During his five years at the New York Fed, Geithner presided over "an era of unbridled and ultimately disastrous risk-
taking by the financial industry," while wining-and-dining with all the
titans. So are we surprised that Geithner's calendars show the top execs
of Goldman Sachs, Citigroup, and JP Morgan being the select group he's
always on the phone with? (At least 80 contacts during Geithner's first
seven months.)[65]

At the treasury, Geithner's chief of staff is Mark Patterson, who a year
earlier was a Goldman Sachs lobbyist fighting against a bill Senator
Obama introduced to try and rein in compensation for execs. Patterson is
now the main man administering the bailout dough.[66] William Dudley,
new president of the New York Fed, is another Goldman alum. Is it coincidental that, by being allowed to become a bank holding company,
Goldman's main overseer is now the New York Fed? I doubt they'll be ter-
ribly concerned about things like the $54.7 million Goldman CEO Lloyd
Blankenfein took home in compensation in '07.[67]

As for the health care debate: Insurance industry lobbyists are opposing
reform at a record pace, having spent an astounding $32 million on TV ads
as of October.[68] Have you ever heard of the MLR? That stands for "Medical
Loss Ratio": "the fancy term used by health insurance companies for their
slice, their take-out, their pound of flesh, their gross—very gross—profit.
The 'MLR' is the difference between what you pay an insurance company
and what that insurer pays out to doctors, hospitals and pharmacists for
your medical care." The MLR is about to top a quarter trillion dollars a
year. AIG has "kicked up their Loss Ratio by nearly 500 percent."[69]

Are we that selfish a nation where health care can be such a divisive
issue? Where is mainstream America today? To me, the doctor issue is a
human right. I don't care if you're an illegal alien or whatever, if you're sick
you should be able to have treatment. It amazes me that we've got people
out there holding signs and making our president look like a Nazi, because
he supports a change in the system. Here's another point: If government-
run health care is so bad, does that mean we've been screwing over our
veterans for close to a hundred years? My father would go nowhere else but
to the Veterans Administration hospital. The one here in Minneapolis is
state-of-the-art, brand-new, and completely government-run, and I don't

see anyone protesting about that! If it's good enough for the veterans, shouldn't it be the same for all of us?

As I write this, unemployment stands at ten percent of our work force, foreclosures are still happening at around 10,000 a day, people defaulting on their credit cards has hit a record, and across the country the states are having to slice crucial services to the bone. As governor, when we had a budget that went over what we'd allocated, I gave checks back to the people. That was a true stimulus package. When people at home have more money in their pockets, they tend to spend it. Cutting taxes also stimulates the economy, as much as Democrats hate the sound of it. In this case, the taxes coming out of our pockets are just making the rich get richer. "Nine of the financial firms that were among the largest recipients of federal bailout money paid about 5,000 of their traders and bankers bonuses of more than $1 million apiece for 2008."[70] For the fiscal year that ended in October 2008, the IRS audited only about four out of every hundred Americans who showed income of $1 million and up. IRS data also showed that the income of the 400 wealthiest individuals in the country hit an average of $263 million in 2006. Within a decade, their share of our nation's wealth almost doubled—to more than 22 percent.[71]

Meantime, the offshore tax havens haven't gone away. Citigroup, for example, has 91 subsidiaries in Luxembourg and another 90 in the Cayman Islands (out of 427 units in 23 countries altogether).[72] The Caymans are part of Great Britain, and more than 12,000 "companies" operate out of a single building there. The Caymans lay claim to being the fifth largest center of bank deposits in the world; while it's true that the shares, bonds, and cash are technically on the islands, they're actually headquartered back in New York. The $1.9 trillion in bank deposits, although it's invested in the U.S. and abroad, remains invisible to the IRS. If you ever wondered why Enron paid no taxes, that's because they created hundreds of these paper companies. Oh, and Dick Cheney's Halliburton subsidiary, KBR, pays at least 21,000 of its employees through subsidiaries in the Caymans.[73]

That's called globalization, I guess. Just like IBM sending its laid-off American workers overseas to countries like India "where your skills are in demand."[74] Fed Chairman Bernanke is also a board member of something called the Bank for International Settlements, based in Basel, Switzerland. The BIS encouraged all the speculative investment banking that led to our current debacle. Carroll Quigley, in *Tragedy and Hope*, wrote that the BIS was created as the apex of "a world system of financial control in private hands able to dominate the political system of each country and the economy of the world as a whole." The goal being control "in a feudalist fashion by the central banks of the world acting in concert, by secret agreements arrived at in frequent private meetings and conferences."

Based inside the BIS is a new agency called the Financial Stability Board. It's proposed to "strengthen" and "institutionalize" a mandate to "promote global financial stability." Sounds good, but some see this as the "latest sinister development in a centuries-old consolidation of power by an international financial oligarchy." Third World countries who can't pay off their debts would be required to sell off their national assets to private investors. The board has oversight over all "systematically important" financial institutions, instruments, and markets. (Like gold, oil, and food maybe?) Yet there's no treaty involved, merely a private committee looking out for national sovereignty. Seems like the fulfillment of what banker Mayer Rothschild said back in 1791: "Allow me to issue and control a nation's currency, and I care not who makes its laws."[75]

Thomas Jefferson warned the country back in 1815: "The dominion which the banking institutions have obtained over the minds of our citizens . . . must be broken, or it will break us."[76] Is it naïve to think about banking returning to the austere, staid practice of simply taking deposits and making conservative loans at low interest rates to qualified borrowers, under rigid regulations administered by moderately paid federal employees? Wouldn't that greatly reduce systemic risk? Here's what some smart economists think we need to do:

- Reinstate the Glass-Steagall Act and wall off commercial banking from investment bank gambling, and require strict leverage limits.
- Insulate the federally insured depositors from reckless investment schemes with no social utility whatsoever like these "credit default swaps" that are entered into by entities that don't own the underlying bonds.
- Withdraw the massive handouts and taxpayer-backed guarantees given to prop up specific banks and financial institutions, and use these funds to instead support the struggling homeowners and

defaulting borrowers who form the root of this crisis. This will reduce the record rate of foreclosures and put a floor under asset prices at a sustainable level, which will in turn stabilize financial institutions that are still hemorrhaging from increasing foreclosures and loan defaults. In other words, bottom-up, not top-down economic support.

- Let the already-insolvent banks go bankrupt and begin removing the bad debt from the system. We need a sound banking system, but there is no reason we need the specific banks we have now. There are plenty of regional and community banks in this country which avoided exposure to risky mortgage and credit derivatives, and which would gladly replace the market share held by the too-bloated-to-fail banks for loans issued to small businesses and consumers, if they were able to compete in a truly free market against these subsidized behemoths. In short, why doesn't the public demand a financial system that serves the people rather than enslaves us to a treadmill of debt?

The national debt is basically what the government owes from years of borrowing money to pay off the yearly deficits (the amount by which spending exceeds revenue from taxes and the like). Back in 1791, our national debt was $75 million; today it rises by that amount every hour or so.[77] During the years of Bush-II, the national debt increased by over 65 percent to nearly $10 trillion! Now there's talk among some of our creditors (like China, which as of November 2007 held $390 billion of our debt) about replacing the dollar as the world's reserve currency.[78] But we keep right on spending money we don't really have, to players who don't deserve it. A Congressional Oversight Panel report early in 2009 said the Bush Administration had overpaid the banks by tens of billions for stocks and other assets in the bailout.[79] Our economy has been captured by an alien power—not the Klingons, but the Kleptos. We can't go on like this. A much worse disaster than we faced in 2008 is in the wind, without something real being done about this mess that the government–Wall Street conspiracy created.

Can we still heed the words of Andrew Jackson, when he said to a delegation of bankers in 1832: "Gentlemen, I have had men watching you for a long time, and I am convinced that you have used the funds of the bank to speculate in the bread-stuffs of the country. When you won, you divided the profits amongst you, and when you lost, you charged it to the bank. You tell me that if I take the deposits from the bank and annul its charter, I shall ruin ten thousand families. That may be true, gentlemen, but that is your sin! Should I let you go on, you will ruin fifty thousand families, and that would be my sin! You are a den of vipers and thieves. I intend to rout you out. . . ."

I'm ready to see a rout that restores our Republic to the principles of Jefferson and Jackson. How about you?

WHAT SHOULD WE DO NOW?

When the average American is on the edge of losing it all, at the same time the "fat cats" are getting even fatter, it's time to call their bluff, folks. We need to realize first that we've become a corporatized state, one that our government is beholden to while the majority of us are held hostage by it. We should be demanding that President Obama put people in charge who weren't part of the problem. We should be battering at the gates of Goldman Sachs and AIG, and the Federal Reserve too, letting the pillagers take the fall they deserve.

CHAPTER FOURTEEN

THE SECRET PLANS TO END AMERICAN DEMOCRACY

THE INCIDENT: The two terms of George W. Bush saw passage of the Patriot Act, the Foreign Intelligence Surveillance Act, and other similar laws in the wake of 9/11. Afghanistan and Iraq were invaded, and detention centers for terrorists established.

THE OFFICIAL WORD: The erosion of civil liberties, including wiretapping and torture and suspending habeus corpus, is necessary in order to prevent the spread of terrorism on our shores.

MY TAKE: The federal government, and elements of the military, have used 9/11 as an excuse to put in place the means to impose martial law and lock up dissenters in "camps" if they deem it necessary. Our Constitution and Bill of Rights have never been in greater peril than now. The technology exists to further erode our democracy, and basically make slaves of those who won't go along with the program.

"With a fascist the problem is never how best to present the truth to the public but how best to use the news to deceive the public into giving the fascist and his group more money or more power. American fascism will not be really dangerous until there is a purposeful coalition among the cartelists, the deliberate poisoners of public information. . . . They claim to be super-patriots, but they would destroy every liberty guaranteed by the Constitution."
—Henry Wallace, vice president of the United States, 1944

What transpired during the Bush-II years has been coming out in dribs and drabs, so as not to unduly alarm the populace. President Obama wants to look forward and put all that behind us, but when our own government has sanctioned torture and even murder in the name of "national security," I don't see how we can. We need accountability from our government, and if that means even a Cheney or Rumsfeld standing trial for war crimes, so be it.

The Senate Armed Services Committee came out with a report in April 2009 that said: "The abuse of detainees in U.S. custody cannot simply be attributed to the actions of 'a few bad apples' acting on their own. The fact is that senior officials in the United States government solicited information on how to use aggressive techniques, redefined the law to create the appearance of their legality, and authorized their use against detainees."[1]

I was waterboarded during my navy training at SERE (Survival, Escape, Resistance and Evasion) School, to know what it's like in case we ever became POWs, and it *is* a method of torture. Cheney's word for it is "enhanced interrogation." Well, you give me Dick Cheney and a waterboard for an hour, and I'll have him confessing to the Sharon Tate murders. Not too long ago, the ACLU managed to pry loose government documents including a CIA manual about what they call "extraordinary rendition." It describes the "capture shock" that happened before a detainee got put on the flight to some overseas prison. Little techniques like being shackled, and bound up in blindfolds and hoods so you couldn't see or hear. After which you'd get stripped down and shaved and have your picture taken. Not to mention "walling," defined as slamming somebody's head against the wall but with certain "protective measures" so they don't die.[2] You get the picture.

We all remember the gruesome images of Abu Ghraib, but the CIA admits having destroyed hundreds of hours of "coercive interrogation" videotapes that took place in secret prisons.[3] Don't you find it pretty sadistic that they'd even want to make movies of all this? These are measures I've always associated with the KGB or the Nazis. Come to find out from a Senate Armed Services Committee report on prisoner abuse that they even created an experimental "battle lab" for the torture program at Guantánamo, in a throwback to MK-ULTRA.[4]

What galls me more than anything is how they used torture in pursuit of lies to justify their actions. First of all, Bush and Cheney pressured lawyers at the Department of Justice to produce memos authorizing them to do whatever they wanted and call it legal.[5] Then, in the weeks just before we invaded Iraq and the first couple months of our occupation, there turned out to be major spikes in the harshest torture techniques. It was all part of an attempt to link Saddam Hussein to al-Qaeda. Major Paul Burney, who was part of the Guantánamo interrogation team, told investigators: "The more frustrated people got in not being able to establish this link, there was more and more pressure to resort to measures that might produce more immediate results."[6]

After Ibn Al-Shaykh Al-Libi was captured, the CIA "rendered" him to Egypt (the term reminds me of what we do to slabs of beef). There he was tortured into making a false confession that Saddam had gotten information about use of chemical and biological weapons from a couple of al-Qaeda operatives. Al-Libi was a supposed suicide in a Libyan jail in May 2009.[7] Speaking of al-Qaeda, I recently came across this point: "Should the members of the 9/11 Presidential Commission not have been informed that two of the 'key witnesses' upon whom their report was based had provided the information to the report's conclusions only after being waterboarded a total of 266 times?"[8]

How low would these guys stoop? We've learned since Bush left office of a meeting he had with Tony Blair to talk about how the United Nations inspectors weren't going to find any Weapons of Mass Destruction, but why not go ahead anyway? A memo written early in 2003 has Bush telling Blair of a U.S. plan "to fly U2 reconnaissance aircraft painted in U.N. colors over Iraq with fighter cover." If Saddam fired at them, he'd be in violation of the U.N. resolutions and that would be ample justification to invade.[9] Sounds like a transplant of Operation Northwoods to me.

We may never know how many detainees died in our custody in secret prisons. We do have fresh evidence, though, of an "executive assassination ring" that was revealed by investigative journalist Seymour Hersh in March 2009. Hersh spoke of an independent special wing called Joint Special Operations Command that reported directly to Cheney's office. Word was that a three-star admiral eventually ordered it stopped because so many "collateral deaths" were happening. It pains me to say that among the unit's trainees were young men from the Navy SEALS.[10]

By the summer of '09, word was out about a clandestine CIA program to assassinate al-Qaeda members. The private company enlisted was identified as Blackwater,[11] which started out protecting our brass in Iraq. Today, even though the Iraqi government has kicked them out, they're still under contract to our own government for "black ops." I read a chilling book about Blackwater by Jeremy Scahill that I highly recommend. They're in the vanguard of privatization of our armed forces. It's astounding to consider that we have more private soldiers (74,000) than uniformed troops (57,000) in Afghanistan, as of summer 2009.[12]

Blackwater—which recently changed its name to the more innocuous-sounding Xe Services—is run by Erik Prince, who one former employee says "views himself as a Christian crusader tasked with eliminating Muslims and the Islamic faith from the globe."[13] After getting some bad press for mowing down 17 Iraqi civilians on a crowded street in 2007,[14] the company set about to clean up its image. They don't call themselves mercenaries anymore, but "global stabilization professionals." Their Web site claims a corporate vision "guided by integrity, innovation, and a desire for a safer world." They sponsor NASCAR events and have performed dramatic parachute landings at college football games. Blackwater, as Erik Prince puts it, "is going to be more of a full spectrum" operation.[15]

Hmmmm, wonder what "full spectrum" means. One arm of Blackwater is called Total Intelligence Solutions, run by J. Cofer Black, who used to head up the CIA's counter-terrorism branch. The company has bid for a $15 billion Pentagon contract to "fight terrorists with drug-trade ties." They've got an offshore affiliate, Greystone Ltd., in Barbados. And, while Iraqi civilians are suing Blackwater for murders and other war crimes, the Obama Administration has replaced them with a new outfit called Triple Canopy, giving the company a billion-dollar contract to provide private security services in Iraq. Not only did they hire some of Blackwater's finest, but some company employees have claimed Triple Canopy has used stolen cars and weapons taken from Iraqis to lift their profits on certain contracts to more than 40 percent.[16] Meantime, Blackwater also remains on our government payroll to arm drone aircraft in Afghanistan, among other lucrative missions.[17]

After Katrina devastated New Orleans in 2005, Blackwater got itself a mission there, too. About 150 of its mercs fanned out around the city in full battle gear, carrying automatic assault weapons and with guns strapped to their legs. When Jeremy Scahill talked to four of the men, they described their work as "securing neighborhoods" and "confronting criminals," on behalf of Homeland Security.[18]

I find it so disturbing that our country is allowing professional mercenaries to take over protection of our nation. If that's the case, what do we need the military for at all? In Iraq, Ambassador Bremer went over and absolved them of anything they did. They could literally commit murder and just walk away. If, because of terrorism, laws don't matter anymore, then we're no better than the terrorists. We can't just have the law when it's convenient.

But this is only one of a host of assaults on our Constitution and the Bill of Rights since the events of 9/11. We would do well to review elements of the USA Patriot Act, passed by Congress a month after the attacks. Among other things, the new law made it a crime for anybody to contribute money or material support for a group that appeared on the Terror Watch List. It allowed the FBI to monitor and tape-record conversations between attorneys and clients, once considered privileged. It let the FBI order librarians to turn over information about people's reading habits. And it opened the door for government surveillance on our e-mails and snail-mails.[19]

So it's no surprise that the Bush Administration soon embarked on an illegal wiretapping program, a story that the *New York Times* sat on for a year before finally publishing it. The National Security Agency (NSA) set up a secret room in downtown San Francisco under the auspices of AT&T, where the NSA could tap into the telcom giant's fiber-optic cables. These weren't just part of AT&T, but connected their network to Sprint, Global Crossing, and other companies (including Qwest, which had refused to play ball). According to former AT&T technician Mark Klein, the result was "a complete copy of the data stream." It all went through NSA headquarters at Fort Meade, ten miles outside D.C., where the agency has a "colossal Cray supercomputer, code-named the 'Black Widow.'" (Don't you love all these "black" designations?) This super-computer is capable of scanning "millions of domestic and international phone calls and e-mails per hour . . . performing hundreds of trillions of calculations per second, [it] searches through and reassembles key words and patterns, across many languages."[20] They targeted certain journalists and basically vacuumed in all the domestic communications of Americans, including faxes, phone calls, and Internet traffic.[21] Code-named Pinwale, the NSA's secret database even scooped up the private e-mails of former President Clinton.[22]

What's truly outrageous is that all this was legalized when Bush signed into law the FISA Amendments Act of 2008 (FISA stands for Foreign Intelligence Surveillance Act). That's right, Congress gave the NSA still more power to ferret out supposed terrorist patterns in our private communications. "This gives AT&T, Verizon, and the rest a hearty signal to go on pimping for the government." After writing that column, Nat Hentoff, who'd been with the *Village Voice* since it started in the mid-1950s, got laid off.

Snooping through our telecoms was only the beginning. Even after Congress held back funding for the "Suspicionless Surveillance" program developed by a new Total Information Awareness department (don't you just love the labels?), Bush apparently kept it going anyway. This was broader than the warrantless wiretaps, giving law enforcement the right to inspect our credit cards and bank transactions on the off-chance we might be tied in to terrorists.[23]

In shooting an episode called "Big Brother" for my TV series, my son Ty and I came to Minneapolis to film a little B-roll. We went downtown to First and Washington Avenue. There wasn't one camera, there were four—on every single street corner! A middle-aged guy came by on a bike and I stopped him to ask if he'd ever noticed this. He said, "No, what are they filming?" I told him, "I don't know, but obviously they're watching us, they've got every direction covered."

I found out that private corporations provide the money to buy the cameras. The city says, "Great, it doesn't cost us a thing," and the taxpayers say, "Great, my taxes don't go up." But are the corporations doing this out of the goodness of their heart, to make a safer America? The cameras are all run by computer. One thing that automatically triggers them is when four or more people are together: "Must be up to something, let's film them." We were all outraged and stunned when we read George Orwell's

1984 in school. But I'm afraid he was a prophet. Big Brother *is* watching, and it's happening in subtle ways.

I imagine few of you have heard of InfraGard. A year ago, I was happily ignorant that it existed. Their brochure describes a "collaborative effort" between government and private industry to protect our "critical infrastructures" like banking and finance, agriculture and food, telecommunications, transportation systems, and the like. "An Infra-Gard member is a private-sector volunteer with an inherent concern for national security," says the brochure. Their members connect to a national network of Subject Matter Experts, SMEs for short, and communicate through local chapters with federal law enforcement and government agencies.[24]

It looks completely up-and-up. As of early 2008, InfraGard had 86 chapters around the country, representing more than 23,000 figures in private industry. Over 350 of the Fortune 500 companies are said to be involved. If they follow what the pamphlet says, these are patriotic Americans who meet with agents from the FBI and Homeland Security to help protect the rest of us. Okay, fine and dandy. But I see this as ripe for massive abuse, and I despise the premise of members watching other people and reporting what they see to the government. I learned they have a couple of meetings a month, and every group has its own "handler," who is an FBI agent.

I met personally with two of the upper echelon of InfraGard in Oklahoma City. I posed to them a hypothetical situation: Say your agricultural expert saw something that disturbed him, would the Standard Operating Procedure be for him to call the local police? Nope, it would be the "handler." Again, a matter of the feds superseding everything else. Maybe these are just a bunch of good-old-boys who want to seem important; they can run around with their InfraGard ID cards and impress their buddies at the club. And maybe the FBI sits back and says, "Well, this saves us a ton of money, we don't need agents out there because we've got these knuckleheads doing it."

But this "handler" business is right out of CIA cloak-and-dagger. As head of a corporation, say you have someone working for you that happens to take a different political viewpoint, you can then call your "handler" and the FBI will begin systematic harassment of that person? Infra-

Gard members supposedly receive warnings about alleged terrorist threats before the rest of us, and in return can ask the FBI to investigate disgruntled or annoying employees.

Members also learn what their responsibilities are during periods of an emergency or even martial law. I asked one fellow I talked to, a former sheriff: "At any of your meetings, have you ever been told of a circumstances where you guys could use lethal force?" He said, no, that's never been discussed. But we were told by a whistleblower that, in the event martial law was ever declared, they would be granted that capability. They could protect whatever aspect of the infrastructure they were involved with, and have permission to shoot to kill, without fear of prosecution. So we're going to potentially turn loose a bunch of cowboys with guns, who don't even know Miranda rights? That's a pretty scary proposition.[25]

And it's another step down the road to something like this: A month after Bush left office, a memo entitled "Authority for Use of Military Force to Combat Terrorist Activity Within the United States" came to light. Soon after 9/11, the Justice Department secretly gave the go-ahead for the military to attack apartment buildings or office complexes inside the country and, if necessary to combat the terror threat, suspend press freedoms guaranteed by the First Amendment. "Military action might encompass making arrests, seizing documents or other property, searching persons or places or keeping them under surveillance, intercepting electronic or wireless communications, setting up roadblocks, interviewing witnesses or searching for suspects." As Kate Martin, director of the Center for National Security Studies think tank, put it bluntly: "In October 2001, they were trying to construct a legal regime that would basically have allowed for the imposition of martial law."[26] Constitutional scholar Michael Ratner was even more blunt. He called the legal arguments "Fuhrer's Law" and added: "The memos revealed how massive the takeover of our democracy was to be. . . . [they] lay the groundwork for a massive military takeover of the United States in cahoots with the president. And if that's not a coup d'etat then nothing is."[27]

Such plans date back a ways. During an earlier period of racial unrest and anti–Vietnam War protests, in 1968 the Pentagon came up with Operation Garden Plot. It was updated most recently in 1991, and activated briefly during the L.A. riots in 1992. The idea was for flexible "military operations in urban terrain," using various kinds of high-tech weaponry and in concert with "elite" militarized police units, that would be ready to stop "disorder," "disturbance," and "civil disobedience" in America.[28]

Then, during the Reagan years, Oliver North organized Rex-84—short for "readiness exercise" 1984 (I guess somebody had been taking their Orwell seriously)—that envisioned using the Federal Emergency Management Agency (FEMA, created in 1979) to round up and detain in camps as many as 400,000 "refugees" in case of "uncontrolled population movements" coming across our border from Mexico.[29] When North was asked during the Iran-Contra hearings about his work on "a contingency plan in the event of emergency, that would suspend the American constitution," chairman Daniel Inouye ruled that this "highly sensitive and classified"matter shouldn't be discussed in an open hearing.[30]

So who do you think was doing some of the top-level planning of this along with North? Donald Rumsfeld and Dick Cheney, along with Vice President Poppa Bush, under something called the National Program Office.[31] "Rumsfeld and Cheney were principal actors in one of the most highly classified programs of the Reagan Administration." Congress would have no role in the event of a "national security emergency."[32]

Ten months *before* 9/11, immediately upon the second Bush Administration taking control, Pentagon chief Rumsfeld approved an updated version of the Army's COG plan. COG stands for Continuity-of-Government. The idea has been around since the Fifties and the possibility that the Russians would drop a nuke on us.[33] In May 2001, Bush put Cheney in charge of a terrorism task force and opened a new Office of National Preparedness within FEMA.[34] The guy Bush had named to head FEMA was Joe Allbaugh, who'd managed the Bush-Cheney campaign in 2000 and helped out with the dirty tricks "19th Floor Riot" that brought a halt to the ballot recount going on in Miami-Dade County.[35]

After 9/11, the COG plans went operational. Here's what the *Washington Post* reported six months later: "President Bush has dispatched a shadow government of about 100 senior civilian managers to live and work secretly outside Washington, activating for the first time long-standing plans to ensure survival of federal rule after catastrophic attack on the nation's capital. . . . Known internally as the COG, for 'continuity of government,' the administration-in-waiting is an unannounced complement to the acknowledged absence of Vice President Cheney from Washington for much of the past five months."[36]

Under the new Homeland Security office, another plan called ENDGAME was established. Its goal was to place "all removable aliens" and "potential terrorists" in detention facilities.[37] Attorney General John Ashcroft came right out and announced his wish that such "enemy combatants" be put in camps scattered around the country. In January 2002, the Pentagon submitted a proposal for deploying troops on our streets and, that April, the Northern Command (NORTHCOM) was set up to implement this.[38] "The command will provide civil support not only in response to attacks, but for natural disasters," according to the Pentagon's announcement.[39] (In September 2005, NORTHCOM conducted a highly classified exercise in D.C. called Granite Shadow.)[40]

Bear in mind that the Posse Comitatus Act of 1878 specifically outlaws the military acting like cops on our own soil. Bush also put through an executive order that changed the 1807 Insurrection Act, giving himself much greater powers in the event of something he might label as "insurrection." (The Constitution lets habeas corpus be suspended during such an occurrence.)[41] This marked "a fundamental change in military culture," according to Paul McHale, an assistant secretary for homeland defense. Before 9/11, he says, this "would have been extraordinary to the point of unbelievable."[42]

All through the Bush years, this kind of "preparedness" kept building. Early in 2006, as part of ENDGAME, Homeland Security awarded a $385 million contract to KBR—a subsidiary of Cheney's old company, Halliburton—to get going on "temporary detention and processing facilities" in case there was "an emergency influx of immigrants, or to support the rapid development of new programs" with a natural disaster.[43] (Think Katrina, which saw the first "round-up" of citizens, held not only in the football stadium in New Orleans but shipped out to other detention centers.)

Shortly before the midterm elections, the Military Commissions Act of 2006 made it through Congress. This went so far as to permit the indefinite imprisonment of anybody who happened to give money to a charity on the Terror Watch List, or even someone who spoke out against these kinds of policies.[44]

Several more unbelievable dictums took effect in 2007, even after the Democrats regained control of Congress. The Violent Radicalization and Homegrown Terrorist Prevention Act of 2007 passed the House, 404 to 6, aimed at setting up a commission to "examine and report upon the facts and causes" of domestic extremism. The National Counterterrorism Center already has more than 775,000 "terror suspects" on its list. The Animal Enterprise Terrorism Act expands the definition of terrorism to include those who "engage in sit-ins, civil disobedience, trespass, or any other crime in the name of animal rights." Section 1042 of the 2007 National Defense Authorization Act provided the executive branch power to impose martial law in response to "a natural disaster, a disease outbreak, a terrorist attack or any other condition in which the President determines that domestic violence has occurred to the extent that state officials cannot maintain public order." And the White House itself quietly put in place National Security Presidential Directive 52 to make sure Continuity-of-Government was intact, providing authority to cancel elections or suspend the Constitution in the event of a national emergency.[45]

Then what did we see in the course of the 2008 presidential election year? First of all, mass arrests at the Republican Convention in St. Paul, including journalists arbitrarily thrown in the clink while filming the demonstrators. The 3rd Infantry Division 1st Brigade Combat Team was trained to do crowd control in Iraq, but on October 1, between 3,000 and 4,000 of them got deployed in the U.S., ready to manage "unruly individuals" in case of a national emergency.[46] One scenario envisioned by the Pentagon was civil unrest as a result of financial meltdown. They'd cooperate with FEMA on plans with code names like Vibrant Response and EXCALIBUR.[47]

In November 2008, the U.S. Army War College came out with a study saying the military should be ready for a "violent, strategic dislocation inside the United States" that could be provoked by "unforeseen economic collapse," "purposeful domestic resistance," "pervasive public health emergencies" (swine flu?), or the "loss of functioning political and legal order." The "widespread civil violence would force the defense establishment to reorient priorities in extremis to defend basic domestic order and human security. . . . Under the most extreme circumstances, this might include use of military force against hostile groups."[48]

And guess what, friends, it's already happening. There was a story recently in the Salinas, California paper, about how violence and terrorism experts from the Naval Postgraduate School had been recruited to help combat the gang subculture in the agricultural town. U.S. Representative Sam Farr, a Democrat, was quoted: "The Naval Postgraduate School is trying to figure out how to stop violence anywhere in the world, why not start in our own backyard." Except for one thing, Congressman: it's illegal.[49]

Another story, in the *Washington Post* no less, tells of how the military anticipates having 20,000 uniformed troops inside the U.S. by 2011, trained to help state and local officials respond to a nuclear terror attack or some other domestic catastrophe. This is part of a "long-planned shift in the Department of Defense's role in homeland security."[50] Already, an active-duty unit called the Chemical, Biological, Radiological/Nuclear and Explosive Consequence Management Response Force is stationed at Fort Stewart, Georgia.[51]

And do you know about the "fusion centers?" These are much like InfraGard, but more blatant. There are about seventy "fusion centers" around the U.S.—places where local law enforcement, the private sector and the intel community can share information in the fight against terrorism. One in West Texas finds it "imperative" to report on lobbying groups. Another in Virginia has declared that American universities, singling out several black colleges, have become "radicalization nodes" for potential terrorist activity. In September 2009, Homeland Security announced that these "fusion centers" would now have access to classified military intelligence in Pentagon databases.[52]

I've gone to some lengths to trace these developments since 9/11, because I'm a lot more afraid of this than an assault by al-Qaeda. What's going on inside our military also frightens me. More and more, we're seeing an army run by Christianist extremists and an accompanying cadre of what can only be described as neo-Nazis. Since the endless "war on terror" began, our armed services have been turning a blind eye to their own military statutes. Here's how a Department of Defense report stated it in 2005: "Effectively, the military has a 'don't ask, don't tell' policy pertaining to extremism." White supremacists are walking as enlisted men around our bases. There are the Hammerskins at Fort Hood and the Celtic

Knights in Texas. One spokesman for the National Socialist Movement bragged about encouraging members to sign up for the military: "We can use the training to secure the resistance to our government."[53]

Newsmax is an online Web site controlled by the ultra-right media baron Richard Mellon Scaife, who used to pay people to dig up dirt on Bill Clinton. Recently, one of *Newsmax*'s columnists (John L. Perry) wrote about a "gaining" possibility that the military would stage a coup to "resolve the Obama problem." It sounded like a page right out of the financial barons' plot to overthrow FDR. The coup would be "civilized" and "bloodless," with a "patriotic general" getting together with the president to let him keep making speeches while a new system of "skilled, military-trained, nation-builders" did "the serious business of governing and defending the nation."[54] Pulitzer-winning journalist Seymour Hersh has also warned that the military is "in a war against the White House— and they feel they have Obama boxed in."[55]

Meantime, you've got news commentators like Glenn Beck warning about a looming insurrection. According to the FBI, there have been 5.5 million requests for background checks on potential gun buyers over the past year or so.[56] The Southern Poverty Law Center reports "unmistakable signs of a revival of what in the 1990s was commonly called the militia movement." It's estimated that 50 new militia training groups have sprung up over the last couple years.[57] There are people out there offering prep for what's coming, like the Front Sight Firearms Training Institute founded by Dr. Ignatius Piazza: "the Millionaire Patriot, wants YOU armed and trained and he is putting his money where his mouth is"—ready to help you get a concealed weapon permit that's good in 30 states.[58]

I suppose, given all the illegal activity that the non-elected Bush Administration engaged in since the millennium, we can't be too surprised at the reaction. A government that played on people's worst nightmares to achieve its own ends creates a culture not only of fear, but mistrust to the point of insurrection—which is what they secretly seem to have been longing for.

I went recently to Corcoran, Kansas, where a civilian is building state-of-the-art underground condos for wealthy people. I think they've got 12 units up for sale. These are being built on what used to be sites for launching nuclear missiles, so they were designed to withstand a nuclear attack. They go down 15 stories with about 15 feet of hardened concrete. They're planned as self-sustaining. They'll grow their own food and raise fish. They've figured out how much everyone can eat per day, to sustain them up to five years. They'll each have a pool, a workout room, and a movie theater.

I asked one buyer, "Well, you live in Florida, if the shit hits the fan, how are you going to get here?" He told me, "We have contingency plans." But if all the electricity's gone, you're going to walk? "If we have to," he said. And you figure people are going to stand out there and hand you food while you make your journey? "We have contingency plans," he said again.

A different fellow I interviewed has been a bunker builder for 20 years, for rich people who want a safe shelter under their house to safeguard against hurricanes or tornadoes. He told me about a certain material that only a couple of vendors sell. In the course of the last decade, when he's tried to get it, he couldn't. Because the government has bought them out. He said the government is building massive bunkers as fast as they possibly can. Why? What do they know that they're not telling the rest of us?

I'm not suggesting that President Obama is a part of such a scheme. He may not even be privy to it. But in the event of a "national emergency," the bunkers would ensure Continuity of Government. Meantime, in a martial law scenario, all the technology is in place to impose government's will on the people. James Bamford, an author who specializes in what the National Security Agency is up to, says they're even developing an artificial intelligence system designed to know what people are thinking! Here come the thought police![59]

Think about what our so-called technological advances really mean. Early in 2009, the National Security Archive in D.C. obtained an "Information Operations Roadmap" under a Freedom of Information Act request. This was signed by Rumsfeld in 2003, and it calls for electronic warfare, in the form of computer network attack specialists and Psyops troops whose specialty is manipulating the beliefs of an enemy. At the Pentagon's request, a private company called the Lincoln Group planted hundreds of articles in Iraqi newspapers in support of U.S. policy. "Information intended for foreign audience, including public diplomacy and

Psyops, is increasingly consumed by our domestic audience. Psyops messages will often be replayed by the news media for much larger audiences, including the American people." (CIA and FBI computers have already been used to edit Wikipedia entries on things like the Iraq War and Guantánamo.)[60] If that's not Big Brother enough, the document closes with the recommendation that the Pentagon ought to pursue an ability to "provide maximum control of the entire electromagnetic spectrum . . . disrupt or destroy the full spectrum of globally emerging communications systems, sensors, and weapons systems dependent on the electromagnetic spectrum." Which translates into being able to KO every telephone, networked computer, and radar system anywhere on the planet.[61] Darth Vader, your time may be coming.

Under the radar, a provision was slipped into the Violence Against Women Act reauthorization bill at the end of 2005. It's the DNA Fingerprint Act, meaning that if you get arrested at a demonstration on federal property, they can take a sample of your DNA and keep it on permanent file.[62] This fits nicely with a billion-dollar FBI project to have a massive computer database containing individuals' physical characteristics. They call this biometrics, and it gives the government a brand-new opportunity to identify folks at home and abroad. They're storing digital images of faces, fingerprints and palm types in a climate-controlled underground facility in Clarksburg, West Virginia. They'll soon be crime-stopping even by analyzing the way we walk and talk. [63] At some airports, people who aren't line-standers at the metal detectors are taking advantage of the "opportunity" to have their irises scanned to prove they've passed a background check (that's called Next Generation Identification).[64]

In 2008 a three-judge appeals court, reversing a lower court's finding, ruled that federal border agents don't need any special reason to search laptops, cell phones, or digital cameras for evidence of crimes.[65] Since Bush had already called for some high-tech measures to crack down on illegal immigration from Mexico, a company called VeriChip came up with a way to "chip the foreigners." It's a Radio Frequency Identification Tag, RFID for short, encapsulated in glass and injected hypodermically into your skin. The ID number can be read right through your clothes, by radio waves, from close range. Tommy Thompson, who headed up Health and Human Services under Bush, joined VeriChip's board after he left the administration and soon was out there extolling the merits of getting chipped as a means for Americans to link up to their medical records. The Pentagon has been entertaining talk of the RFIDs taking the place of the old military "dog tags." It's also being marketed as a possible future way to make payments by combining the chip with your credit card.[66]

Microchips are already everywhere. They're putting chips in our credit cards, our cars, department store clothing tags, library books, literally everything but us—and I figure we're not far behind. I disconnected the North-Star on my vehicle as soon I bought it. I'd rather have to break my window to get my keys, rather than have them know my location every time I drive anywhere. The RFID technology enabling both objects and people to be wirelessly tagged and tracked is on the edge of being a billion-dollar industry. Back in 2003, the Defense Department and Wal-Mart teamed up to move RFID along by mandating their suppliers to put these radio tags on all their crates and cartons. Unlike barcodes, RFID chips don't fall under federal regulations—and they can be read, without knowledge of the holder, through just about anything except metal and water.

Big corporations are excited about using miniaturized computers along with radio antennaes to electronically "sniff" you. In 2005, American Express applied for a patent describing how RFID-embedded objects that shoppers carry could send out "identification signals" picked up by electronic "consumer trackers." In return, the shoppers could be sent video ads offering them "incentives" to buy the products they'd seemed interested in. In 2006, IBM received patent approval for an invention it dubbed "Identification and tracking of persons using RFID-tagged items." Yet another patent (NCR Corporation) described using camouflaged sensors and video cameras to film your facial expression at counter displays, "which allows one to draw valuable inferences about the behavior of large numbers of shoppers." Proctor & Gamble went so far as to seek a patent to check out what you're examining on a lower shelf of the store.

"With tags in so many objects, relaying information to databases that can be linked to credit and bank cards, almost no aspect of life may soon be safe from the prying eyes of corporations and governments," says Mark Rasch, who used to head the computer-crime unit at the Justice Department. By putting sniffers in the right places, companies can invisibly "rifle through people's pockets, purses, suitcases, briefcases, luggage . . . and possibly their kitchens and bedrooms . . . anytime of the day or night."[67]

Under our Constitution and Bill of Rights, government is not allowed to do certain things. Corporate America doesn't fall under those same rules. So the government is getting the private sector to do the dirty work, violations that they can't be held accountable for. Then the corporations simply take the information they've acquired and turn it over to the government. You might say, what else could they learn? Well, things like this: say you've got health care coming up. If they know everything you buy in the store, they might say, "Here's a candidate for diabetes, look how he eats, let's pass this along because you could be a risk."

I know I was surveilled when I was governor of Minnesota. To this day, every time I start appearing on national TV or radio, all of a sudden my phones get weird—you hear clicks on the other end—and my wife can't get online as quickly and things disappear from her computer. Is this happenstance? It always seems to coincide with when I take a high profile. If you're at all a dissenter, apparently you will be observed and put under surveillance.

Doesn't it also concern *you* that "We the Rabble" could be looking at a corporatized, militarized future where we're tracked down by radio-tags and herded into camps for undesirable citizens who won't go along with the program? Not to worry if you're part of the elite. The insurance giant AIG has pioneered a special service for customers living in upper-class zip codes. During the 2007 wildfires in Southern California, its Private Client Group paid big bucks to AIG's Firebreak Spray Systems to have their homes hosed down with a fire retardant—sometimes while the next-door neighbor went up in flames. A start-up company called Sovereign Deed, tied into the mercenary outfit Triple Canopy, has since developed our first privatized national disaster response center with a "country-club type membership fee."[68]

Do you realize that, since 2002, there has been a 47 percent increase in American workers classified as security guards? And that as high as one quarter of our labor force is now centered around protection instead of production?[69] That's a culture increasingly based on fear. And, as Benjamin Franklin said in 1775, "Those who give up essential liberty to obtain a little temporary safety, deserve neither liberty nor safety."

We don't *have* to put up with this. When everything is built on lies, it's built on nothing, isn't it? It's a house of cards waiting to fall. I'd like to believe that we as a people *can* handle the truth. But we don't have a free media anymore. They're corporatized and controlled. The proof is in the pudding, when Bush got caught paying off journalists to espouse the administration's line. You don't see much investigative reporting like we had in the old days.

So where do We the People start? I say, by demanding prosecution of the politicians who condoned torture on their lying road into Iraq. And by a new, legitimate investigation into what happened on September 11, a tragedy that's been used ever since to justify all the lies and undermine our democratic freedoms. With President Obama, we voted for a fresh start, but now we've got to hold *his* feet to the fire and get to the bottom of what's happened to our country over these recent decades.

I've not written this book because I get off on talking about conspiracies. I've written it because, until we face the terrible reality of the assassinations and the governmental drug dealing and the stolen elections and the rest—until we look at how, slowly and insipidly, the most venal of men took control of our nation, we don't stand a chance of putting things back on track. I'm not saying that knowledge sets us free, but it does force us to wake up and realize that we're on the brink of losing everything the founders of our country stood for and bequeathed to us.

> *"Single acts of tyranny may be ascribed to the accidental opinion of a day; but a series of oppressions, begun at a distinguished period and pursued unalterably through every change of ministers, too plainly prove a deliberate, systematic plan of reducing [a people] to slavery."*
>
> —Thomas Jefferson: *Rights of British America*, 1774

> *"Cherish . . . the spirit of our people, and keep alive their attention. Do not be too severe upon their errors, but reclaim them by enlightening them."*
>
> —Thomas Jefferson, 1787

Words to live by. Thank you, Mr. Jefferson.

CHAPTER 15

LYME DISEASE: A GERM-WARFARE EXPERIMENT GONE AWRY

THE INCIDENT: Lyme disease was first recognized in 1975, after large numbers of children living near wooded areas of Lyme, Connecticut, were diagnosed with juvenile rheumatoid arthritis. Today, Lyme disease is the most common tick-carried chronic ailment in the Northern Hemisphere, with at least 20,000 more Americans being infected every year.[1]

THE OFFICIAL WORD: Lyme disease may have spread from Europe to the U.S. in the early 1900s, but it wasn't recognized until recently as a distinct illness. The disease is spread mainly by deer ticks that attach to human skin.

MY TAKE: Lyme disease originated at a top-secret germ warfare laboratory located on Plum Island, right across Long Island Sound from the mainland Connecticut town where it was first detected. Our government has gone so far as to admit that experiments with ticks have taken place at Plum Island, but denies any connection to Lyme disease. That's a flat-out lie.

"In vast laboratories in the Ministry of Peace, and in experimental stations, teams of experts are indefatigably at work searching . . . for breeds of disease germs immunized against all possible antibodies."
—George Orwell, 1984

The first I heard about Plum Island was a phone call from a guy named Kenneth King, a Ph.D. expert on bio-warfare and the author of a book called *Germs Gone Wild*. He began by telling me: "There were about 200 high containment germ lab facilities in 2001, and there are now at least 1,356 plus many more off the books. We now have a kind of military-academic-industrial complex that is devoted to hyping the fear of bio-terror so that they will continue to get the funds."

Dr. King went on to say, "They're taking the approach that a terrorist might create some new pathogens, so we'll go ahead and do it ourselves to see if it's possible. Then once we've done it, maybe we can dream up a defense against it." I asked what these labs are actually researching and he said, "A whole bunch of things, some of it very reckless. We have a clear indication that accidents are occurring regularly" and are being concealed from the public. They're doing bio-weapons research masquerading as animal studies—and these germs and viruses (supposedly restricted to animals) are crossing over to humans.[2]

Dr. King recommended that I check out Plum Island, where the lab was started by the Army and U.S. Department of Agriculture (USDA) back in 1954 and since 9/11 has been run by Homeland Security. Even though it's off-limits to the general public, a Connecticut passenger ferry runs right past the facility, making it completely exposed to a potential terrorist attack. For an episode of my truTV show, *Conspiracy Theory*, I figured I'd see how close a former governor might get. That's a story I'll get to momentarily, but first a little history:

Guess who the prime mover was in setting up the germ-warfare lab at Plum Island? A former Nazi scientist named Erich Traub, who'd been brought to the U.S. under top-secret Project PAPERCLIP after World War Two along with about two thousand other German researchers. This was at the start of the Cold War, and the idea was to grab these Dr. Strangelove types before the Soviet Union did. Traub had formerly worked under Heinrich Himmler, who ran Hitler's SS, and he'd been lab chief at a secret Nazi bio-warfare lab looking into animal diseases. That seems to have been the model for Plum Island.[3]

Here's what Justice Department attorney John Loftus had to say in his 1982 book, *The Belarus Secret*: "Even more disturbing are the records of the

Nazi germ warfare scientists who came to America. They experimented with poison ticks dropped from planes to spread rare diseases. I have received some information suggesting that the U.S. tested some of these poison ticks on the Plum Island artillery range off the coast of Connecticut during the early 1950s."[4]

A former director of Plum Island, Dr. Jerry Callis, doesn't believe Lyme disease came from there but admitted this much: "Plum Island experimented with ticks, but never outside of containment. We had a tick colony where you take them and feed them on the virus and breed the ticks to see how many generations it would last, on and on, until it's diluted."[5]

That's what Callis told Michael Christopher Carroll, author of the 2004 book *Lab 257*. Carroll also writes about a document that turned up in the files of ex-Congressman Thomas Downey, a 1978 internal research paper from the USDA titled "African swine fever." Turns out Plum Island was experimenting with Lone Star ticks and the Cayenne tick, feeding them on viruses and testing them on pigs in 1975 and 1976—exactly when Lyme disease first showed up across from the island. At that time, the Lone Star tick was otherwise only found in Texas. Nobody can explain how it's since happened to migrate all across the Eastern seaboard. Along with its cousin, the deer tick, the Lone Star variety is known for spreading Lyme disease.[6]

Think about how little it would take—a single tick infected by our scientists with a man-made disease escaping from the lab, crawling up a blade of island grass, and chowing down on a small bird that flies back and forth from Plum Island to Lyme, Connecticut. That bird carrying the exotic germ lands on a wild deer, where a deer tick also happens to reside. In turn, the disease starts getting passed on to more birds, deer, and mice, and before long to humans.

Homeland Security says on their website "About Plum Island Animal Disease Center" that "the PIADC does not and has not performed research on Lyme disease."[7] Sounds to me like they're hedging a bet. Back when they were doing those experiments, nobody yet *called* it Lyme disease. The website does say that the facility is the only place in the United States where foot-and-mouth disease and Rinderpest viruses can be studied. But I don't get why the Centers for Disease Control openly stated a few years back that a new lab in Texas would be looking at "potential bioterrorism agents"

including anthrax, cholera, desert fever, tularemia, *and* Lyme disease.[8]
Somebody's not coming clean about all this.

In 2003, the Government Accountability Office (GAO) put out a report
about terrorism and Plum Island. They called it a substantial risk that "an
adversary might try to steal pathogens" from the lab and use them against
people or animals in the U.S. A camel pox strain being researched could
be turned into "an agent as threatening as smallpox," and the Venezuelan
equine encephalitis virus they were studying could be "developed into a
human bio-warfare agent." According to the GAO, Plum Island "was not
designed to be a highly secure facility."[9]

In the summer of 2010, I decided to check out Plum Island for myself. I'd
been told about virus outbreaks, infected workers, and contaminated raw
sewage being flushed into Long Island Sound. I'd also heard about a terrorist known as "Lady al Qaeda" (Aafia Siddiqui). When she was captured in
Afghanistan in 2008, she had handwritten notes in her possession about a
"mass-casualty attack" and a list of targets: Statue of Liberty, Empire State
Building, Brooklyn Bridge, Wall Street—and the Plum Island Animal Disease Center.[10]

So at Orient Point, I looked to charter a fishing boat to make the mile-
and-a-half journey out to the 840-acre facility. Well, it took us awhile to
shove off. None of the captains I approached at first would take me, for fear
of losing their licenses. Apparently, Homeland Security had laid down the
law. I couldn't help wondering why they'd care, unless something diabolical
was really going on out there. Finally I wrangled a boat, but the Coast Guard
was following close behind.

My navigator was Jim McCoy, who worked in the bio-level-3 containment area before he blew the whistle on dangerous safety violations. McCoy
said there was basically no security monitoring inside there and, when
he interrupted a meeting of bigwigs one day to say so, it cost him his job.
He said it was "unknown what they're developing" on Plum Island. As we
approached, I asked McCoy what the buildings I could see were all about.

"They used to keep their livestock in pens there," he said. "There was talk
when I worked at the lab that cows that had been injected with a virus got
out and got into the pen with all the other cows, and they had to kill all the
cows. The long building with all the stacks sticking up, that is the bio-con-

tainment laboratory. In the event of a power failure to the island, generators will kick on, and that is something that didn't happen in December of 2002. There was a period of four hours when they lost power from the mainland. During this time, they had no ventilation to the bio-containment area, to ensure that the viruses were being kept under negative pressure. The people were going around putting duct tape on the outside doors on the bio-containment area, trying to contain what might be getting out into the atmosphere. But duct tape doesn't stop viruses."[11]

We were just digging in when we noticed we had company. It followed us all the way around the island. The Coast Guard was on our tail again, and security vehicles were shadowing us on the island. We were as close as we were going to get, and we decided to turn back. I found it curious—here I was, a former governor, a former mayor, a former Navy SEAL with a top-secret security clearance. Yet I can't go on Plum Island; instead, my every move is being shadowed. Where I come from, if you're the one paying the money, that makes you the boss. How come we the people aren't the boss anymore? Aren't we the ones paying the salaries of these people? And yet they deprive us of knowing what they do on this island.

I headed on to Washington, D.C., to see Timothy Bishop, the congressman whose district includes Plum Island. He thought that what I'd encountered was simply "an increased level of security," and had nothing to do with intimidation of fishermen or me. When I told him about Erich Traub and the tick experiments that went on there, Congressman Bishop replied: "If that was what was going on there, and I was convinced that was going on there, that would bother me. But I don't believe that's what's going on there." So he didn't think Lyme disease originated at Plum Island and spread across the water? "I do not accept that." He said they weren't working on animal-borne diseases that could spread to humans and added, "I accept what I've been told."[12]

That was the difference between Representative Bishop and myself—I don't just accept what I've been told. I staked out another guy in Washington, Dr. Roger Breeze, who used to direct the Plum Island lab and is today a chief scientist in the Biological Weapons program. Lo and behold, Dr. Breeze indicated that Plum Island *does* in fact work on animal diseases that can infect humans. (So it seems Congressman Bishop was told a bunch of b-s.) And Breeze let slip that nobody working out there can visit a zoo or a pet store because they might be harboring an infectious disease—and security is on the honor system! That's one for the books!

One thing I'll say for Dr. Breeze: he sure wasn't enthusiastic about a plan to close down Plum Island and move the whole works out to Kansas, right in the heart of our nation's food supply. Wouldn't it be far more devastating if a toxic germ got loose out there in cattle country? "I agree with you," he said, "but the Congress decides what it wants to do."[13] Later I saw Breeze quoted as saying that such a move "goes against every aspect of the safety program for the last 50 years."

No matter. The new National Bio and Agro-Defense Facility (NBAF) in the university town of Manhattan, Kansas, looks like a done deal. We're talking big bucks, folks. This is a $725 million project, expected to be fully operational by 2018. Kansas State University already won a $12 million grant from Homeland Security for being a "Center for Excellence" in animal disease defense.[14]

But why isn't anyone paying attention to a 146-page report issued by the National Research Council in November 2010? Homeland Security's risk assessment report came up way short, it said. Based on Homeland Security's study, the Council estimates that there is a *70 percent chance* that an accidental release of foot-and-mouth disease could happen at some point during the facility's 50-year lifetime. It's highly contagious to cloven-hoofed animals and would cause between $9 billion and $50 billion in economic harm, with the risks and costs potentially being "significantly higher" than that![15]

Think about it: almost 10 percent of our nation's cattle are within a 200-mile radius of the NBAF. In the county around the NBAF alone, there are probably about 400,000 livestock. Professor Tom Manning, who's pretty much a voice-in-the-wilderness fighting to stop this from being built, told us: "It takes so few virus particles to affect animals. The consequences of infection are just horrendous to the whole economy, because this immediately shuts down exports of beef to the rest of the world."[16]

We're talking about being in the middle of "tornado alley," and Manning hasn't seen any data that the door seals will be designed to withstand the pressure drop from a tornado. And he points out that "some of the releases at

Plum Island have been from the failure of the door gaskets." So if a foot-and-mouth outbreak occurred, they'd first do a quarantine, and then slaughter all the affected cattle.

If you ask me, combine sheer greed with our tax dollars and you've got a bio-warfare industry that's out of control. Germ labs like Plum Island pose a bigger threat to our country than any terror group, in my opinion. Consider the toll taken by Lyme disease. It's the fastest-growing infectious illness in America after AIDS, with a cost to society measured in the billions. Anybody who goes outdoors can acquire it, and very often it can be months, years, or even forever that it goes undiagnosed while rendering a person chronically ill and sometimes totally disabled.

With more than 1,300 of these germ labs across the country, that means one of them is probably upwind from *you*. At any moment, you and I could wind up the victims of an attack or a careless accident, something you can't see, hear, or even know about. Do you really want to take that chance? Think about it. And if you have a pet, make sure you check it for ticks.

WHAT SHOULD WE DO NOW?

Have any Lyme disease victims considered a class-action lawsuit against the government, demanding to know the facts about what our defense-and-ag types were working on at Plum Island during the 1970s? Also, where is the outrage about shifting this kind of "dirty work" to the central part of our country where the majority of our food supply comes from? Once upon a time, Kansas was the birthplace of the Populist movement. Maybe it's time to resurrect it!

CHAPTER 16

THE GULF OIL SPILL: A PRE-PLANNED DISASTER?

THE INCIDENT: On April 20, 2010, an explosion rocked an offshore oil platform in the Gulf of Mexico called the Deepwater Horizon, killing eleven workers and gushing nearly five million barrels (205 million gallons) of petroleum into the water before the well was officially sealed on September 19. Marine habitats, as well as the fishing and tourism industries, were devastated by the biggest oil spill in American history.

THE OFFICIAL WORD: A huge bubble of methane gas escaped the well and ignited after shooting up the drill pipe past several seals that were supposed to suppress it. A report issued in January 2011 by a presidential commission blamed the accident largely on poor decisions and other "management failures" by the three companies involved— oil lease-holder British Petroleum (BP), rig owner Transocean, and cement contractor Halliburton. BP lost billions in clean-up costs.

MY TAKE: Certain corporate bigwigs actually made out like bandits in profiting from our all-time worst environmental disaster. The toxic dispersants used to "contain" the spill were already known to cause terrible health problems for workers, dating back to the Exxon Valdez oil spill in 1989. The Gulf spill might even have been allowed to happen as part of a long-range plan to depopulate the region and leave it to the oil companies.

"I hear comments sometimes that large oil companies are greedy companies or don't care, but that is not the case with BP. We care about the small people."

—BP Chairman Carl-Henric Svanberg,
speaking to reporters in Washington, June 16, 2010.

Not long after the toxic oil started spewing into the Gulf, I got a call from a couple of investigative journalists while I was working on a second season of my show, *Conspiracy Theory*, for truTV. Sherri Kane and her partner, Dr. Leonard Horowitz, laid out some startling information—that BP *knew* the rig was going to blow. She'd come across evidence indicating that the whole Gulf Oil disaster was planned.

Some of this sounded crazy, but a lot of conspiracy theories do until you take a deep breath and start looking below the surface of what the media are feeding us. First, there was the fact that Tony Hayward, BP's CEO at the time, had cashed in about one-third of his holdings in the company, 223,288 shares, on March 17, a little over a month before the explosion. He then paid off a mortgage on his family's mansion in Kent, England—and avoided losing more than 423,000 pounds when the BP share price plunged after the spill began (by June, about 30 percent).[1] Coincidence? Maybe, but BP was already having a lot of problems with its exploratory drilling at that particular spot in the Gulf, so surely there was inside speculation on what might happen.

Here was another one Kane and Horowitz had uncovered: on April 14, six days before the explosion, the Management Boards of the Eurex Stock Exchanges decided to introduce an equity option on shares of Transocean Ltd., the biggest offshore drilling contractor in the world and owner of the Deepwater Horizon rig, effective as of April 20! Do the math, folks. This is called a "put-option" among the inside traders, which is like buying insurance on your stock price. In other words, those traders had a full day to dump their "uninsured" stock in Transocean at the highest price possible, before the rest of Wall Street could respond to the explosion. As Kane and Horowitz wrote, they "knew no matter how far the stock dropped, it could be sold at the original 'strike price' (also called the 'put option') anytime before April 20, 2012."[2] Horowitz told me we're talking millions in profits from this. Kane called it "crisis capitalism, actually creating a problem and offering the solution for it."

According to these two journalists, another player was involved, a name that really raised a red flag for me. That was Halliburton, the energy "services" corporation with 50,000 employees and dual headquarters in Houston and Dubai, formerly run by Dick Cheney. Halliburton was in charge of reinforcing the BP oil well with cement. Except, according to an investigator with the presidential commission trying to figure out what happened, Halliburton had used a cement mixture that the company knew was unstable![3] They even *told* BP about one of the four failed tests on cement used to seal the bottom of the well, only days before the well was activated.[4] (Of course, BP and Transocean went ahead and operated the well even after a pressure test indicated it wasn't stable enough to handle the explosive mix of oil and gas.)[5]

Eleven days before the blast, Halliburton just happened to buy a Houston-based company called Boots & Coots in a cash-and-stock deal valued at about $240 million. They'd already done a lot of work with Halliburton during the Iraq War, and Boots was well known for putting its foot down on some of the world's biggest oil and gas fires. Under its contract with BP, the 700-person company would focus "on oil spill prevention and blowout response."[6] Of course, after the merger and the Gulf spill, they made a ton of money.

So the evidence was stacking up that everyone connected with the rig had something to gain from the disaster. My team and I headed for the Gulf coast. An environmental attorney in Florida, Mike Papantonio, revealed more evidence that inside players knew the spill would happen. "It's one thing that they were negligent, but it was far more than that," Papantonio said. "They knew that the blowout preventer had been malfunctioning weeks before it actually blew up. First of all, it could have been prevented with what we call an acoustic switch that ignites the blowout preventer from a distant site. If all things go bad on a rig, if the explosion has taken place and people are jumping over the side to save their lives, somebody from a distant site can hit a button and it will cause the blow-out preventer to engage. In other countries, there's a law that you have to have an acoustic switch. The reason we don't have that in the United States is because lobbyists have thrown so much money into the process, and we had a vice-president, Dick Cheney, who gave the oil industry these huge passes on what they had to comply with as far as regulations. One of those things was the acoustic switch."[7]

In Louisiana I met with Adam Dillon, a former cop who spent ten years in U.S. Army special ops. He was hired by a BP clean-up operation to keep an eye on the spill several weeks after it happened, "like an observer and con-

troller over the entire shoreline operation for Grand Isle," as he put it. Dillon got fired after he says he "found something of grave importance to these
people." What happened was, he ended up flying around in airplanes all day
looking for oil and that's when he realized "the massive scale....For everything we saw on the surface, there was a hundred times more than that *under*
the surface. And a lot of the numbers just were not adding up, with what
we were briefing to the media. I took these pictures to the people with BP
that were supposed to be in charge of constantly updating the information,
and within twenty-four hours of that happening I was gone." First, though,
Dillon's bosses took him into a trailer for an exit interview that was more
like the interrogations he'd run as a police officer and a soldier in Iraq. They
wanted to copy the hard drive off his laptop and all the personal contracts
off his iphone—but they couldn't intimidate him.[8]

I went with Dillon to the BP Command Center, but we weren't allowed
in. Some security guys started hanging out by the deputy sheriff, checking
us out. Dillon told me, "I've been in military installations that did not have
as much security as this place does." But before they made it over to us, a PR
man for BP came around offering to take me for a boat ride into the Gulf
and display how well they were cleaning up the oil. I had my suspicions, but
figured it would be worth the risk.

Our first stop was their own little beach. I said to the guy that there were
obviously areas far worse than this one. "Yes, as the current comes in and
out, you don't ever know," was his reply. So how long could this go on, for
years? "I don't think so, I think mother nature in its time is gonna take care
of it." Sounded like they were positioning themselves to get off the hook by
blaming mother nature. I asked about the stuff they were using to get rid of
the oil. "Some type of dispersant, I'm not sure what the chemical make-up
was." Well, was the dispersant dangerous? "I couldn't tell you," he said. He
couldn't tell me?! This guy must be living under a rock.

The dispersant was called Corexit and what it actually does is break the
slick into little globules, smaller tar-balls of oil that sink to the ocean floor.
The oil is still there, you just can't see it. Back in Grand Isle, everybody
knew how toxic it is. David Arnesen, a local fisherman enlisted to help in
the clean-up, had been splashed with Corexit like a lot of other guys down
here. "I've been out there in the middle of it for the last hundred days and

I've been sick the whole time," Arnesen said. He'd not only had sinus problems and non-stop earaches, but "brown stuff running out of my ears."⁹ And Arnesen was far from the only suffering worker. Many of the first responders had reported shortness of breath, disorientation, fatigue, and a feeling of being drugged.

Yet when I mentioned Corexit to BP's next mouthpiece, he said: "It's an EPA-approved dispersant that's used for situations like this." Okay, but truth be told, on May 20 the EPA had ordered BP to look for less toxic alternatives and later told them to scale back their use of Corexit. After all, the EPA's website listed human health warnings for Corexit 9527A, including avoiding prolonged breathing of vapors and contact with the eyes. I read aloud to the PR man what scientists said, that Corexit contains arsenic, cadmium, chromium, mercury, and cyanide. What's going to happen to the oil when you add those poisons into the mix? The BP spokesman said: "Again I would say that that product, whatever its constituents are, was approved for that use by the EPA." So what about the EPA's recent order, did BP keep on using Corexit? "To the best of my knowledge, no." But witnesses claimed there were still C-130s going out at night, dropping this stuff into the ocean so it couldn't be seen during the day. "I have no knowledge of that.... Throughout this entire process, it's really been one of extremely good cooperation between the EPA and BP."

By the beginning of July 2010, close to two million gallons of Corexit had been sprayed into the Gulf—a chemical mix that's been banned in the U.K.¹⁰ and that our EPA called a chronic and acute health hazard, with a formula pinpointed as a primary cause of the lingering health problems for cleanup workers after the 1989 Exxon Valdez spill in Alaska. In fact, according to an interview aired on CNN, the average lifespan of the Valdez cleanup crew is fifty-one—and most of them are now dead!¹¹

So what's the deal here? Why, when there are far less lethal and more effective alternatives on the market, did BP continue using Corexit? Well, if you check out testimony from a congressional hearing on May 19, 2010, you learn that Corexit is manufactured by the Nalco Holding Company, one of whose board members is Rodney F. Chase, and who also happens to be a former Deputy Group Chief Executive of BP and one of *their* board members for eleven years! He retired from BP in 2003 after thirty-eight years with the company, and two years later joined the board of Nalco![12] Wonder if Mr. Chase still holds shares in both outfits? Because Nalco sure made some big bucks off the clean-up.

The dangers of Corexit go far beyond the water. As the water in the Gulf heats up, it goes through a phase transition that changes it from a liquid to a gas, which is readily absorbed by clouds and released as toxic rain![13] Four times more poisonous than oil, it's spreading through the air like a weapon of mass destruction. And BP gave the federal government one big fat middle finger to the idea of coming up with something different.

Then again, the government's relationship with BP has been cozy for a long time and that hasn't necessarily changed so much since Bush-Cheney left town. Think about this one: back in 2007, when Stephen Chu was still at Stanford, the Lawrence Berkeley National Laboratory that he ran was given $500 million from BP to establish a new bio-science research facility. At the time, Chu announced that now that they were partnered with BP, "we'll have the resources we need to carry out some of the things we want to do in order to help save the world."[14] Today, Chu is Obama's Secretary of Energy, and his department's Undersecretary for Science is none other than Dr. Steven E. Koonin, who was BP's chief scientist between 2004 and early 2009 and worked with Chu to establish the new lab with BP's money.[15]

I started hearing rumors that the Gulf oil spill might even be a lot more sinister than goosing the corporate bottom line. In New Orleans, I made my way to the Ninth Ward, the neighborhood that got destroyed after Katrina when the levees burst. A lawyer and environmental activist named Alfred Webre met me by the levee that's supposed to keep the place from flooding again. He told me: "Our analysis, as shocking as this may seem, is that Katrina was a test or a run-through. The ultimate goal is that this region would become a petroleum servicing area."

Phase one of the depopulation plan, according to Webre, was blowing up the levees. With the destruction of lives and property, the powers-that-be got 150,000 people to leave the state. It was Webre who first clued me in about the huge grant that BP had given to Steven Chu's lab, and the BP exec who joined Chu at the Department of Energy. Webre's take was that it's all about a corporate takeover of our government. He said the Army Corps of Engineers had been co-opted, along with FEMA—both agencies engaged in imple menting the depopulation of New Orleans and the Gulf Coast! They want to get rid of fishermen and ordinary people, the lifeblood of this country.

It turned out the evidence for this possibility was hidden in plain sight. One of my team got hold of an Army Corps document called the Mississippi Coastal Improvements Program. Back in 2007, the Corps first proposed the largest federal buyout in the history of our country, a $1.2 billion plan to purchase 17,000 properties along Mississippi's Gulf Coast and relocate the home-owners. Many of the homes and businesses on this land had been wiped out by Katrina, but a lot of these residents had been trying to rebuild—and they sure didn't like the idea of their communities coming to a permanent end.[16]

We found out this might be part of a much larger $40 billion plan to take the "Coastal Improvements" up into Louisiana. So I arranged a meeting with Dr. Susan Rees, who heads up the Army Corps' Mississippi program. She brought along a PR man, Patrick Robbins. When I asked what was going on down here, Rees nodded and said: "We have developed a comprehensive program where we will relocate people. Some of these houses along the coast have been here for over 150 years." I thought to myself, must not be so easy moving families with roots that deep. I pressed Rees to reveal more. "Obviously after Katrina," she said, "it was sort of a wake-up call that maybe this is not the area we want to spend the rest of our lives in."

I asked, what about corporations and the oil industry, will they be asked to move out too? Robbins chimed in: "No, this is strictly residential." To which Rees added: "This is for the people." Uh huh, so what will happen to fishing down here? "If you look at our program," Robbins said, "in addition to the buyouts, there is a lot of environmental restoration that is proposed." But won't it all get wrecked again if a big storm comes in? "This is a national discussion that has begun," Rees said.

I wondered how they answered a judge who asserted that gross negligence by the Army Corps led to the levee breaks in New Orleans after Katrina? Robbins responded, "That is a national issue for the Corps of Engineers, we can't discuss it." Hmm, I thought they *were* the Corps. Okay, time to go for the jugular. I brought up the multi-billion dollar programs to depopulate the area so they could turn it loose to the oil companies.

"No, we don't have $40 billion, that's incorrect," Rees said. And they didn't anticipate the program ever going to that figure? "I can't answer that question," Robbins said. There seemed to be a lot of important issues they couldn't answer. I showed them an article I'd come across about allocating $40 billion to move people out. "No, that's not true," Robbins said.

"Not yet," Rees said.

"Not yet," Robbins repeated.[17]

First they deny such a figure exists, then Rees lets slip that the $40 billion plot maybe isn't fiction after all. Getting rid of all us undesirables, ruining the environment—all so the oil companies can keep drilling.

They say the well's been capped and everything is going to be fine. Well, here are some of the results so far from the Gulf oil disaster: petroleum is still washing up along the shorelines of all four coastal states, even in areas they'd said were cleaned up. Different teams of independent scientists say that eighty percent of the oil still remains, on the ocean floor and suspended in plumes in the water column. Nearly 7,000 animals have been found dead, but that's only a portion of the affected wildlife.[18]

Meanwhile, remember that $20 billion fund that BP set aside for compensating victims of the spill? Well, 91,000 claims have been filed, and there's been precisely *one* final payment as of January 2011. That's $10 million that went to a business partner of BP's that they won't even name![19] And a federal judge has said that Kenneth Feinberg, the lawyer who's administrating the settlement fund, has to let potential claimants know about his ties to BP. The judge said this "full disclosure. . . . will at least make transparent that it is BP's interests" that Feinberg is representing. By the way, he was the mediator who also oversaw claims by victims of September 11.[20]

WHAT SHOULD WE DO NOW?

Let's start by demanding a real investigation into the behind-the-scenes financial finagling that went on among BP, Transocean, and Halliburton executives, as well as the Corexit connection. Not to mention the $40 billion plan to de-populate the Gulf region. What we really need is for the federal government to take action and put a permanent ban on offshore drilling in fragile areas like the Gulf, and shift their focus to alternative energy sources for powering our future. These oil giants have had control of our destiny for long enough!

EPILOGUE

"TRUTH BEING THAT WHICH IT IS CAN NEVER BE DESTROYED"

I close this book with that quote from Gandhi. Because, after I'm long gone, I believe there needs to be a record that some people thought things other than just the status quo of what the government has put out for us all to believe. I think it's a duty we have to humanity. Even if we're wrong, we're right enough to have an alternate opinion. You may not believe everything that's been written in this book, but it's certainly scary. Even thinking that a lot of it *could* be true is scary enough.

I've covered a lot of ground in *American Conspiracies*, most of it not pleasant to consider. But we can't simply look the other way about the dark side of our history. And there's been no shortage of "dark," over this last half-century or so. After the Second World War where my father, my mother, and millions of others distinguished themselves, in our leaders' well-meaning effort to contain Communists and now terrorists, they unleashed something equally threatening. I guess you could call it power run amuck.

It's not a new element, really. You see it in the plot to assassinate Abraham Lincoln, and the big-money forces that wanted to overthrow Franklin D. Roosevelt. When President Kennedy set out to challenge the status quo on many different fronts, he paid the price with his life. The same was true for the three other great American leaders of the 1960s: Malcolm X, Martin Luther King Jr., and Robert Kennedy. Then Nixon became, in a way, a victim of some of the same forces he'd helped come to power in the Fifties, like the CIA. And the CIA's ultimate experiment in controlling human behavior, Jonestown, followed at the close of the seventies.

With the rise of Reagan—not a face that belongs on Mount Rushmore—we saw the first of the neo-cons' successes in ripping off an election, or at least making sure the incumbent president couldn't properly fulfill his mandate. Dealing drugs, as a crucial element of our political landscape, came to the fore during the Reagan years. I decided not to delve into the right wing's ongoing efforts to sabotage Bill Clinton's presidency, culminating in setting him up to take the fall with Monica Lewinsky, but it's no stretch to add that to the list of conspiracies.

The last chapters in this book are, in my view, the most painful and frightening of all. Since the dawn of the new millennium, our democracy has eroded to the point where it's hanging on by a bare thread. You can trace this directly to the times that George W. Bush and his cronies stole the 2000 and 2004 presidential elections from their opponents, and also to the tragic events of 9/11 that unleashed their assault on our freedoms in the name of protecting them. What's happened to our economy grew out of that, and now we're standing at the abyss looking at the still-in-place plans to end America as we've known it since 1776.

It's about time people understand that, like anything in life, there's more than one side to any story. This book presented an opportunity to tell the other sides to many stories and then say, you be the judge. Look at the big picture over time, and try to do so with clear judgment, without letting your emotions make the determination or your patriotism interfere.

I consider myself a patriot, loyal to the values that built this country that I served as best I could as a Navy SEAL, a mayor and a governor. But I'm outraged when I hear about people like Van Jones being dismissed from his government position for signing a petition calling for an unbiased investigation into 9/11. What is our country turning into, when you can't dissent from any official opinion? That's again why I felt so compelled to write this book, because it's bigger than even these stories—bigger, in that we're not allowed to talk about them, or criticize.

Also, we've got to have a more open government. Why can't those 10,000 documents on Able Danger be released? The old excuse of "national security"? Shouldn't there be some elected board that would say, "Okay, tell us why this falls under national security and we'll make the determination whether it truly does, or is this simply a political cover-up?" When the government starts keeping too many secrets for us, that's a big step on the road to losing more of our liberties.

I'm sure I'll be attacked as the messenger disseminating this information. Well, it's not based on my opinion, folks, it all came from documentation. It was a matter of putting together the pieces that the media no longer pays attention to. So let the powers that be come at me. I'm not backing down. I'll continue to fight against the "special interests" that have taken a choke-hold on our democracy. If you want good government, you've got to have an involved citizenry. You've got to have people willing to tell— and hear—the truth, much as this might shatter our illusions and trouble our sleep.

Do you ever think that maybe our country needs a Truth Commission, to understand the crimes that were committed "in our name" over these recent decades? My hope is that some of you will stand with me in calling for accountability. The only way we can truly move forward is to come to grips with a recent past that's brought us to the brink of losing it all.

Maybe we ought to put ourselves in the position of the little Vietnamese farmer who did nothing but raise his rice. They handed him an AK-47 and in came the powerful United States, and we dropped more armaments on Vietnam than we did in World War II. We threw everything we had at this little rice farmer—and we couldn't beat him, could we? When push came to shove, he outlasted us. Why? Because he had the resolve for freedom. That Vietnamese farmer wanted to self-govern, not be part of colonialism. Maybe we, in the United States, should start viewing our government as colonialists. Now the rest of us, in our own country, are becoming the colony. And somehow, some way, we've got to reclaim our nation.

FURTHER READING

THE LINCOLN ASSASSINATION

Blood on the Moon: The Assassination of Abraham Lincoln, by Edward Steers Jr., The University Press of Kentucky, 2001.

Lincoln and Booth: More Light on the Conspiracy, by H. Donald Winkler, Cumberland House: Nashville, Tennessee, 2003.

FDR AND THE BANKERS

The Plot to Seize the White House, by Jules Archer, Skyhorse Publishing, 2007.

Tragedy and Hope: A History of the World in Our Times, by Carroll Quigley, G.S.G. & Associates, 1975.

THE KENNEDY ASSASSINATION

JFK and the Unspeakable: Why He Died and Why It Matters, by James W. Douglass, Orbis Books, Maryknoll, N.Y., 2008.

Harvey and Lee: How the CIA Framed Oswald, by John Armstrong, Qasar, Ltd., Arlington, Texas, 2003.

Legacy of Secrecy: The Long Shadow of the JFK Assassination, by Lamar Waldron with Thom Hartmann, Counterpoint: Berkeley, 2008. (Also covers later assassinations of the sixties.)

Brothers: The Hidden History of the Kennedy Years, by David Talbot, Free Press, 2007.

The Man Who Knew Too Much, by Dick Russell, Carroll & Graf, revised edition 2003.

On the Trail of the JFK Assassins, by Dick Russell, Skyhorse Publishing, 2008

Not In Your Lifetime, by Anthony Summers, Marlowe & Co., N.Y., 1998 updated edition.

The Assassinations, Ed. by James DiEugenio and Lisa Pease, Feral House, Los Angeles, 2003. (Also covers other assassinations of the sixties.)

THE ASSASSINATION OF MALCOLM X

The Judas Factor: The Plot to Kill Malcolm X, by Karl Evanzz, Thunder's Mouth Press, N.Y., 1992.

Conspiracys: Unravelling the Assassination of Malcolm X, by Baba Zak A. Kondo, Nubia Press, Washington, D.C., 1993.

THE ASSASSINATION OF MARTIN LUTHER KING

An Act of State: The Execution of Martin Luther King, by William F. Pepper, Verso, London, 2008 updated edition.

Truth at Last: The Untold Story Behind James Earl Ray and the Assassination of Martin Luther King Jr., by John Larry Ray and Lyndon Barsten, The Lyons Press, Guilford, Ct., 2008.

The Martin Luther King Assassination: New Revelations on the Conspiracy and Cover-Up, 1968–1991, by Dr. Philip H. Melanson, Shapolsky Publishers, N.Y., 1991 updated version.

THE ROBERT KENNEDY ASSASSINATION

Who Killed Bobby?: The Unsolved Murder of Robert F. Kennedy, by Shane O'Sullivan, Union Square Press, N.Y. & London, 2008.

The Robert F. Kennedy Assassination: New Revelations on the Conspiracy and Cover-Up, by Philip H. Melanson, Shapolsky Publishers, N.Y., 1991.

The Assassination of Robert F. Kennedy, by William W. Turner and Jonn G. Christian, Random House, N.Y., 1978.

WATERGATE REVISITED

The Arrogance of Power: The Secret World of Richard Nixon, by Anthony Summers with Robbyn Swan, Viking, 2000.

Secret Agenda: Watergate, Deep Throat and the CIA, by Jim Hougan, Random House, 1984.

JONESTOWN AND CIA MIND CONTROL

Was Jonestown a CIA Medical Experiment?: A Review of the Evidence, by Michael Meiers, Studies in American Religion, Vol. 35.

The Search for the "Manchurian Candidate": The CIA and Mind Control, by John Marks, Norton PB, N.Y., 1991.

1980 ELECTION

October Surprise, by Barbara Honegger, Tudor Publishing, N.Y. & L.A., 1989.

October Surprise: America's Hostages in Iran and the Election of Ronald Reagan, by Gary Sick, Crown Publishers, 1991.

GOVERNMENT AND DRUG DEALING

Dark Alliance: The CIA, the Contras and the Crack Cocaine Explosion, by Gary Webb, Seven Stories Press, 2003 (second edition).

Cocaine Politics: Drugs, Armies and the CIA in Central America, by Peter Dale Scott and Jonathan Marshall, University of California Press, 1998.

Drugs, Oil and War: The United States in Afghanistan, Colombia, and Indochina, by Peter Dale Scott, Rauman and Littlefield, 2003.

Powderburns: Cocaine, Contras and the Drug War, by Celerino Castillo and Dave Harmon, Sundial, 1994.

The Big White Lie: The Deep Cover Operation That Exposed the CIA Sabotage of the Drug War: An Undercover Odyssey, by Michael Levine, Thunder's Mouth Press, 1994.

BUSH AND STOLEN ELECTIONS

Loser Take All: Election Fraud and the Subversion of Democracy, 2000–2008, Edited by Mark Crispin Miller, Ig Publishing, Brooklyn, N.Y., 2008.

Fooled Again: The Real Case for Electoral Reform, by Mark Crispin Miller, Basic Books, 2007 paperback.

The Best Democracy Money Can Buy, by Greg Palast, Plume Book, 2003 revised American edition.

SEPTEMBER 11

The New Pearl Harbor Revisited: 9/11, the Cover-Up and the Exposé, by David Ray Griffin, Olive Branch Press, Northampton, MA., 2008.

9/11 Contradictions: An Open Letter to Congress and the Press, by David Ray Griffin, Olive Branch Press, 2008.

The Road to 9/11: Wealth, Empire, and the Future of America, by Peter Dale Scott, University of California Press, 2007. (Includes material related to Continuity of Government plans.)

THE WALL STREET CONSPIRACY

The Creature from Jekyll Island: A Second Look at the Federal Reserve, by G. Edward Griffin, American Media Fourth Edition, 2002.

Secrets of the Temple: How the Federal Reserve Runs the Country, by William Greider, Simon & Schuster, 1989.

The Shock Doctrine: The Rise of Disaster Capitalism, by Naomi Klein, Metropolitan Books, 2007.

The Return of Depression Economics and the Crisis of 2008, by Paul Krugman, Norton, paperback 2009.

The Ascent of Money: A Financial History of the World, by Niall Ferguson, Penguin, 2008.

THE SECRET PLANS TO END AMERICAN DEMOCRACY

Family of Secrets: The Bush Dynasty, the Powerful Forces that Put it in the White House, and What Their Influence Means for America, by Russ Baker, Bloomsbury Press, 2009.

American Dynasty: Aristocracy, Fortune, and the Politics of Deceit in the House of Bush, by Kevin Phillips, Viking, 2004.

Blackwater: The Rise of the World's Most Powerful Mercenary Army, by Jeremy Scahill Nation Books, 2008 revised and updated edition.

The End of America: A Letter of Warning to a Young Patriot, by Naomi Wolf, Chelsea Green Publishing, 2007 paperback edition.

LYME DISEASE: A GERM-WARFARE EXPERIMENT GONE AWRY

Carroll, Michael Christopher. *Lab 257: The Disturbing Story of the Government's Secret Germ Laboratory.* New York: Harper Collins, 2005.

King, Kenneth. *Germs Gone Wild: How the Unchecked Development of Domestic Bio-Defense Threatens America.* New York: Pegasus, 2010.

NOTES

Chapter One

1 Lincoln attending *Marble Heart*: *Lincoln and Booth*, by H. Donald Winkler, Cumberland House: Nashville, Tennessee, 2003, p. 38.

2 Plot in Baltimore: *Blood on the Moon*, by Edward Steers Jr., University Press of Kentucky, 2005 paperback edition, pp. 17–18.

3 Biological warfare plot: Ibid., pp. 47–48.

4 Dahlgren papers: Ibid., p. 45.

5 Booth and Knights: Winkler, p. 44.

6 Early plots: Ibid., pp. 50–53.

7 No more kidnapping: Steers.

8 Booth meeting conspirators: Steers, pp. 110–112; Winkler, p. 99.

9 Drunk customer to Booth: Winkler, p. 102.

10 "highest sources in Washington": Ibid., p. 95.

11 Booth and assassination: Ibid., pp. 112–114.

12 Carter, Reagan, and Mudd: Ibid., p. 127.

13 Mudd responsible for coconspirators: Ibid., p. 149.

14 Atzerodt on Booth and Mudd: Ibid., p. 149.

15 Mudd later years: Ibid., p. 138.

16 Corbett on shooting Booth: Steers, p. 204.

17 *Unsolved Mysteries* theory: Ibid., p. 246, 250.

18 Bates's story: Ibid., pp. 246–250.

19 Booth body ID: Ibid., pp. 265–267.

20 Stanton's dragnet: Winkler,

21 Stanton prior knowledge: Winkler, p. 120–121.

22 Booth diary: Ibid., pp. 289–292.

23 Congressman Conness: Ibid., pp. 290–292.

24 John Surratt: Ibid., pp. 235–248.

25 *Come Retribution* theory: Ibid., p. 14.

26 Atzerodt lost confession: "George Atzerodt's Lost Confession," http://home.att.net/~rjnorton/Lincoln82.html.

27 Other theories on assassination: Ibid., Lincoln74.html.

Chapter Two

1 Basis of chapter: *The Plot to Seize the White House*, by Jules Archer, Hawthorne Books, New York, 1973. Except where otherwise noted, all material quoted is from this book.

2 American Liberty League: Archer, p. 160.

3 Quigley on Round Table Groups: *Tragedy and Hope*, by Carroll Quigley, The MacMillan Co., New York, 1966, p. 950.

4 Cecil Rhodes: Quote in Griffin, p. 271, citing *The Anglo-American Establishment: From Rhodes to Cliveden*, Books in Focus, New York, 1981, pp. ix, 36.

5 Front for Morgan: *Tragedy and Hope*, pp. 951–952.

6 Quigley on goal of global financiers: *Tragedy and Hope*, p. 324.

7 Media: Ibid., p. 953.

8 Quigley on suppression: letters cited in *The Creature from Jekyll Island*, by G. Edward Griffin, American Media, Westlake Village, California, 24th printing May 2009,

pp. 268–269. Griffin notes that the letters were first published in Summer 1976 issue of *Conspiracy Digest*, published by Peter McAlpine.

9 Rockefeller quote: *The Bilderberg Group*, by Daniel Estulin, TrineDay, 2009, North American Union Edition, p. 61.

10 Prescott Bush and plot: http://carnival-of-anarchy.blogspot.com/2008/01/smedley-butler-and-business-plot.html; "BBC: Bush's Grandfather Planned Fascist Coup in America," by Paul Joseph Watson, July 24, 2007, http://prisonplanet.com.

11 Walker and money men: *American Dynasty*, by Kevin Phillips, Viking, New York, 2004, p. 179.

12 "part of this cabal": Ibid., p. 180.

13 Union Banking/Thyssen: Ibid., p. 180.

14 Brown Brothers Harriman merger: Ibid., p. 184.

15 Relationships with Nazis: Ibid., p. 192.

16 Prescott Bush and Nazis: Ibid., pp. 38–39.

17 "German embroilments": Ibid., p. 39.

18 Butler on war: Archer, p. 220.

Chapter Three

1 "Magic bullet": There are numerous sources on this, but one good one is *Not In Your Lifetime*, by Anthony Summers, updated edition, Marlowe & Co., New York, 1998, pp. 31–33.

2 Cyril Wecht: "Why Did Feds Persecute Celebrity Expert Cyril Wecht? Who's Next," by Andrew Kreig, www.huffingtonpost.com, October 18, 2009.

3 Humes burning autopsy notes: *On the Trail of the JFK Assassins*, by Dick Russell, Skyhorse Publishing, 2008, p. 280 (interview with Douglas Horne).

4 Zapruder film to CIA lab: Ibid., p. 293.

5 Oswald prints on rifle: Summers, pp. 44–45.

6 LBJ on Oswald: Telephone recordings of Johnson White House, http://wwww.theatlantic.com/doc/200406/holland.

7 Nixon on Warren Commission: Nixon tapes, http://news.bbc.co.uk/2/hi/americas/1848157.stm.

8 Hoover on assassination: Summers, p. 376.

9 HaleBoggs: http://www.texasmonthly.com/preview/1998-11-01.feature23.

10 Oswald as FBI informant: *The Man Who Knew Too Much*, by Dick Russell, Carroll & Graf, New York, 1992, p. 68.

11 Oswald at Stripling: *Harvey and Lee*, pp. 98–99. Dick Russell also interviewed Frank Kudlaty and received verification for this story.

12 Hoover imposter memo: FBI File No. 105–82555, addressed to: Office of Security, Department of State.

13 Slawson quote: *New York Times*, February 23, 1975.

14 Harvey and Lee name shifts: Russell, *On the Trail* pp. 127–128.

15 Robert Oswald: Ibid., p. 128.

16 Harvey and Lee: Ibid., pp. 128–129.

17 Height discrepancies: *Khrushchev Killed Kennedy* by Michael H.B. Eddowes (Dallas, TX, self-published, 1975), pp. 18, 96–97.

18 Groody story: told to author Jim Marrs.

19 Oswald burial: Russell, *On the Trail* pp. 130–132.

20 Burroughs on two Oswalds in theater: *JFK and the Unspeakable*, by James W. Douglass, Orbis Books, Maryknoll, N.Y., 2008, pp. 291–93.

21 Bernard Haire on two Oswalds: Ibid., p. 293.

22 Media and cover-up: This story is all drawn from Russell, *On the Trail*, pp. 34–40, "The Media, the CIA, and the Cover-up."

23 Media and *JFK* film: Fairness and Accuracy in Reporting (FAIR) report.

Chapter Four

1 Gordon Parks, "I was a Zombie Then—Like All [Black] Muslims, I Was Hypnotized," *Life* magazine, March 5, 1965, p. 28.

2 Sources for the chapter: I'm drawing heavily on an excellent article by James W. Douglass ("The Murder and Martyrdom of Malcolm X"), in a book called *The Assassinations* that I gave a cover endorsement for when it came out in 2003. Douglass summarizes the investigations recounted in several other books: *The Judas Factor*, by Karl Evanzz (1992), *Conspiracys: Unravelling the Assassination of Malcolm X*, by Baba Zak A. Kondo (1993), and the much earlier book by Louis E. Lomax, *To Kill a Black Man* (1968). Lomax was working on a documentary film alleging that the American intelligence community—specifically the FBI and CIA—had a hand in Malcolm X's assassination, when he died after the brakes on his car suddenly failed while he was driving to the studio on July 31, 1970.

3 FBI watching Malcolm X in prison: March 16, 1954, FBI report, captioned MALCOLM K. LITTLE, cited in *Conspiracys: Unravelling the Assassination of Malcolm X*, by Zak A. Kondo, Nubia Press, Washington, D.C., 1993.

4 Police inspector comment: *The Autobiography of Malcolm X*, as told to Alex Haley, Ballantine Books, New York, 1973, p. 309.

5 "neutralizing Malcolm X": FBI HQ file on Elijah Muhammad; FBI NY file on Malcolm X, cited by Karl Evanzz, *The Judas Factor: The Plot to Kill Malcolm X*, Thunder's Mouth Press, N.Y., 1992, p. 186.

6 John Ali background: "The Murder and Martyrdom of Malcolm X," by James W. Douglass, in *The Assassinations*, edited by Jim DiEugenio and Lisa Pease, Feral House, 2003, pp. 378–379.

7 "dark night of social disruption": Evanzz. pp. 226–227.

8 Ulasewicz: Douglass, p. 390.

9 Roberts with Malcolm X: Ibid., pp. 390–391.

10 Assassins come together: Ibid., p. 392.

11 John Ali on "life in danger": Evanzz, pp. 247–48.

12 Malcolm X on "resources": *Ghosts in Our Blood*, by Jan Carew, Lawrence Hill Books, Chicago, 1994, p. 39.

13 CIA report/knowledge: Evanzz, p. 254.

14 Hoover on "social revolution": Evanzz, p. 258.

15 John Lewis: *Walking with the Wind*, by John Lewis, Simon & Schuster, N.Y., 1998, p. 288.

16 Louis Farrakhan: Douglass, p. 400.

17 "bad rap sheet": *The Death and Life of Malcolm X*, by Peter Goldman, University of Illinois Press, 1979 second edition, p. 261.

18 French knowledge: Douglass, p. 404, citing Eric Norden, "The Murder of Malcolm X," *The Realist*, February 1967, p. 12.

19 Firebombing of house: Douglass, p. 406.

20 "dry run": Douglass, p. 407.

21 "marked for death": Haley, p. 428; Evanzz, p. 293.

22 Assassination day: Douglass, citing numerous sources, pp. 411–415.

23 Trial and Hayer confession: Douglass, p. 413.

24 Background on suspects: Appendix to Kondo, pp. 203–04.

25 Ali-Hayer meeting:" Douglass, p. 411. The author notes, "Hayer denied this to Peter Goldman, per Goldman p. 432."

26 Ameer death: Evanzz, pp. 314–15.

Chapter Five

1 King family and Ray: "Dexter King visits James Earl Ray in prison; says he believes Ray is innocent," *Jet*, April 14, 1997.

2 Civil trial: http://www.maryferrell.org/wiki/index.php/Martin_Luther_King_Assassination.

3 FBI and King: Final Report of the Select Committee to Study Government Operations with Respect to Intelligence Activities, Book III, cited in *Legacy of Secrecy*, p. 550.

4 Hoover's logs: "The Martin Luther King Conspiracy Exposed in Memphis," by Jim Douglass, Spring 2000, *Probe Magazine*, at http://www.ratical.org/ratville/JFRK/MLKconExp.html.

5 Brown on evidence: Ibid.

6 Shot from bushes: Ibid.

7 Judge Joe Brown: "A King-Sized Conspiracy," by Dick Russell, *High Times* magazine, 1999, http://www.dickrussell.org/articles/king.htm.

8 Justice Department memo: *Legacy of Secrecy*, by Lamar Waldron with Thom Hartmann (Counterpoint: Berkeley, Ca., 2008), p. 513.

9 Ray in New Orleans: Ibid., p. 541.

10 Sartor killed: Ibid., p. 514.

11 Jowers and Liberto: "The Martin Luther King Conspiracy Exposed in Memphis," op. cit.

12 Jowers and rifle: Ibid., portions also recounted in "A King-Sized Conspiracy," Russell.

13 Ibid., "… exposed in Memphis." Testimony of William Hamblin. Ray's attorney, William Pepper, believed Hamblin, rather than Jowers's account.

14 Liberto witnesses: Ibid., citing testimony of Lavada Addison and her son Nathan Whitlock.

15 Ibid.

16 McCollough: *An Act of State*, by William F. Pepper Verso, 2008 edition, pp. 73–74.

17 Army intelligence: William F. Pepper talk on his book, *An Act of State*, in San Francisco, Feb. 4, 2003. http://www.ratical.org/ratville/JFK/WFP020403.html.

18 Pepper quote: Ibid.

19 Gelber lead: FBI Headquarters file, Murkin King Section 10; Birmingham to director with copies to Memphis, L.A., Mobile/response to Miami report of April 6, 1964.

20 Hoover edict: FBI Headquarters File, Murkin King Section 10, director to SAC's in Birmingham, Memphis, and Los Angeles. Order to hold ID checks and leads.

21 Ray phone call: *Legacy of Secrecy*, p. 604.

22 Judge Gelber later stated that Dade County state attorney files on the Milteer case—literally thousands of pages—had somehow disappeared from a warehouse in Miami.

23 Ray brother and Stoner: Ibid., p. 697.

24 William Bradford Huie, *He Slew the Dreamer*, New York: Delacorte Press, 1970, pp. 91–97. (The original title for

Huie's book was *They Slew the Dreamer*—until he decided to go with the Ray-as-lone-assassin scenario).

25 Ray and hypnosis: *Legacy of Secrecy*, p. 559.

26 Von Koss and intelligence work: Letter from Bernard Fensterwald Jr. to Harry Arons, Association to Advance Ethical Hypnosis, April 29, 1970, in Committee to Investigate Assassination archives, Washington, D.C.

27 Ray brother: *Legacy of Secrecy*, p. 561.

28 Ray's mental condition: *Truth At Last*, by John Larry Ray and Lyndon Barsten, Lyons Press, Guilford, Ct., 2008, pp. 23 and 27.

29 General's response: Ibid., p. 26.

30 Kimble and McGill: Ibid., pp. 84–85.

31 Ray phrases: Ibid., p. 104.

Chapter Six

1 Number of shots: "40 Years after RFK's Death, Questions Linger," *San Francisco Chronicle*, June 3, 2008; Van Praag interview on blip.tv (viewable on Internet).

2 Bullet locations: *Chronicle*, ibid. Van Praag co-wrote a book about the assassination called *An Open and Shut Case*.

3 Noguchi finding: Ibid.

4 District Attorney's office on ballistics: *Legacy of Secrecy*, Waldron and Hartmann, p. 684.

5 Cesar statements to police: Article by Lisa Pease in *Probe*, March–April 1998, Vol. 5, No. 3.

6 Security guard: Ibid.

7 H&R 922: Van Praag interview on blip.tv.

8 Another gunman: *Legacy of Secrecy*, p. 640.

9 Polka dot dress lady: *Legacy of Secrecy*, p. 634.

10 Sharaga report: *The Assassination of Robert Kennedy*, by William W. Turner and Jonn G. Christian, Random House: New York, 1978, p. 76.

11 Sirhan on girl: Ibid., p. 193, quoting interview with Turner.

12 Pease article.

13 LAPD and CIA: *Legacy of Secrecy*, p. 678, quoting William Turner.

14 Pena and Hernandez: Article by Pease.

15 Missing evidence: *Legacy of Secrecy*, p. 685.

16 Philip Melanson quoted on missing evidence: Ibid.

17 Sirhan files: *Legacy of Secrecy*, p. 650.

18 Sirhan and gun: Ibid., pp. 652–653.

19 Sirhan sightings: *Legacy of Secrecy*, p. 659.

20 Estabrooks article: "To 'Sleep'; Perchance to Kill?", *Providence Evening Bulletin*, May 13, 1968 (Colgate University Archives).

21 CIA assassin program: *The Man Who Knew Too Much*, by Dick Russell, Carroll & Graf, N.Y., 1972, p. 380.

22 CIA and hypnosis: *The Search for the "Manchurian Candidate,"* by John Marks, W.W. Norton, N.Y., 1991, p. 202.

23 Spiegel on Sirhan/hypnosis: "Hypnosis: Flight from Reason or Floating Toward Bethlehem?", by Dick Russell, *Harper's Weekly*, June 28, 1976.

24 Teletype: *Who Killed Bobby?*, by Shane O'Sullivan, Union Square Press, N.Y./London, 2008, p. 381.

25 Diamond on Sirhan: Ibid., p. 382.

26 Simson-Kallas on Sirhan: Ibid., p. 385.

27 Sirhan to Simson-Kallas: Ibid., p. 384.

28 FBI agent on programming: *R.F.K. Must Die*, by Robert Kaiser, Overlook Press 2008 edition, pp. 355–356, also posted

on www.maryferrell.org. Today, Kaiser writes in the epilogue to a new edition of his book that he believes "the Manchurian Candidate aspect" to be what happened. "I hold it now, maybe ninety-five percent certainty," Kaiser says, "that he really didn't remember shooting Robert Kennedy, that he probably killed Kennedy in a trance and was programmed to forget that he'd done it, and programmed to forget the names and identities of others who might have helped him do it."

29 Spiegel quote: Ibid., p. 392.

30 Bryan and Sirhan: Ibid., pp. 398–400.

31 William Kroger: *The Robert F. Kennedy Assassination*, by Philip H. Melanson, Shapolsky, N.Y., 1991, p. 208.

32 Kroger interviews with Russell: Personal conversation (the interviews have not been published).

33 Selection of attorneys: *Legacy of Secrecy*, pp. 663–664.

34 Melanson on trial: Ibid., p. 656.

35 Sirhan on Cooper: told to author Dan Moldea.

36 Sirhan to Cooper: Ibid., p. 682.

37 Sirhan and money: Ibid., p. 652.

38 Sirhan and mob ties: Ibid., p. 651.

39 Mob involvement: Ibid., p. 671–672.

40 Morales: Ibid., p. 676.

41 Pepper and regression therapy: *Who Killed Bobby?*, p. 492.

Chapter Seven

1 Most of the material in this chapter was developed by my collaborator, Dick Russell, over the course of 20 years of research.

2 Liddy on Watergate: "G. Gordon Liddy: Voice of Unreason," *Independent*, November 22, 2004, http://mediamatters.org/items/2 00411230004?offset=20&show-1.

3 Haldeman on Nixon and Bay of Pigs: *The Ends of Power*, by H.R. Haldeman with Joseph DiMona, Dell, New York, 1978, pp. 67–70.

4 Haldeman-Ehrlichman conversation: As recounted by Haldeman in his memoir.

5 Ehrlichman and documents: Ibid., pp. 53–54.

6 First Anderson column on plots: January 18, 1971, syndicated. It's also believed that Nixon hated Anderson because of a story the columnist broke just before the 1960 election, about a secret loan from Howard Hughes to Nixon's brother Donald.

7 Maheu and O'Brien: One matter that Nixon would obviously have been concerned about was O'Brien's possible knowledge of a $100,000 illegal campaign contribution that had come to him from Hughes, using Nixon's best friend "Bebe" Rebozo as the go-between.

8 Anderson second column on Rosselli: February 23, 1971, in the *Washington Post*: "Castro Stalker Worked for the CIA."

9 Maheu/Mitchell meeting: *The Arrogance of Power*, by Anthony Summers with Robbyn Swan, Viking, N.Y., 2000, p. 197.

10 Hunt investigating JFK assassination: 1975 interview given by Hunt.

11 Ellsberg–Frances FitzGerald friendship: Recounted by Jim Hougan in the book, *Secret Agenda*.

12 Nixon-Helms conversation: "Richard Nixon's Greatest Cover-Up," by Don Fulsom, http://crimemagazine.com/03/richardnixon,1014.htm (audiotape of Nixon-Helms-Ehrlichman session is available on www.nixontapes.org). See also, *The Arrogance of Power* by Anthony Summers, Viking, 2000, pp. 176–178.

13 McCord and anti-Castro operations: Enrique (Harry) Ruiz-Williams was a Bay of Pigs veteran who later became a key figure in AM/WORLD or C-Day, a plan to overthrow Castro and take back the island, scheduled for November 1963. Williams has said that both McCord and Hunt became his CIA "handlers" that year. *The Fish Is Red*, a history of the exile movement, reported that "Hunt became Williams's link to the Langley headquarters, while McCord liaisoned with brigade veterans at Fort Jackson." Tad Szulc's biography of Hunt (*Compulsive Spy*) described how Hunt and McCord each played a role in "Second Naval Guerrilla," another name for the proposed Cuban invasion in 1963. Ruiz-Williams recalled, "Both of them said to call [them] Don Eduardo. Both Hunt and McCord." That was a pattern, as *Secret Agenda* pointed out, that would repeat itself during Watergate, when "McCord would be arrested and booked under a Hunt alias, 'Edward Martin,' producing a phony ID on which the birthdate was identical with Howard Hunt's own." McCord's phony ID, issued by the CIA to Hunt, disappeared immediately after McCord got fingerprinted by Washington police.

14 Sturgis on break-in: *True* magazine, August 1974, p. 74.

15 McCord fire and CIA contract agent: A former official with the FBI, Lee Pennington was also a director of the ultraconservative American Security Council.

16 Nixon on Hunt as "double agent": *Memoirs*, by Richard Nixon, Grossett & Dunlap, N.Y., 1978, pp. 643–44.

17 Nixon on Hunt "scab": www.ajweberman. com/tape.htm (New Nixon Tapes).

18 *Los Angeles Star* on Boggs: November 22, 1973.

19 Gray and Hunt files: "Dirty Politics— Nixon, Watergate, and the JFK Assassination," http://mtracy9.tripod. com/kennedy.html.

20 FBI memo about Ford informing on Warren Commission: Written to Hoover from Cartha "Deke" DeLoach, disclosed in 1991 by the *Washington Post*.

21 FBI probing Hunt's residence: Author Tad Szulc.

22 McCord to Caulfield: Letter of Dec. 21, 1972, http://educationforum.ipbhost. com/index.php?showtopic=4558.

23 Helms destroying documents: *Legacy of Secrecy*, by Lamar Waldron with Thom Hartmann, Counterpoint, Berkeley, 2008, p. 724.

24 Morgan on assassination: Interview with Dick Russell, 1976.

25 McCord helping Fensterwald: Article in *Los Angeles Times*.

26 Jaworski and CIA conduit: From *Wall Street to Watergate*: North American Conference on Latin America, November 1973, p. 30.

27 Theft of Hughes documents: "The Great Hughes Heist," by Michael Drosnin, *New Times Magazine*, January 21, 1977.

28 Hunt claims on assassination: "Blowing Smoke From the Grave: E. Howard Hunt and the JFK Assassination," by Don Fulsom, www.crimemagazine.com/07/ howard-hunt_jfk-assassination,0606-7. htm citing article in *Rolling Stone*.

Chapter Eight

1 Lyman Kirkpatrick CIA memorandum: *Foreign and Military Intelligence, Book I, Final Report of the Select Committee to Study Governmental Operations with Respect to*

Intelligence Activities, U.S. Senate (April 26, 1976), p. 390.

2 Holsinger quote: "Slain Congressman to be Honored," *San Mateo (Calif.) Daily Journal*, November 12, 2008.

3 Writers looking into "broader conspiracy": One is Jim Hougan, author of the Watergate classic, *Secret Agenda*, among other books. Hougan wrote a long article, "The Secret Life of Jim Jones: A Parapolitical Fugue," that came out in a British publication (*Lobster 37*) in Summer 1999. More light was shed by Peter Levenda, in volume two of his *Sinister Forces* series in 2006. And for those who really want to dig deep into the muddy waters, there's *Was Jonestown a CIA Medical Experiment?*, by Michael Meiers, in *Studies in American Religion*, Volume 35 (1988).

4 Temple assets: John Judge, in a piece about "The Jonestown Banks" (August 1982) wondered: "Was the Jonestown empire built with the same dirty money that came from the Banco Ambrosiano, the Nugan Hand Bank and other international conduits of cash for the men who trade in narcotics, espionage, human flesh and death?"

5 Body counts: *Sinister Forces, Book Two: A Warm Gun*, by Peter Levenda, TrineDay, Waterville, Oregon, 2006, p. 223.

6 Cyanide: Ibid., p. 224.

7 Disappearing samples: "The Secret Life of Jim Jones: A Parapolitical Fugue," by Jim Hougan, *Lobster 37*, Summer 1999. Also on www.jimhougan.com.

8 Handling of bodies: *New England Journal of Medicine*, "Law-Medicine Notes: The Guyana Mass Suicides: Medicolegal Re-evaluation," by William J. Curran, J.D., L.L.M., S.M. Hyg., June 7, 1979, cited in Hougan.

9 Removal of medical tags: *Newsweek*, December 4, 1978. Robert Pastor denied the article's account.

10 Bracelets and bodies: *Sinister Forces*, p. 224.

11 Survivors treated at Langley-Porter: Hougan article.

12 Langley-Porter research: *Mind Wars*, by Ron McRae, St. Martin's Press, 1984, p. 136.

13 Ryan letter to CIA: October 10, 1978. San Francisco Mayor Moscone was reportedly involved in funding of the rehab program.

14 Ryan and Vacaville research: *Sinister Forces*, p. 207.

15 Ryan's investigation: Researcher John Judge was the first to suggest this, in his 1985 article, "The Black Hole of Guyana" (http://www.ratical.org/ratville/JFK/JohnJudge/Jonestown.html).

16 Jones as informant: Hougan article.

17 Jones-Mitrione relationship: *Sinister Forces*, p. 176.

18 Jones and 201 file: Hougan article.

19 Jones and Cuba: Hougan article.

20 Two Jones passports: Hougan article.

21 Jones-Mitrione socializing: Autobiographical fragment found at Jonestown.

22 Jones and Mitrione in Brazil: Ibid.

23 "suspected CIA conduit" Invesco: Hougan writes: "The firm was owned and operated by men and women whose connections to criminals such as Ronald Biggs [involved in England's Great Train Robbery] and spooks like Fernand Legros—and to gangster-spooks such as Christian David—deserve serious scrutiny."

24 Jones's interest in occult: Hougan article.

25 Temple alliances: Ibid.

26 "target populations": *Individual Rights and the Government's Role in Behavior*

Modification, 1974 Government Printing Office report.

27 Jones and Guyana; Reverend Smith: *Sinister Forces*, p. 210.

28 State Department officer quote: Ibid., p. 214 (Frank Tunniminia).

29 Larry Layton and father: *Sinister Forces*, p. 195.

30 Dwyer: Hougan article.

31 James Adkins: e-mail from Hougan to Dick Russell, June 30, 2009.

32 Zombie-like killers: *White Night*, by John Peer Nugent, Rawson/Wade Publishers, 1979, p. 197.

33 Body not matching Jones: Michael Meiers.

34 Questions about Jones's identification: "The Black Hole of Guyana," by John Judge.

35 Holsinger on Jonestown: www. friendsofliberty.com.

36 Survivors' lawsuit: *The Jonestown Genocide*, by Robert Sterling, online page.

37 Ryan children lawsuit: *Sinister Forces*, p. 227.

38 Gritz on Jonestown and MK-ULTRA: interview with Adam Parfrey.

39 Sign at Jonestown: Hougan article.

Chapter Nine

1 Casey approach: cited in "The Case for a Conspiracy," by Joseph E. Persico, *New York Times Book Review*, December 22, 1991.

2 Hashemi and Carter: "The Ladies' Room Secrets," *The Consortium for Independent News*, by Robert Parry.

3 July meeting: *Defrauding America*, p. 202, citing a CIA informant to author Stich.

4 Bribes: Stich, p. 196.

5 Bani-Sadr on secret deal: First described it in a letter to the U.S. Congress (December 17, 1992) identifying Reza Passendideh as the Khomeini nephew.

6 Bani-Sadr letter: cited in "October Surprise: Time for Truth? Part 2," by Robert Parry, *Consortium News*, 1997.

7 Carter, hostages, and Reagan leak: "The Election Story of the Decade," by Gary Sick, *New York Times*, April 15, 1991.

8 $3 million deposit: "The Ladies' Room Secrets."

9 Bush's whereabouts: Stich, p. 201.

10 Bush airplanes, Ibid., p. 203.

11 Gary Sick on Bush in Paris: "The Election Story of the Decade."

12 Ben-Menashe book: Ibid., p. 199.

13 Brenneke testimony: Ibid., p. 200.

14 Russian investigation: "Russia's PM & October Surprise," by Robert Parry, *The Consortium*, May 17, 1999.

15 Gates and Iran/Iraq: "The Secret World of Robert Gates," by Robert Parry, www. consortiumnews.com/2006/110906. html. The NSC's Howard Teicher submitted the affidavit in federal court in Miami in 1995.

16 Bush at CIA: Cited in Peter Dale Scott, "Deep Events and the CIA's Global Drug Connection," www.globalresearch.ca.

17 Iran's shift: Sick article.

18 Israeli shipment: Ibid.

19 Banker's claim: Robert Denis and Ernest Backes, *Revelation$*, Les Arénes Publishers, 2001. Backes said copies of his files also went to the National French Assembly.

20 Bani-Sadr on documents: interview with Barbara Honnegger, cited at Wikipedia, "October Surprise Conspiracy Theory."

21 Chardy and Honegger: Stich book, pp. 197–198.

22 Ben-Menashe arrest and Eitan quote: quoted in *I/F Magazine*, "Israeli Spy Cover-Up Crumbles," by Jack Colhoun, September–October 1999. Citing Gordon Thomas, *Gideon's Spies: The Secret History of the Mossad*.

23 Ben-Menashe and Israelis: Ibid.

24 BCCI and Barcella: "October Surprise X-Files (Part 4): The Money Trail," by Robert Parry, *The Consortium*.

25 BCCI and Iran: *In These Times*, "For the Record" by Joel Bleifuss, March 8, 1993.

26 Barcella quote: *In These Times*, "Mr. Fixit," by Joel Bleifuss, February 22, 1993, citing the book on BCCI, *False Profits*.

27 House findings: "October Surprise conspiracy theory," Wikipedia (online).

28 Donald Gregg: Stich, p. 245.

29 Andelman testimony: "Fact Finders: U.S.-Iran: 20 Years of Secrets," *I/F Magazine*, November–December 1999.

30 Russian report: "Russia's PM & October Surprise," by Robert Parry, *The Consortium*, May 17, 1999.

31 Steven Emerson: www.steveemerson.com.

32 Clinton: *I/F Magazine*, November–December 1999 article.

Chapter Ten

1 Statistics on prisons: "Will Obama End 'War on Drugs?', by Sherwood Ross, June 1, 2009, www.truthout.org.

2 Banks and drug money: Chapter by Peter Dale Scott, "Drugs, Anti-Communism and Extra-Legal Repression in Mexico," p. 187, in *Government of the Shadows*, edited by Eric Wilson, Pluto Press, 2009.

3 Heroin smuggling: "The Cocaine Connection," by Vince Bielski and Dennis Berstein, *Covert Action*, Summer 1987, quoting Alfred McCoy, author of *The Politics of Heroin*.

4 Heroin in bodies: Rodney Stich, *Defrauding America*, p. 296.

5 Nugan Hand bank: "The Australian Heroin Connection," by Jerry Meldon, *Covert Action*, Summer 1987.

6 Reagan and Nicaragua: "Reinventing Reagan?", by John Lampert, April 29, 2009, www.truthout.org.

7 Memorandum of Understanding: "Hyde's Blind Eye: Contras & Cocaine," *I/F Magazine*, November–December 1999.

8 Hitz report: *The Consortium*, October 26, 1998.

9 Levine and Castillo: "Hyde's Blind Eye"

10 Reagan statement on Contras: "U.S. Concedes Contras Linked to Drugs, But Denies Leadership Involved," Associated Press, April 10, 1986.

11 Reagan Administration report: April 17, 1986. North memo: quoted in "Hyde's Blind Eye."

12 Wanda Palacio testimony: "Congress Puts Contra-Coke Secrets Behind Closed Doors," by Robert Parry, *I/F*, July–Aug. 1999.

13 Kerry quote: "Cocaine Connection," *Covert Action*, Summer 1987.

14 Anti-Drug Abuse Act: *CounterPunch*, June 15–30, 1998.

15 Kerry report: April 13, 1989, Government Printing Office.

16 *Times* and Kerry report: "CIA: We Knew All Along," *CounterPunch*, October 15–25, 1998. The series was written by Keith Schneider.

17 *Post* and *Time*: "R.I.P. Gary Webb—Unembedded Reporter," by Jeff Cohen, December 13, 2004, www.commondreams.org. The *Time* correspondent was Laurence Zuckerman.

18 Stone and Noriega: "A Talk with Manuel Noriega," *The Nation*, January 24, 1994.

19 Noriega: Stich, *Defrauding America*, p. 307.

20 Seal smuggling billions: 1986 letter from the attorney general of Louisiana to U.S. Attorney General Edwin Meese.

21 Mena, Arkansas and Seal: "The Crimes of Mena," by Sally Denton and Roger Morris, online at www.theforbiddenknowledge. com. Barry Seal's story became the subject of an HBO film in 1991 called *Doublecrossed*.

22 Gary Webb series: Ibid. See also Webb's book, *Dark Alliance*.

23 Pincus and CIA: "WaPo Covered for CIA in Iran-Contra Crack Scandal," *Huffington Post*, June 29, 2009.

24 *LA Times* slant: Cohen article.

25 Gates comment: Stich book, p. 400.

26 Gates and BCCI: www.historycommons. org. Complete 9/11 timeline: BCCI. Citing article in London's *Financial Times* in 1991.

27 Pakistani president and drugs: Report by Alfred McCoy.

28 Kerry investigation and cooperation: "with the key exception of the Federal Reserve," Senator Kerry later told the Foreign Relations Committee.

29 Largest Islamic bank: Owned 77% at the time by Sheikh Zayed bin Sultan Al Nayhan, president of the United Arab Emirates.

30 Bin Laden: www.historycommons.org, BCCI timeline, citing United Press International story March 1, 2001.

31 Peter Dale Scott: "Afghanistan: Heroin-Ravaged State", May 8, 2009, on Global Research Web site.

32 Pentagon refusal to bomb drug labs: Pakistani journalist and best-selling author Ahmed Rashid.

33 Karzai's brother: "Brother of Afghan Leader Said to be Paid by C.I.A.," *New York Times*, October 28, 2009.

34 Marshal Fahim and drugs: *New York Times*, August 27, 2009, "Accused of Drug Ties, Afghan Official Worries U.S."

35 Expert: Loretta Napoleoni.

36 Traffickers targeted: *New York Times*, August 10, 2009, "Drug Chieftains Tied to Taliban are U.S. Targets."

37 Peter Dale Scott: chapter in *Government of the Shadows*, p. 173.

38 Haro bust: Scott, p. 176.

39 Honduran supplier: Scott, p. 184.

40 Mexico corruption: Ibid.

41 Salinas, Citibank, Lehman: Scott, p. 186.

42 Profits flowing south: "Obama Targets Mexican Cartels," *Washington Post*, April 16, 2009.

43 Drug war deaths: "Vast U.S. Illegal Drug Market Fuels Mexican Cartels," by David Crary, Associated Press, May 26, 2009.

44 Guns from U.S.: Truthout Web site, June 19, 2009.

45 Plan Mexico: "U.S.-Trained Death Squads?", *Mother Jones* magazine, July–August 2009.

46 Obama effort: "Obama Targets Mexican Cartels."

47 Obama policies: "Will Obama End 'War on Drugs?'" by Sherwood Ross, June 1, 2009, www.truthout.org.

48 Drug figures: "Vast U.S. Illegal Drug Market Fuels Mexican Cartels."

49 Marijuana on public lands: "High Sierras," *Mother Jones* magazine, July-August 2009.

Chapter Eleven

1 John Ellis and Fox: "Because Jeb Said So: What Really Happened on Election Night in Florida," by David W. Moore, in *Loser Take All*, edited by Mark Crispin Miller, Ig Publishing, Brooklyn, 2008, p. 36.

2 Volusia County "mistake": *Loser Take All*, "Diebold and Max Cleland's 'Loss' in Georgia," by Robert F. Kennedy Jr., p. 66.

3 Voter delays; photo IDs; missing ballots: "The Stolen Presidential Elections," www.michaelparenti.org.

4 Felon purge in Florida: Greg Palast, *The Best Democracy Money Can Buy*, Plume paperback, 2003, pp. 11–21.

5 *Post* story: Ibid., p. 19.

6 Russert comment: Ibid., p. 39.

7 Absentee ballots: "Did Bush camp encourage military personnel to vote after Election Day?", by Jake Tapper, www.salon.com, March 5, 2001.

8 Mob and recount: "The Five Worst Republican Outrages," by Wayne Barrett, www.villagevoice.com, December 19, 2000.

9 Scalia on decision: Miller piece, *Loser Take All*, p. 40.

10 Later articles showing Gore victory: cited in Miller article, *Loser Take All*, p. 37.

11 *Times* and *Post* on 2004 election: "Was the 2004 Election Stolen?", by Robert F. Kennedy Jr., posted June 1, 2006 at www.rollingstone.com.

12 Kennedy on election: Ibid.

13 Voting machine companies: "Diebold and Max Cleland's 'Loss' in Georgia," *Loser Take All*, p. 66.

14 Vote shift: "The Suspicious, Disturbing Death of Election Rigger Michael Connell,"

by Bob Fitrakis and Harvey Wasserman, www.freepress.org/departments/display/19/2008/3320, December 21, 2008.

15 Ohio events: Kennedy article.

16 Lou Harris: Ibid.

17 Blackwell and Conyers: Fitrakis and Wasserman article.

18 Suit against Blackwell: *King Lincoln Bronzeville Neighborhood Association v. Blackwell*.

19 Missing Ohio records: "2004 Ballots Not Preserved," *Cincinnatti Enquirer*, August 12, 2007.

20 Background on lawsuit: Cliff Arnebeck interview with Dick Russell, August 21, 2009.

21 Arnebeck on Spoonamore: Interview with Dick Russell, August 2009.

22 Spoonamore background: "Cyber Security Expert Says KingPin Attack Benefited Bush," www.epluribusmedia.net, October 30, 2008.

23 SMARTech: "Chattanooga Takes Center Stage in Connecting Voters for President," *Chattanooga Times Free Press*, March 19, 2004.

24 Contract between Ohio, GovTech: "Statement of Work Under State Term Schedule Number 533384-1, Secretary of State Contract Number 180."

25 Spoonamore on Ohio setup: Interview with Dick Russell, August 21, 2009.

26 Bush/Rove/Blackwell meeting: "Are Rove's Missing E-mails the Smoking Guns of the Stolen 2004 Election?", by Bob Fitrakis and Harvey Wasserman, *The Free Press*, April 25, 2007.

27 Connell managing: Mark Crispin Miller on *Democracy Now!*, www.truthout.org, December 25, 2008.

28 Triad: "Proof of Ohio Election Fraud Exposed," on www.michaelmoore.com, December 2004.

29 Connell admission: Court deposition, 2008.

30 Conyers letter: "Ballot Scamming," www.americanfreepress.net.

31 Connell background: "Who is Michael Connell? Why He Should be Investigated by Congress," document prepared for House Judiciary Committee, provided Dick Russell, 2009.

32 Spoonamore on Connell: Russell interview.

33 Roy Cales: "Who is Roy Cales and What's his Connection to Mike Connell?", epluribusmedia.net, August 6, 2008.

34 Cales resignation: "Arrest of Florida CIO Prompts Resignation," *Washington Technology*, September 4, 2001.

35 Connell and Ohio computers: House Judiciary Committee document.

36 Rove and Connell subpoena: "Cyber Security Expert Says KingPin Attack Benefited Bush."

37 Pre-election predictions: "Obama Hasn't Closed the Sale," by Karl Rove, *Wall Street Journal*, October 16, 2008; www.rove.com/election, November 2008.

38 Spoonamore on election counter-hacking '08: interview with Russell.

39 Connell plane crash: "The Suspicious, Disturbing Death of Election Rigger Michael Connell," by Bob Fitrakis and Harvey Wasserman, December 21, 2008.

40 Connell canceling flights: www.cbsnews.com/stories/2008/12/23.

41 Arnebeck on Connell's death: interview with Dick Russell, August 21, 2009.

Chapter Twelve

1 John Farmer book: *The Ground Truth: The Story Behind America's Defense on 9/11*, 2009.

2 Charles Lewis on 9/11 and LAX: interview with Dick Russell, July 2, 2009. See also: "What I Heard LAX Security Officials Say During the 9/11 Attacks," at www.911truth.org.

3 Fighter jet intercepts: *Loose Change*, documentary about 9/11, 2007 version.

4 Defense Secretary approval: http://911review.com/means/standdown.html.

5 Mineta story and Cheney: *The New Pearl Harbor Revisited*, by David Ray Griffin, Olive Branch Press, 2008, pp. 91–94.

6 Barry Jennings on explosions: "Summary of Evidence of Controlled Demolition at World Trade Center," by David R. Wayne and Greg Garrison, November 25, 2008.

7 Tower design and aircraft statistics: *Loose Change*.

8 NIST report and molten metal: Ibid.

9 Nano-thermite report: Press release from Political Leaders for 9/11 Truth, April 21, 2009, quoting Harrit on Danish TV2 News. Asked why he thought this was responsible for the buildings' collapse, Harrit said: "Well, it's an explosive. Why else would it be out there?"

10 Gage on building collapses: www.ae911truth.org/.

11 Steel debris shipped: *Loose Change*.

12 Lewis on missile hitting Pentagon: Russell interview.

13 Location of strike: *Loose Change*.

14 Pentagon attack: Both Wittenberg and Stubblebine are interviewed in the *Zero* documentary, viewable online.

15 Stubblebine on Pentagon: www.youtube.com video interview.

16 Lack of damage and debris: Griffin, *The New Pearl Harbor Revisited*, pp. 63–64.

17 Colonel Nelson on Pentagon crash: E-mail communication with coauthor Dick Russell.

18 Hanjour experience and maneuver: Griffin, ibid.

19 Disappearance of financial information: Arlington County After Action Report.

20 Operations and budget information: Griffin book.

21 Olson calls: Griffin, pp. 60–61.

22 Wittenberg on Flight 77: *Zero*.

23 Operation Northwoods: www.whatreallyhappened.com/northwoods.html quoting from *Body of Secrets*, by James Bamford, Doubleday, 2001, p. 82 and following.

24 Charles Lewis on Pennsylvania plane: Russell interview.

25 Pennsylvania crash site: *Loose Change*, including footage from CNN.

26 Voice recorder, mayor's comment, jets scrambled: *Loose Change*.

27 Bush, Rumsfeld, and Rice denials: *The New Pearl Harbor*, p. 134.

28 Bush intelligence briefing: Declassified April 2004, viewable online.

29 Rice warned by Tenet: "Two Months Before 9/11, an Urgent Warning to Rice," *Washington Post*, October 1, 2006, p. A17.

30 Cofer Black: Ibid.

31 Rice response: "Rice: No Memory of CIA Warning of Attack," Associated Press, October 2, 2006.

32 Israel warning: "What did Israel know In advance of the 9/11 Attacks?", By Christopher Ketcham, *Counterpunch*, 2007 Vol. 14, Nos. 3 and 4. The story first appeared in the *British Sunday Telegraph* (September 16, 2001).

33 French warning: "September 11 01: The French Knew Much About It," by Guillaume Dasquie, *Le Monde,* April 16, 2004.

34 Susan Lindauer warning: "Susan Lindauer Reveals Facts about 9/11 Warning," by Michael Collins, March 3, 2009. Also, "911 Prediction Revealed at Lindauer Hearing in NYC," by Michael Collins, June 19, 2008, www.scoop.co.nz.

35 FBI list: Ibid.

36 Hijackers alive and well: *Zero*, Italian documentary about 9/11, viewable online.

37 Bin Laden videos and lack of evidence: *Loose Change*.

38 Evidence left behind: *Loose Change*.

39 Atta's movements: *Zero*.

40 CIA and hijackers: cited in Scott, from *The Looming Tower*, by Lawrence Wright.

41 Background on terrorists/CIA and visas: *Zero*.

42 Edmonds bombshell: As a guest on Mike Malloy radio show.

43 Edmonds on bin Laden and U.S.: "Bombshell: Bin Laden worked for US till 9/11," July 31, 2009, www.dailykos.com.

44 Chartered planes: "FBI's 9/11 Saudi Flight Documents Released," by Matt Renner, June 22, 2007, www.truthout.org.

45 Ahmad wire transfer to Atta: *The New Pearl Harbor Revisited*, p. 222.

46 Graham book: *Intelligence Matters*, published 2004, cited in *The New Pearl Harbor Revisited*, pp. 224–5.

47 U.S. and Saudis: One of Bush's brothers, Marvin, was on the board of a company called Securacom (since renamed Stratesec). Its board chairman is Wirt D. Walker III, who happens to be a cousin of

both Marvin and W. Securacom provided security for both the World Trade Center and the Dulles International Airport, where Flight 77 originated before supposedly crashing into the Pentagon. Stratesec has both Kuwaiti and Saudi investors, and W's uncle Jonathan is a board member of the Riggs bank. "Saudi Princess Haifa al Faisal, the wife of Saudi Ambassador to the US Prince Bandar, used a Riggs account to funnel money to Omar al Bayoumi and Osama Basnan, two Saudi students in California associated with two of the 911 hijackers." (Wayne Madsen article, "Marvin Bush Employee's Mysterious Death," www. democraticunderground.com.)

48 Shaffer on Able Danger: Interview with Dick Russell, September 19, 2009.

49 Able Danger's discoveries: *The New Pearl Harbor Revisited*, pp. 179–80.

50 Colonel Shaffer: Ibid, p. 180.

51 Attempts to tell story: Ibid., pp. 181–185.

52 Griffin quote: Ibid., p. 195.

53 Clarke on Iraq: *Washington Post* op-ed, May 31, 2009.

54 Zelikow and 9/11 Commission: *The New Pearl Harbor Revisited*, pp. 238–9, citing Philip Shenon's 2008 book *The Commission*.

55 Zelikow and report on "catastrophic terrorism": *The New Pearl Harbor*, p. 243.

56 Zelikow and Iraq: Ibid., p. 245.

57 Zelikow and Rove: "NYT's Reporter Claims Rove Influenced 9/11 Commission Report," by Max Holland, Washington Decoded, January 30, 2008, www. truthout.org.

58 Clarke on Zelikow: Ibid., p. 248, citing Shenon book.

59 Government minders: "Newly Released Memo: Government 'Minders' at 9/11 Commission interviews 'Intimidated' Witnesses," May 1, 2009, www.opednews. com.

60 *Washington Post* on commission: Cited in "The 9/11 Commission Rejects own Report as Based on Government Lies," http://www.salem-news.com/araticles/ september112009/911_truth_9-11-09. php.

61 Kean/Hamilton on CIA obstruction: "Stonewalled by the CIA," by Thomas H. Kean and Lee H. Hamilton, *New York Times*, January 2, 2008.

Chapter Thirteen

1 Roosevelt quote: Forum, February 1895. Mem. Ed. XV, 10; Nat. Ed. XIII, 9.

2 "perverse set of incentives": "Former Wall Street Player Reveals the Inside World Behind Shady Bailouts to Bankers," by Joshua Holland and Nomi Prins, www. alternet.org, October 30, 2009.

3 AIG employees & assets: "The 10 Worst Corporations of 2008," *Multinational Monitor*, Nov.–Dec., 2008.

4 AIG intelligence background: "The Secret (Insurance) Agent Men," *Los Angeles Times*, September 22, 2000. See also, *The Shadow Warriors: OSS and the Origins of the CIA*, by Bradley F. Smith, Basic Books, 1983.

5 AIG and Helliwell: *The War Conspiracy*, by Peter Dale Scott, Bobbs-Merrill, 1972.

6 Barbados company: See www. fromthewilderness.com, report by Michael Rupert.

7 AIG and aircraft: "Deep Politics of AIG: OSS, CIA, Drug Money Laundering," at www.ronpaulforums.com.

8 AIG recent history: "AIG is a 'special case,'" by Wayne Madsen, September 23, 2008, http://onlinejournal.com.

9 AIG in Asia: *L.A. Times* article, op.cit.

10 Greenberg and CIA: Madsen article.

11 Goldman Sachs's formula: "The Great American Bubble Machine," by Matt Taibbi, *Rolling Stone*, July 9–23, 2009.

12 Creation of Federal Reserve: *The Journey to Jekyll Island*, by G. Edward Griffin, American Media (24th printing, May 2009), p. 23. The meeting on Jekyll Island took place in November 1910.

13 JFK and Federal Reserve: "President John F. Kennedy, the Federal Reserve and Executive Order 11110," by Cedric X, *The Final Call*, Vol. 15, No. 6, January 17, 1996.

14 Greenspan on Federal Reserve: "AIG A Gold Standard for Fiascoes," by Rhonda Swan, March 20, 2009, *Palm Beach Post*.

15 Reagan era: "Reagan Did It," by Paul Krugman, *New York Times*, June 1, 2009.

16 Glass-Steagall Act: "Shattering the Glass-Steagall Act," by William Kaufman, September 19, 2008, www.counterpunch.org; "Wall Street's Best Investment," by Robert Weissman and James Donahue, *Multinational Monitor*, January–February 2009.

17 "bar-room brawl": L. William Seidman, a longtime Republican adviser.

18 Bush Administration and economy: "White House Philosophy Stoked Mortgage Bonfire," *New York Times*, December 21, 2008.

19 "red flags" at SEC: "Report Details How Madoff's Web Ensnared S.E.C.," *New York Times*, September 3, 2009, citing a new report by the SEC's inspector general.

20 SEC ignoring expert: "First the Swindle, Now the Whitewash," by Eamonn Fingleton, *CounterPunch*, Sept. 16–30, 2009.

21 Company hotline: "SEC Alerted About Allen Stanford in 2003: Report," February 27, 2009, www.reuters.com.

22 SEC and Madoff: "SEC's Madoff Miss Fits Pattern Set With Piquot," by Gary J. Aguirre, *Bloomberg*, February 2, 2009; "SEC Whislteblower Speaks on Madoff Fraud," by Matt Renner, Dec. 22, 2009, www.truthout.org.

23 Spitzer investigation: Madsen article, op.cit.

24 Luxury spa retreat: "More pigs at the trough," by Arianna Huffington, July 28, 2009, www.truthout.org.

25 Cassano's unit: *Market Ticker*, by Karl Denninger, March 31, 2009.

26 Office of Thrift Supervision/housing market: "The Big Takeover," by Matt Taibbi, *Rolling Stone*, www.truthout.org, March 23, 2009.

27 Paulson and SEC: "Obama's Top Econic Adviser is Greedy and Highly Compromised," by Matt Taibbi, April 10, 2009, www.alternet.org.

28 Goldman "lending lust": "It's time to enshrine Hank Paulson as national hero," by Matt Taibbi, June 8, 2009.

29 "strongest in decades": Ibid.

30 Oil and commodities: Taibbi article, *Rolling Stone*.

31 Industry subsidies: "Former Wall Street Player Reveals the Inside World Behind Shady Bailouts to Bankers," Alternet, op.cit.

32 John Thain: Taibbi, "The Great American Bubble Machine" (area rug); "Why an A**Hole Is Always in Charge," by Greg Palast, January 25, 2009.

33 Paulson-Blankfein calls: "Paulson's Calls to Goldman Tested Ethics During Crisis," *New York Times*, August 9, 2009.

34 Goldman check: "Former Wall Street Player," Alternet.

35 Spitzer on "inside job": "The Real AIG Scandal," by Eliot Spitzer, March 18, 2009, www.slate.com.

36 $40 billion outstanding: "Why big US, Foreign Banks Got Billions from AIG Bailout," by Greg Gordon and Kevin G. Hall, McClatchy newspaper, April 6, 2009, www.truthout.org.

37 AIG's overseas paybacks: "AIG a gold standard for fiascoes," by Rhonda Swan, op.cit.

38 AIG losses: Taibbi article.

39 AIG bonuses: Taibbi article, op.cit.

40 Cassano fired but salaried: *Market Ticker*, op.cit.

41 Total financial support in trillions: www.sigtarp.gov/reports/congress/2009/July2009_Quaraterly+Report+to+Congress.pdf (p. 134).

42 $1.1 trillion; quote: "The Greatest Swindle Ever Sold," by Andy Kroll, May 26, 2009, originally at TomDispatch.com, www.truthout.org. Economist quoted is Dean Baker, who co-directs the Center for Economic and Policy Research in Washington.

43 Big banks: "Banks 'Too Big to Fail' Have Grown Even Bigger," by David Cho, *Washington Post*, August 28, 2009.

44 Lewis/Cohan op-ed: "The Economy Is Still at the Brink," *New York Times*, June 7, 2009.

45 Federal Reserve and economists: "Priceless: How the Federal Reserve Bought the Economics Profession," by Ryan Grim, *The Huffington Post*, September 7, 2009.

46 Ron Paul and bill: www.ronpaul.com.

47 Federal Reserve: "Dismantling the Temple: How to Fix the Federal Reserve," by William Greider, *The Nation*, August 3–10, 2009. Greider is also author of the classic *Secrets of the Temple: How the Federal Reserve Runs the Country*.

48 Bonuses to execs: "Letting the Banking Rats out of the Bag," by Robert Scheer, August 11, 2009, www.truthdig.com.

49 Goldman employee earnings: "A Year After a Cataclysm, Little Change on Wall St.," by Alex Berenson, *New York Times*, September 12, 2009.

50 Goldman profit surge: "Goldman to Make Record Bonus Payout," by Philip Inman, June 21, 2009, www.guardian.co.uk.

51 Liddy and Goldman: "AIG Chief Owns Significant Stake in Goldman," *New York Times Dealbook*, April 17, 2009.

52 Durbin on banking lobby: "Top Senate Democrat: Bankers 'Own' the U.S. Congress," by Glenn Greenwald, April 3, 2009, www.salon.com.

53 $5 billion: Sidebar to "Wall Street's Best Investment," *Multinational Monitor*, op.cit.

54 Senators and Banks: "Senators Held Stock in Bailed-Out Banks," by Reid Wilson and Kevin Bogardus, June 13, 2009, www.truthout.org.

55 TARP quote: "Good Billions After Bad," by Donald R. Barlett and James B. Steele, *Vanity Fair*, October 2009.

56 TARP report: "Thievery Under the TARP," by Robert Scheer, April 22, 2009, www.truthout.org.

57 TARP quote: "no problem here": "Good Billions After Bad," by Donald R. Barlett and James B. Steele, *Vanity Fair*, October 2009.

58 TARP program: Ibid.

59 GE Capital: "How a Loophole Benefits GE in Bank Rescue," by Jeff Gerth and Brady Dennis, originally in ProPublica and *Washington Post*, June 29, 2009, www.truthout.org.

60 Goldman as Obama donor: Taibbi, "The Great American Bubble Machine," op.cit.

61 Obama contributions: Center for Responsive Politics.

62 Summers and earnings: "Awake and Sing!", by Frank Rich, *New York Times*, April 12, 2009.

63 Summers crusade: "Larry Summers, Tim Geithner, and Wall Street's Ownership of Government," by Glenn Greenwald, April 4, 2009, www.salon.com.

64 Geithner's proposal: "Member and Overseer of the Finance Club," by Jo Becker and Gretchen Morgenson, *New York Times*, April 27, 2009.

65 Geithner's phone contacts: "When Wall St. Calls, Geithner Answers," www.cbsnews.com/stories/2009/10/08/business/main5371216.shtml%20.

66 Geithner chief of staff: "Obama's top economic adviser is greedy and highly compromised," by Matt Taibbi, April 10, 2009, www.alternet.org.

67 Blankenfein compensation: "AP Study Finds $1.6 billion went to bailed-out bank executives," December 22, 2008.

68 TV ad spending: Organizing for America release, October 24, 2009, citing Associated Press.

69 "Medical Loss Ratio": "The S-Word and Dr. Kevorkian's Accountant," by Greg Palast, October 15, 2009, www.truthout.org.

70 Bonuses to traders: "Bankers Reaped Lavish Bonuses During Bailouts," *New York Times*, July 31, 2009. Citing a report by New York attorney general.

71 IRS and wealthy Americans: "Tempo of Audits Drops for Wealthy," by Lynnley Browning, March 23, 2009, www.nytimes.com.

72 Citigroup tax havens: "Report: Over 8 in 10 Corporations Have Tax Havens," by Ken Thomas, January 16, 2009, citing GAO report.

73 Caymans as tax haven: "Lax Little Islands," by David Cay Johnston, *The Nation*, June 1, 2009.

74 IBM workers: "IBM offers to move laid off workers to India," by Paul McDougall, *Information Week*, February 2, 2009.

75 The BIS: "The Bloodless Coup of the Global Financial Stability Board: From Guidelines to Rules," by Ellen Brown, June 24, 2009.

76 Jefferson warning: Letter to James Monroe, January 1, 1815.

77 National debt, 1791: www.brillig.com/debt_clock/faq.

78 Budget deficit, dollar situation: "The American Empire is Bankrupt," by Chris Hedges, June 14, 2009, www.truthdig.com.

79 Bush overpayment: "Bush Overpaid Banks in Bailout, Watchdog Says," Associated Press, February 6, 2009.

Chapter Fourteen

1 Senate report: "The Stomach-Turning Truth About Bush's Torture Programs," by Scott Horton, April 28, 2009, www.alternet.org.

2 Torture manual: "New CIA Docs Detail Brutal 'Extraordinary Rendition' Process," by Scott Horton, August 28, 2009, www.huffingtonpost.com.

3 CIA videotapes: "Trail of Torture Tapes," by Nat Hentoff, *Village Voice,* December 27, 2007.

4 "Battle Lab": "CIA Experiments on US Soldiers Linked to Torture Program," by Jeffrey Kaye, www.truthout.org.

5 Pressuring Justice Department: "What the New Jim Comey Torture E-mails Actually Reveal," by Glenn Greenwald, June 7, 2009, www.salon.com.

6 Major Burney on interrogations: "The Stomach-Turning Truth," op.cit.

7 Torture and death of Al-Libi: "New Revelations About the Torture and Alleged Suicide of Ibn Al-Shaykh Al-Libi," by Andy Worthington, June 19, 2009, www. pubrecord.org.

8 Waterboarding of 9/11 Witnesses: "Why Didn't Pelosi Speak Out Against Torture," by Robert Scheer, May 15, 2009, Truthdig, www.alternet.org.

9 Bush-Blair meeting: "Confidential Memo Reveals US Plan to Provoke an Invasion of Iraq," June 21, 2009, www.guardian. co.uk.

10 "executive assassination ring": "Investigative Reporter Seymour Hersh Describes 'Executive Assassination Ring,'" by Eric Black, March 11, 2009, www. newsfromunderground.com.

11 Assassination and Blackwater: "CIA Sought Blackwater's Help to Kill Jihadists," by Mark Mazetti, August 20, 2009, *New York Times.*

12 Privatization in Afghanistan: "Flushing Blackwater," by Jeremy Scahill, *The Nation,* August 31, 2009, www.truthout. org.

13 Erik Prince as "Christian Crusader": Ibid.

14 Blackwater killing Iraqi Civilians: "Blackwater Founder Accused in Court of Intent to Kill," by Jerry Markon, *Washington Post,* August 29, 2009.

15 Blackwater image change: "Blackwater's Business," *The Nation,* December 24, 2007.

16 Triple Canopy: "Former Iraq Security Contractors Say Firm Bought Black Market Weapons, Swapped Booze for Rockets," by T. Christian Miller and Aram Roston, ProPublica, September 21, 2009, www.truthout.org.

17 Blackwater operations: *Nation articles,* Ibid. and op.cit.

18 Blackwater in New Orleans: "Blackwater Down," by Jeremy Scahill, *The Nation,* September 21, 2005.

19 Patriot Act: "Bill of Rights Under Bush: A Timeline," by Phil Leggiere, for Question Authority (on the Web).

20 NSA spying and setup: "Obama's Black Widow," by Nat Hentoff, *Village Voice,* January 7, 2009, www.truthout.org.

21 Targeted journalists: "Whistleblower: NSA Targeted Journalists, Snooped on All U.S. Communications," by Kim Zetter, January 22, 2009, http://blog.wired.com.

22 Clinton e-mails: "NSA Secret Database Ensnared President Clinton's Private Email," by Kim Zetter, June 17, 2009, www.truthout.org.

23 "Suspicionless Surveillance": "Did Bush Continue to Secretly Operate Total Information Awareness?", by Jason Leopold, September 19, 2009, www. truthout.org.

24 Brochure: See www.infragard.net.

25 For more on Infragard, check out: www. democracynow.org, February 11, 2008, interview by NPR's Amy Goodman with *Progressive Magazine* editor Matt Rothschild.

26 Memo on anti-terrorist plans: "Extraordinary Measures," by Michael

Isikoff, *Newsweek*, March 3, 2009, posted on www.truthout.org.

27 Ratner on "Fuhrer's Law": "Do the Secret Bush Memos Amount to Treason? Top Constitutional Scholar Says Yes," by Naomi Wolf, Alternet, March 26, 2009, www.truthout.org.

28 Operation Garden Plot: "Secret Bush Administration Plan to Suspend US Constitution," by Tom Burghardt, Global Research, October 6, 2008.

29 Rex 84: "Rex 84: FEMA's Blueprint for Martial Law in America," by Allen L. Roland, Global Research, August 20, 2006.

30 Iran-Contra hearing: *The Road to 9/11*, by Peter Dale Scott, University of California Press, 2007, p. 184.

31 Top-level planning: Ibid.

32 Rumsfeld/Cheney: Ibid., p. 185, citing author James Mann.

33 COG plan: Dated January 19, 2001, the latest version was headed: "Army Regulation 500-3, Emergency Employment of Army and Other Resources. Army Continuity of Operations (COOP) Program." According to the Web site Wikileaks that published it, there was an addendum: "Destruction Notice: Destroy by any method that will prevent disclosure of contents or reconstruction of the document."

34 New terrorism task force: Ibid., p. 185.

35 Allbaugh at FEMA: *The Road to 9/11*, p. 210.

36 "Shadow government": "Shadow Government Is at Work in Secret," by Barton Gellman and Susan Schmidt, *Washington Post*, March 1, 2002.

37 ENDGAME: "Rule By Fear or Rule By Law?", by Lewis Seiler and Dan Hamburg, February 4, 2008, www.sfgate.com.

38 Troop plan/NORTHCOM: "Secret Bush Administration Plan," op.cit.

39 Northern Command quote: U.S. Department of Defense, "U.S. Northern Command," http://www.defenselink.mil/news/Apr2002/no4172002_200204175.html.

40 Granite Shadow: *The Road to 9/11*, p. 242.

41 Bush defining insurrection: "Thousands of Troops Are Deployed on US Streets Ready to Carry Out 'Crowd Control,'" by Naomi Wolf, Alternet, October 8, 2008.

42 McHale on fundamental change: "Pentagon to Detail Troops to Bolster Domestic Security," by Spencer S. Hsu and Ann Scott Tyson, *Washington Post*, December 1, 2008.

43 KBR contract: First revealed by author Peter Dale Scott, quoted in "Secret Bush Administration Plan," op.cit.

44 Military Commissions Act: "Rule by Fear or Rule By Law?", op.cit.

45 2007 laws and decrees: Ibid.

46 Troops deployed in U.S.: "Thousands of Troops Are Deployed on U.S. Streets," op.cit.

47 Financial meltdown/plan names: "Secret Bush Administration Plan," op.cit.

48 US Army War College study: "Bad News From America's Top Spy," by Chris Hedges, February 16, 2009, www.truthdig.com.

49 Gang subculture in Salinas: "Navy School Takes on Salinas Gangs," by Jack Foley, February 3, 2009, www.thecalifornian.com.

50 20,000 troops by 2011: "Pentagon to Detail Troops to Bolster Domestic Security," op.cit.

51 Fort Stewart unit: "Apparent Plan to Deploy Active-Duty Military Unit Inside the U.S. Draws ACLU Scrutiny," by Marcia Coyle, November 4, 2008, www.law.com.

52 "Fusion centers": "Police to get access to classified military intelligence," http://rawstory.com/08/news/2009/09/16.

53 Extremists in army: "I Hate Arabs More Than Anybody: Desperate Army Recruits Neo-Nazis," by Matt Kennard, Nation Institute Investigative Fund, June 17, 2009, www.alternet.org.

54 Coup against Obama: http://tpmlivewire.talkingpointsmemo.com/2009/09/newsmax-columnist-military-coup-may-be-needed-toresolve-the-obama-problem.php/ (cited by Mark Miller's newsfromunderground on October 2, 2009).

55 Obama and military: "Military Waging War Against the White House," *Huffington Post*, October 23, 2009.

56 Beck/background checks: "Pitchforks and Pistols," by Charles M. Blow, *New York Times* op-ed, April 4, 2009.

57 Rise of militias: "Report: Militia Activity on the Rise in U.S.," by Arthur Bright, *Christian Science Monitor*, August 16, 2009, www.truthout.org.

58 Millionaire Patriot training: e-mail on www.townhall.com

59 Thought police: "Obama's Black Widow," op.cit.

60 CIA/FBI Wikipedia edits: "CIA, FBI Computers Used for Wikipedia Edits," Yahoo! News, August 16, 2007.

61 Pentagon electronic war: "US Plans to 'Fight the Net' Revealed," by Adam Brookes, BBC Pentagon correspondent, January 25, 2009, http://news.bbc.co.uk.

62 DNA Fingerprint Act: Web site of Center for Constitutional Rights.

63 FBI biometrics program: "FBI Prepares Vast Database of Biometrics," by Ellen Nakashima, *Washington Post*, December 22, 2007.

64 Airport iris ID: Ibid.

65 Border searches: "Border Agents Can Search Laptops Without Cause, Appeals Court Rules," By Ryan Singel, *Wired*, April 22, 2008.

66 VeriChip: "VeriChip Injects Itself into Immigration Debate," May 18, 2006, www.spychips.com.

67 RFID tags: "Microchips Everywhere: A Future Vision," by Todd Lewan, Associated Press, January 29, 2008, *Seattle Times*.

68 Saving the wealthy: "Rapture Rescue 911: Disaster Response for the Chosen," by Naomi Klein, *The Nation*, December 19, 2007.

69 Security increase: "How to Profit From a 'Police State," by Jon Markman, MSN Money, November 8, 2007.

Chapter Fifteen

1 20,000 Americans infected: "Frequently Asked Questions About Lyme Disease," www.idsociety.org.

2 Kenneth King: transcript from *Conspiracy Theory with Jesse Ventura*, truTV, aired October 16, 2010.

3 Erich Traub: Michael Joseph Carroll, Lab 257: *The Disturbing Story of the Government's Secret Plum Island Germ Laboratory*, Harper Collins: 2004, pp. 7-11.

4 Belarus Secret: quoted in "Did Lyme disease originate out of Plum Island?", October 30, 2010, www.examiner.com/infections-disease-in-national....

5 Dr. Jerry Callis: Carroll, p. 23.

6 USDA paper: Ibid.

7   Plum Island website: "Did Lyme disease originate....", op.cit

8   Centers for Disease Control: Ibid.

9   GAO report: "Plum Island: A Sitting Duck," by Karl Grossman, July 19, 2010, www.huffingtonpost.com

10 "Lady al Qaeda": Ibid.

11 Jim McCoy: Conspiracy Theory transcript, op.cit

12 Congressman Timothy Bishop: Ibid.

13 Dr. Roger Breeze: Ibid.

14 National Bio and Agro-Defense Facility: "Kansas Bioscience Authority pursues researchers for National Bio and Agro-Defense Facility," *Kansas City Business Journal*, January 5, 2011.

15 National Research Council report: "National Bio and Agro-Defense Facility advances despite critical report," *Kansas City Business Journal*, November 15, 2010.

16 Professor Tom Manning: Conspiracy Theory transcript, op.cit

Chapter Sixteen

1   Hayward selling stock: "BP chief Tony Hayward sold shares weeks before oil spill," London *Telegraph*, June 5, 2010 (www.telegraph.co.uk/finance/newsbysector/energy/oilandgas/7804922/BP-chief-Tony....)

2   Transocean "put option": "Equity Options: Introduction of Equity Options on Transocean Ltd.," www.eurexclearing.com/download/documents/circulars/cf061201oe.pdf

3   Halliburton's unstable cement mixture: "Gulf oil spill update: What's known now about cause and effects," *Christian Science Monitor*, November 9, 2010, www.csmonitor.com.

4   Halliburton telling BP about failed tests: "Halliburton linked to BP oil spill," *The Independent* (Britain), October 29, 2010, www.independent.co.uk

5   BP/Transocean pressure test: "Gulf oil spill update," op.cit.

6   Halliburton purchase of Boots & Coots: "Halliburton planning to buy Boots & Coots," *Houston Chronicle*, April 10, 2010.

7   Mike Papantonio: Conspiracy Theory with Jesse Ventura, "The Gulf Oil Spill," aired December 11, 2010, truTV.

8   Adam Dillon: Ibid.

9   David Arnesen: Ibid.

10 Corexit banned in UK: www.sourcewatch.org/index.php?title=Corexit

11 Exxon Valdez deaths: "Corexit 9500: Cause of death for Exxon Valdez oil spill clean up workers?", Tampa *Examiner*, July 2, 2010: www.examiner.com/gulf-oil-spill-in-tampa-bay/corexit-9500-cause-of-death-for-exxon....:

12 Rodney F. Chase/BP and Nalco: Nalco web-site, Rodney F. Chase biography, http://phx.corporate-ir.net.zhtml?c=182822&p=irol-govBio_pf&ID=139045. See also, "Gulf Oil Spill: BP Grilled Over Choice of Dispersant," *Los Angeles Times*, May 19, 2010.

13 "toxic rain": www.examiner.com, op.cit

14 Steven Chu and BP grant: www.rawstory.com/rs/2010/06/obama-energy-secretary-bp-save-world/

15 Dr. Steven E. Koonin and BP" www.energy.gov/organization/dr_steven_koonin.htm

16 Army Corps Mississippi relocation plan: "Feds Propose Massive Buyout for Mississippi Coast," NPR, November 15, 2007, www.npr.org/templates/story/story.php?storyID=16132092

17 Rees and Robbins: *Conspiracy Theory*, op.cit

18 Figures on Gulf spill: *Christian Science Monitor*, November 9, 2010, op.cit

19 BP compensation: "91,000 Gulf oil spill claims, just 1 final payment," by Brian Skoloff, *Associated Press*, January 31, 2011

20 Kenneth Feinberg: "BP Mediator Feinberg Can't Call Himself Independent, Judge Says," Bloomberg News, February 3, 2011, www.bloomberg.com.